Literary Trails

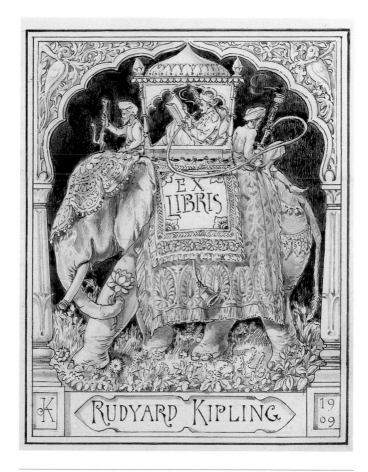

EX LIBRIS

RUDYARD KIPLING

19
09

Literary Trails

BRITISH WRITERS IN THEIR LANDSCAPES

Christina Hardyment

THE NATIONAL TRUST

HARRY N. ABRAMS, INC., PUBLISHERS

First published in Great Britain in 2000 by
National Trust Enterprises Ltd
36 Queen Anne's Gate, London SW1H 9AS

www.nationaltrust.org.uk/bookshop

Distributed in 2000 by Harry N. Abrams, Incorporated, New York

Cataloguing in Publication Data is available from the British Library

ISBN 0 7078 0375 6
ISBN 0 7078 0293 8 (TSP edition)
ISBN 0 8109–6705–7 (Abrams)
ISBN 0 8109–2943–0 (Book Club: Paperback)

Maps by bounford.com
Picture research by Samantha Wyndham, Helen George and Helen Fewster

Designed and typeset by Bridget Heal
Additional composition by SPAN Graphics Ltd
Production by Bob Towell
Printed and bound in China
Phoenix Offset

Front cover: Seven Sisters viewed across Cuckmere Haven, from Seaford Haven in Sussex. (*NTPL/Derry Robinson*)
Back Cover: Thomas Carlyle at his reading desk in the Drawing Room at 24 Cheyne Row, London; painting by Helen Allingham, 1878. (*NTPL/Michael Boys*)
Half title: Rudyard Kipling's bookplate, dated 1909.
Frontispiece: Footpaths meander through the Lake District towards Buttermere, providing access to landscapes that have inspired writers from William Wordsworth to Melvyn Bragg.

Contents

Preface

> Story alone and scenery alone may interest specialists, but the thing that appeals to us all, and charms us, and carries us out of ourselves, is the union of story and scenery. Then you get poetry and romance.
>
> W.G. Collingwood, *Guide to the Lakes*

Literary pilgrimages are among the most ancient forms of tribute which readers pay to the authors who touch their hearts and minds. They have been made since time immemorial to birthplaces, long-term homes and graves; such shrines often endure in folk memory long after a once-fêted genius has been forgotten. Their existence can even make new converts – visiting the enchanting little village of Selborne with its picturesque zig-zag walk was my first introduction to Gilbert White. And few who walk the craggy North Cornish coast and happen upon the little hut tucked under the lip of the cliff at Morwenstow are not tempted to find out more about its eccentric literary vicar Robert Hawker.

The most rewarding of all such journeys are those which relate closely to a writer's invented country. The connection is often indirect. Jane Austen's Hampshire homeland never exactly appears in her novels, but her heroes and heroines were often inspired by her neighbours and their elegant country residences and vicarages south-west of Basingstoke. Strolling between Steventon and Deane, or around her final home at Chawton allows one to understand as nothing else can do how different the pace of events used to be in the eighteenth century; how much time people had to analyse events and cogitate on character.

Some literary landscapes are all but identical to their real life counterparts. Thomas Hardy's Wessex is perhaps the most obvious, but many others exist. Lorna Doone's country is to be found in almost every detail in the hidden valleys of Exmoor in Somerset. The Swallows' and Amazons' 'lake in the north' is there to be sailed on, an ingenious mirror-image amalgam of Coniston and Windermere, in the Cumbrian Lake District. And closer to our own time thriller writers have rooted their

Coniston Water in the Cumbrian Lake District, with the Old Man of Coniston in the distance.

plots significantly in place – what would Daphne du Maurier's *Rebecca* be without the Cornish coast and the brooding, hidden house of Manderley, or Dorothy Sayers' *The Nine Tailors* without its chill Fen landscapes and magnificent churches?

Literary pilgrimages were once only for the rich or for those of gypsy as well as bookish inclinations. Today, thanks to cars, trains, buses and bicycles, almost anyone can enjoy them. The places with which this book is concerned are especially accessible, as many of them are looked after by the National Trust. It is appropriate in this context that the roots of the Trust were profoundly literary. It was the Lakeland of the poets and Ruskin that Canon Hardwicke Drummond Rawnsley and his contemporaries sought to save when the charity was founded in 1895.

The Trust's literary connections have grown stronger over time, sometimes deliberately, sometimes by chance. The great country houses it later acquired often had a history of both direct and indirect patronage of writers. It is also natural enough that the exceptionally beautiful parts of Britain protected by the Trust have continued to inspire modern writers as diverse as Melvyn Bragg and Jack Higgins. Today the Trust can boast of an ever-increasing number of houses that were once the homes of famous authors. Among them are Virginia Woolf's Monk's House in Sussex, Shaw's Corner, George Bernard Shaw's Hertfordshire home, and Benjamin Disraeli's Hughenden in Buckinghamshire.

Above: George Bernard Shaw at lunch in his Hertfordshire home, Shaw's Corner. His desk can still be seen in the study (right).

The main purpose of this book is to highlight this wealth of literary associations, and it is intended as a representative rather than a comprehensive guide to the places of special importance to British writers. There are already several excellent works concerned with 'literary geography', and I have listed them in the bibliography. I should also explain that, since the National Trust for Scotland may well one day produce its very own literary guide, I have, with regret, neglected such vividly topographical North British writers as Sir Walter Scott, John Buchan, S.R. Crockett and Robert Louis Stevenson.

Selectivity has its advantages. Much more detail can be provided on

the themes chosen, and there is plenty of room for self-indulgent digressions on my own favourite authors. Nor is this just a book for the armchair. All the chapters except for the scene-setting first include itineraries and maps of walks, bike-rides, climbs and even one sail, in the hope that readers will enjoy following in the footsteps, pedal tracks or wake of the authors concerned as much as I have done.

The book's eight chapters are self-contained essays which sometimes follow themes across centuries and sometimes focus on a particular individual or type of literature. The first, 'The Pen and The Place', is a down-to-earth affair, intended as an introduction to the main characters of the book as a whole. It looks at the sanctuaries in which authors worked, the tools of their trade and the ingenious methods they employed to attract the elusive muse. There is a lasting fascination in being in the actual room where a writer worked, seeing the small comforts and humble imperfections that make even the most towering literary figures intensely human.

I have always loved the stirring tales of knightly questing and romancing associated with King Arthur's Britain, and no legend has had more influence on our literary traditions. So it seemed right to begin the book proper with an account of the three most famous places connected with King Arthur and his noble Knights of the Round Table – Tintagel, 'Camelot' and Glastonbury. I was less concerned with the reality of Arthur than with the effect of these citadels of chivalry on the writers who became obsessed with a myth which remains of profound cultural significance to Britain: most notably Sir Thomas Malory, Alfred, Lord Tennyson, T. H. White, John Steinbeck and Bernard Cornwell.

Jane Austen is the most famously English of novelists, and the next essay looks at her writings in the context of the places she lived in and visited. She had an extraordinary number of different homes, but made positive use of them as settings, both indirect and direct, for scenes in her novels. Besides exploring her Hampshire homeland, the reader can follow her footsteps through Regency Bath and the new seaside resorts of Devon and Dorset that provided such a breath of fresh air – and romance – for the dutiful Austen sisters.

Next there is a survey of literary salons large and small, ranging from the magnificence of Knole under the Sackvilles to the tea and muffins cosiness of Henry James entertaining at Lamb House, Rye. This essay also considers the way country houses have been used as microcosms of society by novelists as different as Benjamin Disraeli, H.G.Wells and Evelyn Waugh.

The Lake District has long been a haunt of literati, especially of the impoverished sort. But it also has a special kinship with romance, and the 'Muses and Mountains' chapter (which might just as well have been called 'Ladies of the Lakes') concentrates on just this aspect of its hills, lakes and dales. Wordsworth is seen through the eyes of his adoring sister, and Coleridge as a would-be lover. Posthumous affection is offered to the agile and erudite 'fell-climbing philosopheress' Elizabeth Smith by Thomas de Quincey, and to the legendary Maid of Buttermere by Melvyn Bragg. Finally, there is an imaginary dreamgirl: Arthur Ransome's Nancy Blackett.

Chapter Six moves south to Dorset and Cornwall to explore Thomas Hardy's Wessex, surely the most intensely experienced landscape in fiction. I concentrate on two books that are especially connected to landscape: the early novel *A Pair of Blue Eyes*, set on the North Cornish coast where Hardy fell so deeply in love with his first wife, and *Tess of the D'Urbervilles*, a tragic calvary of a book, full of arduous journeyings.

'Bloomsbury by the Sea' concentrates on the intense world of the Bloomsbury set when it left its London heartland and escaped to Sussex and to Cornwall. Virginia Woolf at Monk's House and her sister Vanessa Bell at nearby Charleston were at the heart of the group: no one has written more sensuously about domestic delights than Virginia, or painted them more seductively than Vanessa.

I have always had a greedy appetite for thrillers and detective novels, and Chapter Eight is sheer self-indulgence: an excuse to read lots more

Beatrix Potter and her husband William Heelis on their wedding day in October 1913.

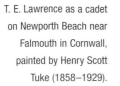

T. E. Lawrence as a cadet on Newporth Beach near Falmouth in Cornwall, painted by Henry Scott Tuke (1858–1929).

of them in order to find out what lies behind the very English obsession with who murdered whom with the candlestick in the library in the vicarage. Were tightly timetabled domestic arrangements peculiarly well-suited to Agatha Christie's devious plots, and is the present enthusiasm for clumsily violent thrillers set in exact landscapes a reflection of today's sloppy housekeeping?

Complementing the eight essays are cameo 'snapshots' of writers at home: Kipling at work on his own ancient British story *Puck of Pook's Hill* at Bateman's in Sussex; Hardy's near neighbour T. E. Lawrence in self-chosen solitude at Clouds Hill in Dorset; Beatrix Potter contentedly becoming Mrs Heelis at Hill Top in Cumbria; Vita Sackville-West looking down from her tower study at Sissinghurst Castle in Kent to the garden she and Harold had created. Finally, to compensate for the many omissions, there is a Gazetteer, which lists the literary connections of Trust properties and lands in each of its various regions.

Over the years I have spent researching and writing the book, I have been helped a little by a lot of people and a lot by a few people. The local knowledge of the many volunteers who staff the Trust properties was invaluable; they have been picking up unconsidered trifles for years and were generous in passing them on. The London Library has the same serendipitous quality: being able to wander its echoing stacks of open

Caricature by Dante Gabriel Rossetti of his sister Christina's tantrum after reading an adverse review of her poetry in *The Times*. The picture hangs in the dining-room at Wightwick Manor in the West Midlands.

shelves always turns up unexpected treasures. Furnished as it now is with a computer search facility as well as its noble old leather-backed volumes, it offers the best of both worlds. Oxford's Bodleian Library has also been invaluable, so too have numerous literary societies and local museums and centres of information.

To travel hopefully is better than to arrive. I may have included my own favourite writers; I have probably left out those of many of my readers. By the time I finished this book, I had become horribly conscious of my own ignorance. As I settled down to proof-read, it struck me that someone somewhere knows more than me about every author in this book, with the possible exception of one. I await their chiding with dread, although I have done what I can to check and double-check my facts. In this context, I am deeply indebted to the many experts who have been kind enough to read relevant parts of the book and to correct at least some of its errors.

Advice, encouragement and information has been essential for such a wide-ranging project. I would like to give especial thanks to Mavis Batey, Nicola and Chris Beauman, Alan Bell, Stuart N. Clarke, Elizabeth Crawford, Oliver Garnett, Martin Haggerty, Jessica Mann, Martin Meredith, Sandy Mitchell, Nicholas Soames, D.J.Taylor, and Professor Charles Thomas. Sailing with Ian Howlett at Medley Sailing Club has been a healthy distraction.

On the professional side, I am very indebted to my agent Gill Coleridge, the National Trust's publisher Margaret Willes, my copy-editor Sarah Dancy, the book's designer Bridget Heal, Trevor Bounford for the admirably clear and simple maps and Samantha Wyndham and Helen George for help with picture research. Most of the burden of marshalling the many different elements of what seemed at times a wildly over-ambitious project has fallen on the shoulders of my editor Helen Fewster. Without her unique combination of generous enthusiasm and tactful goadings, I would probably still be collecting quotations and vaguely dreaming.

The Pen and the Place

The place in which a famous writer wrote and the tools of his or her craft are potent magic. The studies, libraries or humble workhuts of famous writers are always the places in which visitors linger longest if their houses are opened to the public. Most attractive of all is the actual desk or table they used – preferably still displaying aged pens and blotched notebooks, framed photographs and a clutter of loved mementoes. It is as if by visualising exactly where and how a writer worked, something of the mystery of their genius will be revealed. Perhaps, we hope, a little of it might brush off on us. Oscar Wilde certainly acquired Thomas Carlyle's writing desk 'with the hope of recalling memories of Titanic labour'.

A winding stair, a chamber arched with stone,

A grey stone fireplace with an open hearth,

A candle and a written page.

W. B. Yeats, 'My House'

Writing is normally a solitary process, requiring a settled environment, safe from interruption. The earliest and most elegant of such places were the carrels and scriptoria of abbeys, where monks laboured to preserve the written evidences of civilisation before Gutenberg's invention of movable type in the fifteenth century. Besides writing and copying religious texts, they wrote chronicles that form the basis of our knowledge of history. Abbeys were often established on islands that now seem to us exceptionally remote. But in fact communications were far easier by sea than by any other way, and such positions made the abbeys more, not less, accessible to their contemporaries. Lindisfarne on the Northumberland coast, Bardsey Island off the Llŷn peninsula in North Wales and Iona at the tip of Mull were all important missionary centres. Visitors could, however, be hostile as well as friendly. When Saxon and Viking raids made the islands hazardous, monks fled inland to safer, genuinely remote valleys. New, less sociable, orders were established, such as the Cistercians, whose greatest British foundation is Fountains Abbey, hidden deep in Yorkshire in the valley of the Skell.

The monasteries worked out a system whereby the talented worker

William Bell Scott's mural of *The Death of Bede* at Wallington Hall in Northumberland, showing the scriptorium at Jarrow Priory. The Venerable Bede died in 735, just after he had completed his translation of St John's Gospel into Anglo-Saxon.

in their scriptorium was domestically supported by other members of the community. The colleges of Oxford and Cambridge, most of them originally religious foundations, followed the same pattern, and generations of scholars have benefited from the regular regime of quiet study in a room of their own, an opportunity to take exercise in the afternoons (*mens sana in corpore sano*) and communal evening meals to provide society and stimulation. The more recent writers with which this book is primarily concerned also needed both peace and a sense of being domestically supported in order to work well. Achieving a balance between the two, especially in the context of family life, often proved difficult.

When it came to finding a good place in which to live and work, luck was probably the most important factor. It was chance that led Rudyard and Carrie Kipling in 1900 to 'The Very Own House', the mellow old manor house of Bateman's, Burwash, East Sussex. Recognition was instant. 'That's her!' cried Carrie. 'The Only She! Make an honest woman of her – quick!' They lived there for the rest of their lives.

Prosperity also helped in 'suiting alike fancy and necessity' as Henry James put it. Money was no object when Winston and Clementine Churchill bought Chartwell, Kent, and the surrounding 22 acres of land in 1922. Philip Tilden, a popular architect of the day who had just finished a house for Lloyd George, was commissioned to remodel and extend it. 'No client that I have ever had', Tilden later wrote ruefully, 'has ever spent more time, trouble, or interest in the making of his home than did Mr Churchill.'

Sometimes it is a childhood home which has been the ideal place in which to write. Gilbert White lived in the same house, The Wakes, at Selborne, Hampshire, for all but the first eight years of his seventy-three-year life. Hardy's Cottage, Dorset, had been in Thomas Hardy's family for generations before he was born there in 1840. Although he built a more formal mansion nearby at Max Gate to suit his increasing eminence, the humble cottage at Higher Bockhampton always remained

Thomas Hardy at Max Gate by Augustus John (1923). Hardy said of the portrait, 'I don't know if that is how I look, but that is how I *feel*'.

closest to his heart. He wrote his first novels there, and some of his most haunting poems came to him on later visits to it.

If such a home is lost, memories of it can be so powerful that they become a recurring theme in a writer's work. The experiences of William and Dorothy Wordsworth in their childhood home at Cockermouth, Cumbria, now Wordsworth House, are frequently referred to in their poems, journals and letters. As a girl, Vita Sackville-West could not inherit Knole, Kent, a house so close to her heart that she wrote both a history of it and her family (*Knole and the Sackvilles*, 1922) and *The Edwardians* (1930), a novel set in 'Chevron', a thinly disguised Knole. She also wrote the first National Trust guidebook to the house in 1948. Her great friend Virginia Woolf paid tribute to both Vita and her feelings for the house in *Orlando: A Biography* (1928), a time-travelling novel set in part at Knole, and with a sex-switching hero based on Vita and all her Sackville ancestors. The illustrations first envisaged for the book included a photograph of Vita dressed like a Lely portrait and sitting inside a huge gilded frame.

The right house for a writer is not always instantly recognised as such. Carlyle's house in London was constantly declared by its irascible and over-sensitive owner to be impossibly noisy, but it was also immensely convenient, and he and Jane stayed there – though not without frequent complainings. George Bernard Shaw and his wife Charlotte intended the red-brick rectory at Ayot St Lawrence, Hertfordshire, to be a temporary escape from London; they had no idea that they would rechristen it Shaw's Corner and live there for the rest of their long lives.

Writers need very different degrees of isolation. Kipling's study was in the heart of Bateman's, as was Churchill's at Chartwell. Both were exceptionally family-minded; both had remarkable powers of concentration. 'I never had a dull or idle moment from morning to midnight, and with my happy family around me dwelt at peace within my habitation', wrote Churchill. But it was essential for such hub-of-the-house studies to be treated as sacred by spouses, children and servants, never to be invaded except at certain agreed hours. Elsie Kipling recalled that if her father 'was really busy with a piece of work he was utterly absorbed in it and quite oblivious of anything else. [We] learned very early to keep any requests or plans until . . . he "came back".'

More commonly, writers sought greater distance from the rattle of domesticity. Tennyson's first floor library-study at Farringford House, Freshwater, Isle of Wight, is tucked away down a narrow, winding corridor; a spiral staircase directly to the outside gave him a private means of entering and exiting. Disraeli wrote in his 'workshop', as he called his simple but cheerful upstairs room at Hughenden, Buckinghamshire, much more often than in his showy library downstairs.

Vita Sackville-West annexed the tower gateway of Sissinghurst Castle, Kent, and turned it into a sacrosanct writing retreat; her son Nigel says he entered it 'only half a dozen times' while she was alive. Arthur Ransome's study at Low Ludderburn, near Windermere, was in the upper storey of a great barn beside the house. The window faces south with a commanding view of Harter Fell. It was, he wrote in his *Autobiography*, 'the best working room I ever had'; it was here that he wrote *Swallows and Amazons* (1930).

Outbuildings of tiny proportions have proved perennial favourites with writers. They combine the advantage – often a necessity – of being cut off from the main house and its distractions with the convenience and cosiness of remaining relatively close to it, or even, as in George Bernard Shaw's case, umbilically linked to it by telephone. Roald Dahl used to work in a tiny shack in his Buckinghamshire garden with the curtains tightly closed. He liked it because it was 'small, tight, dark – a kind of womb, which no-one ever cleans or dusts'.

One of the most remote of writing retreats is the driftwood hut which Robert Hawker, the eccentric Vicar of Morwenstow, built high in the cliffs about a mile from his rectory. It must once have been a very secret place, tucked below the lip of the cliff fifty yards or so off the path. The door is divided in two, stable-like, to give more shelter from the great storms that lash the coast. Inside, it has a bench at each side and there is no room for a desk. It is a place to think in and make jottings, rather than to write for any length of time.

Perhaps inspired by Hawker, Tennyson built himself a wooden summer-house in Maiden's Croft meadow, just beyond the wood to the south of Farringford House, looking out at the woods and the downland. He decorated it with paintings of dragons and mythical beasts.

George Meredith first slung a hammock in his famous chalet study in the spring of 1877. It was just up the hill from his home, Flint Cottage, on Box Hill, Surrey (see also p.95). Before it was built he had had to write under siege from children, wife, butcher, baker and grocer. 'Once let me be free,' he wrote to a friend, 'and I'll be aloft like the stars of a rocket benignantly brightening and dying in heaven.' When he was working on the veranda, passers-by often heard him carrying on dialogues with his characters. The first book he finished in the chalet was *The Egoist* (1879); he also wrote some of his finest nature poems there.

Virginia Woolf's first 'writing-lodge' at Monk's House, Rodmell, was halfway down its three-quarter-acre garden. At first it was too cold to work there in winter, but later improvements – an oil-stove and a wc – made it 'a palace of comforts'. In 1934 profits from books enabled her to remove to the very bottom of the garden, where she could enjoy the magnificent views across the Sussex Downs. 'I like to have space to spread my mind out', she wrote in her diary in 1926. 'I don't want anyone to come here and interrupt. I am immensely busy.' She worked to a strict pattern, spending long mornings in her hut, then taking a solitary walk before returning to revise what she had written.

Daphne du Maurier liked working in a garden hut well away from her house in Cornwall. It was originally built in 1949 so that she could continue to work without interruptions while the roof of the house was being mended, but she found it so conducive to work that she continued to use it. 'It's ideal', she wrote to her friend Ellen Doubleday. 'It's at the end of the stretch of grass here, that looks down at the far end at the sea . . .

curiously enough, it's just a few yards from the place I've always wanted for my grave.' Photographs of her working there suggest that its furnishings were spartan, with only a dictionary, an ashtray, and a few small loved things on her desk – but perhaps she had tidied up for the camera.

Henry Williamson (1895-1977) spent the Hawthornden Prize money he won for *Tarka The Otter* in 1927 on a couple of acres of copse and down at Ox's Cross, high above Woolacombe in North Devon. On this 'hill of winds', 500ft above sea level, he could look west to Baggy Point, a favourite haunt, south across the Taw Torridge estuary and beyond to Lundy and Hartland Point. The field was his holdfast for the rest of his life, and he built a series of huts and, eventually, in 1974, a proper house there.

W. B. Yeats (1865-1939) discovered 'the old square castle' of Ballylee in 1896 while rambling through Galway, and describes it in *The Celtic Twilight* (1893). He did not buy it until 1916, when he was fifty-one, and moved in with his wife George and his daughter Anne in 1919. It was converted for him by the Dublin architect William Scott, a 'drunken genius' who designed both the simple interiors and the furniture. The tower inspired some of his finest poems – 'The Wild Swans at Coole', 'The Tower' and 'The Winding Stair'. Yeats either wrote in the large ground-floor room – 'the pleasantest room I have yet seen, a great wide window opening over the river' – or in the bedroom directly above, where George had painted the ceiling in blue, black and gold. 'Stone stairs to my surprise are the most silent of all stairs and sitting as I am now upstairs in the Tower I have a sense of solitude and silence', he wrote to Olivia Shakespeare in June 1922.

Coleridge rented his cottage at Nether Stowey, Somerset, in the hope of being able to work without distraction, but a plague of mice, the high spirits of his son Hartley and the many visitors he invited made the cottage itself distracting and noisy. He took to working in his neighbour Tom Poole's 'book-parlour' a peaceful book-lined room which he could reach through a gate between the two gardens. He also used to take long

Coleridge's Cottage: Nether Stowey

View of the rugged
North Devon coast,
a favourite haunt of
Henry Williamson.

walks along the coast and stay overnight at farms; it was probably at Ash Farm at the head of Culbone Combe that he wrote all there was to be of 'Kubla Khan' (1816). All his life he solved the problem of personal domestic interruptions by running away from them, going on long visits to only half-enthusiastic friends or scribbling in the open air.

Life was easier for bachelors. T. E. Lawrence's Clouds Hill, Dorset, even lacked the responsibility of a kitchen. It was, he wrote to his friend Jock Chambers in August 1924, 'very quiet, very lonely, very bare ... Furnished with a bed, a bicycle, three chairs, 100 books, a gramophone of parts, a table. Many windows, oak-trees, an ilex, birch, firs, rhododendrons, laurels, heather. Dorsetshire to look at. No food, except what a grocer & the camp shops provide. Milk. Wood fuel for the picking up.'

When T. H. White gave up schoolmastering at Stowe, Buckinghamshire, he rented a similarly spartan cottage on the estate at Stowe Ridings. He described it as 'snug as a badger's set', and it closely resembled the forest lair where the Wart discovers Merlyn in *The Sword in the Stone*, which was written there in 1938.

'A room of one's own' was, according to Virginia Woolf's famous book of that title, an essential desideratum. But not all great writers either had or needed solitude. Jane Austen is perhaps the most outstanding example of a writer of genius who never seems to have had any private space. At Chawton, Hampshire, she shared a bedroom with her sister Cassandra; she wrote at a tiny three-legged table in the dining-room when nothing else was happening there. Legend has it that she discouraged the use of oil on the squeaky hinge of the hall door so that she would be warned of anyone's approach, and could conceal what she was writing.

Sir Arthur Conan Doyle positively enjoyed writing at a table in a room crowded with friends. Jerome K. Jerome reported that

> He would sit at a desk in his own drawing-room, writing a story, while a dozen people round him were talking and laughing. He preferred it to being alone in his study. Sometimes, without

The cottage at Nether
Stowey in Somerset was
Coleridge's home during
the three years in which
he wrote 'Kubla Khan'
and the 'Rime of the
Ancient Mariner'. He
rarely worked in the
house; it was too full
of domestic distractions.

looking up … he would make a remark, showing he must have been listening to our conversation, but his pen never ceased moving.

Thackeray told a friend that '[I do] most of my composition at hotels or at a club. There is an excitement in public places which sets my brain working'. George Bernard Shaw wrote every day, regardless of where he was. 'I had either to write under all circumstances or not at all,' he explained, 'and I have retained this independence of external amenities to this day. A very considerable part of my plays have been written in railway carriages between King's Cross and Hatfield.' Anthony Trollope, whose day job as Post Office surveyor meant much travelling, also worked in the train:

> I made for myself … a little tablet, and found, after a few days' exercise that I could write as quickly in a railway carriage as I could at my desk. I worked with a pencil, and what I wrote my wife copied out afterwards.

This imperviousness to outside circumstances was unusual. What writers almost always needed was a happy balance between companionship and solitude. The people they lived with often had their work cut out providing such a balance – choosing the right life partner was evidently as important as finding the right writing environment. Kipling's American wife Carrie guarded his privacy jealously when he was at work. A striking portrait shows her as a stern domestic angel, a chatelaine hanging from her waist. Thomas Hardy's second wife Florence was also an able gatekeeper, careful to protect 'the Wessex Wizard' from all but welcome visitors. In their fascinating book *Mothering The Mind* (1984) Ruth Perry and Martine Brownley celebrate the value of such relationships. They also point out that such 'mothers', who include Leonard Woolf and George Henry Lewes, are not necessarily female.

A portrait of Caroline
Kipling (1899) by Philip
Burne-Jones which hangs
over the fireplace in the
study at Bateman's.

The Noisiest Room in the House

Left: Thomas Carlyle outside his house in Cheyne Row. Engraving by Henry and Walter Greaves (1859).

Below: Robert Tait's conversation piece, *A Chelsea Interior,* painted in 1857, shows the Carlyles in their parlour.

Is it not strange that I should have an everlasting sound in my ears, of men, women, children, omnibuses, carriages …steeple bells, door bells, gentleman-raps, two-penny-post-raps, footmen-showers-of-raps, of the whole devil to pay, as if plague, pestilence, famine, battle, murder, sudden death and wee Eppie Daidle were broken loose to make me diversion?

Thomas Carlyle, *Letters*

The Titanic literary labours of Thomas Carlyle were carried out in spite of, rather than because of, his chosen home. At the age of thirty-nine, he and his wife Jane moved to London from Scotland in 1834, renting Number 5 Cheyne Row, a tall narrow house which would remain their home for the rest of their lives. Built in 1708, in Chelsea's first fashionable heyday, it had become one of 'numerous old houses' in the area which Thomas described approvingly as 'at once cheap and excellent'. At the front, it had views through ancient elms to open ground; at the back the outlook was over hayfields to the turrets of Westminster Abbey and the Houses of Parliament.

Our knowledge of the Carlyles' domestic lives is unusually detailed because of Jane's wonderful letters ('I never sit down at night, beside a good fire, alone, without feeling a need of talking a little, on paper, to someone I like', runs one of them). A recurring theme is Carlyle's hypersensitivity to noise. After the peace of his Dumfriesshire farm, London was a shock: clattering

hooves and wheels, harsh shouts from coachmen, street cries, piano-playing and barking dogs from nearby houses.

His own household was often in uproar. Jane was an exacting and thrifty employer with a hot temper; her husband was not much better ('Mr C *exploded* Fanny some fortnight ago', wrote Jane in 1854). They ran through thirty-nine housemaids in thirty-two years, to say nothing of temporary helps. One gave birth to 'a little misfortune' in the china-closet and smuggled it out of the house wrapped in the best table-napkins. But Carlyle hated working in libraries – he was a driving force in the creation of the London Library, from which books could be borrowed and used at home. He experimented with working and sleeping in almost every room in the house, including the kitchen.

In 1854 substantial profits from his books meant he could afford to build a sound-proof study in the attic. It is a womb within a room, with double walls at front and back. It is lit only from above, by a skylight fitted with 'two glazed sashes to run on brass rollers, forming an air chamber between', and a roller-blind. The roof was covered with 'best Bangor slate'. Patent ventilators on each side of the fireplace admitted fresh air. The conversion, designed by Cubitt's, cost £169. 'All the cocks in nature may crow round it, without my hearing a whisper of them!' declared Thomas with excited anticipation.

It didn't work. Through the skylight he heard noises once drowned by more ambient din – river hooters, train whistles and church bells. Jane announced that it was 'the noisiest room in the house'. Thomas said that he loathed the tank-like room, but he did use it for the next thirteen years, while writing his monumental history of Frederick the Great.

Carlyle photographed by
Robert Tait at his writing-
desk in his attic study.

WRITING FURNITURE

So much for settings: what of the practicalities? Desks, chairs, day-beds and lighting arrangements matter enormously. Sitting in comfort with small familiar things at one's fingertips may make all the difference between sustained and intermittent production. Pictures in the initials of medieval manuscripts show that early writing-desks were remarkably sophisticated. They often had high-backed seats with a slope that swung down rather like the tray of a baby's high chair, and could be adjusted to a convenient height and gradient. Books and parchment rolls were either kept in special chests or chained to shelves. We know from a reference made in 1286 by the Franciscan Roger Bacon that by then monks were wearing spectacles if necessary; fragments of an ancient pair have been found at Battle Abbey in Sussex.

Carlyle adopted an arrangement not dissimilar to that of the medieval scribes. He sat in a dining-room carver chair at a small desk with a large hinged flap that swung out towards him. A footstool stood underneath the desk. Light was provided by a candle in a patent candlestick which had a hood that both reflected more light and shielded it from draughts.

Henry James had several different work places: a high desk at which he stood, a swivel-desk attached to his day-bed, and a large knee-hole desk at which he could sit.

Virginia Woolf also liked to use a high desk to write at for a change. She didn't often actually write at the table in her garden workroom; it was too heaped with books and papers. According to her husband Leonard, she sat in a very low chair, its springs collapsed through the base, balancing 'on her knees a large board made of plywood which had an inkstand glued to it, and on the board was a large pad of quarto paper which she had bound up for her and covered herself in (usually) some gaily-coloured paper.'

Churchill sometimes worked at the high, wide writing slope on which his research assistants laid out the archive material they ferreted out for him. But he was a traditionalist at heart. When he had Chartwell rebuilt, he installed a writing-table similar in almost every detail to the one he had described in his only novel, *Savrola*, written in 1897 when he was twenty-three:

> A broad writing-table occupied the place of honour. It was arranged so that the light fell conveniently to hand and head. A large bronze inkstand formed the centrepiece, with a voluminous blotting-pad of simple manufacture spread open before it. The rest of the table was occupied by papers or files. The floor, in spite of the ample wastepaper basket, was littered with scraps. It was the writing-table of a public man.

The table was his own, inherited from his father; it can still be seen at Chartwell, set sideways to the window. His mementoes and necessaries are still in place on it: a silver inkstand and worn green leather blotter, a red-edged calendar, a silver ruler, a small bust of Nelson given to him by Lord Northcliffe, spectacles, a cigar-cutter, a green leather writing-case and a bundle of treasury tags. Propped against a leg of the desk is one of

Churchill's desk, in the study at Chartwell in Kent.

his monthly engagement cards, crowded with appointments and commitments for July 1937.

Kipling's desk was also covered with familiar talismans, most of which can still be seen in his study at Bateman's. He listed them lovingly in his autobiographical *Something of Myself*:

> I always kept certain gadgets on my work-table, which was ten feet long from North to South and badly congested. One was a long, lacquer canoe-shaped pen-tray full of brushes and dead 'fountains'; a wooden box held clips and bands; another, a tin one, pins; yet another, a bottle-slider, kept all manner of unneeded essentials from emery-paper to small screw-drivers; a paperweight said to be Warren Hastings'; a tiny weighted fur-seal and a crocodile sat on some of the papers; an inky foot rule and a Father of Penwipers which a much-loved housemaid of ours presented yearly, made up the main-guard of these little fetishes.

Underneath the table was a vast wastepaper basket into which spoiled sheets of paper were hurled, not always accurately. His walnut workchair was raised on blocks to make it a comfortable height for writing. He faced the long mullioned east window; light also came from a smaller south-facing window to his right. On each side of the table there was a very large globe. His oak day-bed, a crucial part of his writing process, stood like that of so many writers, at right angles to the fire. He lay on it to await the inspiration of his 'daemon'. There is a cigarette burn on its arm; before his doctor advised him to take up a pipe, Kipling used to smoke thirty to forty cigarettes a day. Visitors remember the room bathed in a blue haze of smoke.

In his great barn workroom at Low Ludderburn, Arthur Ransome worked at a very large table, covered with a baize cloth and sometimes extended by putting a folding card-table next to it. His customary *batterie d'écrivain* is described in detail by Hugh Brogan:

There was … a tin of pen-nibs, because he never used a fountain-pen; a typewriter, because he did use that; seal and sealing wax for parcels; mapping pen and pencils, in a china tray, for drawing (a special anti-roll device … was a Turk's Head knot tied in string about the waist of each pencil); an antique Russian ink-well; an ash-tray, also Russian, carved out of wood in the shape of a duck with a hole in its back; a black cat, for luck: a little one of plaster, bought in Egypt, reproducing an ancient figurine; a lucky stone from the top of Coniston Old Man … There were also: two dismountable miniature candlesticks, which had been very useful in unlighted railway carriages on his Russian travels; a miniature telescope; a 'bun' penny; a George III penny; a pocket compass.

Arthur Ransome in his much-loved first floor barn workroom at Low Ludderburn in Cumbria.

Most of these objects can be seen in the Arthur Ransome Room at the Abbot Hall Museum of Rural Life in Kendal, Cumbria. They now stand on a desk Ransome inherited from his father and which he used in later years in less glorious workrooms.

Not all writers liked sitting down at a desk to write. If Wordsworth sat down with a pen, he perspired and got a pain in his chest. Excursions far afield inspired his poetic themes, but for actual composition he used to pace a favourite walk, a flattish stroll along the southern bank of Rydal Water to Red Bank, on the edge of Grasmere, again and again, 'as fast bound within his chosen limits as if by prison walls', reported his sister Dorothy. Afterwards, he needed help in the physical act of setting down his compositions. Dorothy and other 'female devotees', as Coleridge enviously described William's household of dedicated women, were his amanuenses.

Coleridge himself liked 'to compose walking over uneven ground, or breaking through the straggling branches of copse-wood'. It was while walking together in the Quantocks that Coleridge and Wordsworth decided to combine for profit in the writing of a ballad based on the dream that a friend had recounted to Coleridge. Wordsworth, who had

Thomas Carlyle smoking in the garden at Cheyne Row in 1857.

been reading a book about sea voyages, suggested that killing an albatross could make 'the tutelary spirits of these regions take upon them to avenge the crime'. But their approaches to composition were wildly disparate, and in the event it was Coleridge who wrote 'The Rime of the Ancient Mariner'.

Tennyson liked company when he roamed around Freshwater; he would often 'chant a poem he was composing and add fresh lines', reported his son Hallam. He was eighty when he wrote his famous poem, 'Crossing The Bar'. During the twenty-minute crossing from Yarmouth to Lymington, he unfolded a used envelope and jotted the sixteen lines down. At dinner that night, he showed it to Hallam, who said, 'It is the crown of your life's work.' 'It came in a moment', he replied.

Sitting outside on fine days had obvious attractions. Virginia Woolf often moved her writing-chair on to the shady brick terrace in front of her hut. Thomas Carlyle rigged up a cogitation tent in his garden, not least so he could smoke his pipe without being grumbled at by Jane. John Galsworthy used to sit out on the lawn 'with a blotter on his knee and a china inkpot at his feet', according to a nephew. John Masefield always wrote out of doors if he could, 'until the rain makes the ink run, or the frost freezes it on my pen'.

What of writing implements? Charles Dickens used goose-quills and blue ink, occasionally black. He wrote on blue-grey paper measuring 8½ by 7¼in. Disraeli originally used goose-quills, but graduated to steel nibs. One of his favourites had a porcupine quill-holder.

When John Steinbeck came to England to research Arthurian sites for his reworking of Thomas Malory's *Morte d'Arthur*, he threw himself into the spirit of things by living in a medieval house (Discove Cottage at Bruton, Somerset) and inventing a pen that married old and new technology:

The wing quill of a goose is the best for weight and balance, the curve and the texture of the quill is not foreign to the touch like metal or plastics. Therefore I mount the best fillers from ball point pens in the stem of the quill and thus have for me the best of all writing instruments.

Kipling wrote on large pads of blue paper that were specially made for him. Pens were important:

> In Lahore for my *Plain Tales* I used a slim, octagonal-sided agate penholder with a Waverley nib. It was a gift, and when in an evil hour I snapped it, I was much disturbed. Then followed a procession of impersonal hirelings each with a Waverley [nib], and next a silver penholder with a quill-like curve, which promised well but did not perform … I then abandoned hand-dipped Waverleys – a nib I never changed – and for years wallowed in the pin-pointed 'stylo' and its successor the 'fountain' which for me meant geyser-pens. In later years I clung to a slim, smooth black treasure (Jael was her office name) which I picked up in Jerusalem. I tried pump-pens with glass insides, but they were intolerable entrails.

Extract from Carlyle's blotched and barred second manuscript of *The French Revolution*.

In later years, Kipling took to using a typewriter, but he was never very expert at it. He enjoyed drawing – he did the elaborate and fantastical letters for 'How the Alphabet was Made' in the *Just So Stories*.

Henry James dictated to a typist. He had several over the years. Miss Weld, a Rye local, wrote that 'he dictated beautifully … Typewriting for him was exactly like accompanying a singer on the piano'. His sentences 'seemed to spread out across the page like the beautiful architecture of this medieval town'. The sound and rhythm of the typing mattered to him, and he preferred a Remington to any other make. 'During the fortnight when the Remington was out of order, he dictated to an Oliver typewriter with evident discomfort, and found it impossibly disconcerting to write to something that made no responsive sound at all', wrote another secretary, Theodora Bosanquet. James revised his sentences as he dictated, a method which made the end result convoluted and prolix. But he liked what he called his 'Remingtonese'; he felt it increased expressiveness.

G.K. Chesterton dictated – very slowly – to a secretary and very rarely made corrections. According to Jack Hodges (to whose *Makers of the Omnibus* I am indebted for many of the details in this chapter), 'his wife read the proofs' and 'was paid a halfpenny for an omitted comma, a penny for any correction of spelling or style, twopence if she made a suggestion which was accepted, and sixpence if it was particularly good'.

Sir Walter Scott never revised. His narrative 'flowed like fireside talk'. In his prime, Dickens rarely corrected his regular 2,000 words-a-day output, but towards the end of his life he revised assiduously. Hodges recalls 'seeing, in the V&A, the last page of the unfinished manuscript of *Edwin Drood*, found on Dickens's desk when he died. Crossings out, insertions and loops were a moving witness to the toil that composition exacted – even for one of the most prolific professionals – during his later life.'

As only one of Jane Austen's original manuscripts survives, we know very little about how much she revised them, but she read her stories aloud to friends and took advice humbly. There is also the evidence of a letter to Cassandra about *Pride and Prejudice* (29 January 1813): 'I have lop't and crop't so successfully that I imagine it must be rather shorter than S&S [*Sense and Sensibility*]'.

Thomas Carlyle changed his mind frequently, and his alterations and re-alterations of page proofs were the despair of printers. He hated the actual process of writing, working on scrappy bits of paper and frequently despairing of progress. His wife Jane described him as 'fidgetting and flurrying about all the while like a hen in the distraction of laying its first egg'; he once bemoaned the fact that 'after two weeks of blotching and barring I have produced two clean pages'. He frequently tossed a whole morning's work on the fire. It was not, however, his idea to burn the whole finished manuscript of his famous *French Revolution*. That was the work of John Stuart Mill's housemaid, who thought the scruffy heap that Carlyle had given Mill to read was waste paper.

Kipling threw away copiously, seeing first drafts as 'practising, like scales'. The desk would achieve impressive heights of chaos, and both it and Rudyard himself became generously endowed with spots of ink. Ruthless revision was, for him, an essential stage in production, and he employed a special method:

Take of well-ground Indian Ink as much as suffices and a camel-hair brush proportionate to the inter-spaces of your lines. In an auspicious hour, read your final draft and consider faithfully every paragraph, sentence and word, blacking out where requisite. Let it lie by to drain as long as possible…I have had tales by me for three or five years which have shortened themselves almost yearly. The magic lies in the Brush and the Ink. For the Pen, when it is writing, can only scratch; and bottled ink is not to compare with the ground Chinese stick.

Churchill was also an inveterate reviser, circulating his first draft to friends and then revising proofs as often as six times. Speeches were written out in full on octavo sheets held together with treasury tags. They were laid out like blank verse, with phrases, or even individual words, that required special emphasis on separate lines. Pauses and breath marks were all carefully indicated.

The reviser to beat all revisers was William Wordsworth, who believed that 'absolute success…depends on innumerable minutiae'.

Wordsworth informs us he was nineteen years
Considering and retouching Peter Bell…

wrote Shelley of him, concluding caustically:

E.F. Benson, who lived at Lamb House in Sussex after Henry James, also enjoyed the companionship of his dogs. Here Taffy appears with Benson in the garden in the early 1930s.

…Heaven and Earth conspire to foil
The over-busy gardener's blundering toil.

Wordsworth was also quite immune to deadlines, preferring to be poor than to risk publishing anything he was not quite satisfied with. Having finished *The Prelude* in 1805, he spent until 1839 adding small alterations and new touches, then put it away in an iron chest with instructions that it should not be opened until after his death.

Finally, it seems important to mention the need of writers for the silent and undemanding companionship of pets. A whole book could be written on such devoted and faithful familiars; indeed, Virginia Woolf, an enthusiastic dog-owner, did write a whole book about Elizabeth Barrett Browning's dog *Flush* (1933). If it were ever to be written, *Doggies and Moggies as Muses* would star Henry James's dachshunds Tosca and Max, Kipling's string of Aberdeen terriers, Thomas Hardy's well-filled pets' graveyard at Max Gate, Thomas Carlyle's canary Chico and Jane Carlyle's dog Nero. Henry Williamson's many animal companions became the heroes and heroines of his books. It is a curious sidelight on Churchill that he had an aquarium of fish in his study; he was also enormously fond of his swans and geese.

The ultimate in adoration was that given by T. H. White to his red setter Brownie. White was adopted by Brownie while spending the Christmas holidays in the Crown Inn at Tingewick, near Stowe School, where he taught English. She became his inseparable companion, as his roseate paean of praise to her, by Hopkins out of Joyce, conveys.

On the way home from Silverstone I drove with my arm around Brownie, calling her: red setter, sorrel, Indian red, royal sovereign, red-hot poker, sanguine, nut-brown maid, goldfish, marmalade, conker, vixen, crust of bread, 18 carat, carrots, mahogany, chrysanthemum, bloom of rust and blue of shade. In fact, she is my Pocahontas, my nonpareil.

A Living Shrine

A man who has no office to go to – I don't care who he is –

is a trial of which you can have no conception.

George Bernard Shaw, *The Irrational Knot*

Shaw's Corner in Hertfordshire.

Shaw's Corner, at Ayot St Lawrence, Hertfordshire, is well hidden. To get there, take exit 6 off the A1(M) to Welwyn Garden City. Take the road to Codicote, then turn sharp left where a signpost indicates that it is two miles to Ayot St Lawrence. It seems longer; the lanes are narrow and windy and the countryside is as timelessly tranquil as it was in 1906 when George Bernard Shaw, aged fifty, and his wife Charlotte, aged forty-seven, moved in search of peace. The house, formerly a rectory and built of dark red brick in 1898, looks the epitome of sensible domesticity. Inside, it feels comfortable and serious, full of affection rather than romance. It is hard to find any single beautiful object, yet the house overflows with the energy of its former occupants.

Although Shaw had a well-used study in the heart of his house, whenever it was fine he worked in a summer-house hidden away in the garden. It was a haven of peace – not least because although only a few minutes' walk away from the house, his wife Charlotte could truthfully say he was out when unwanted visitors called. A telephone to the house provided a connection to base when necessary.

Spartan as a monk's cell and only six foot square, the hut reflects Shaw's love of invention and contrivance. It was originally slightly suspended from the iron gallows which can still be seen behind it, so it could be turned to catch the sunshine, then wedged still again. Shaw used the hut in both summer and winter: the walls were covered with panels of asbestos to preserve heat, and electricity for a fire and a desk-light came through a thickly insulated cable from the rectory's private generating plant. The work-table is hinged to the wall so that it can be folded down when not in use. Shaw covered it with a fringed woollen cloth when he sat at it in his wicker chair to type – he was one of the first authors to use a typewriter for his first drafts. Beside the table was a large wastepaper basket. Hinged to another wall is a couchette-style bunk on which Shaw lay down after lunch to read and have his afternoon nap. On a shelf was a thermometer, a wind-on calendar, an alarm clock and a toothbrush.

The Shaws did not expect to stay in Ayot St Lawrence as long as they did. They kept a London home as well, where they generally spent the middle of the week. But they grew more rather than less fond of the place. Shaw rechristened the house Shaw's Corner and had a doorknocker made in his own image. It is the first of an extraordinary number of likenesses all over the house. But do not assume too fast from them that Shaw was incurably vain. He was certainly not backwards in coming forward – 'I have advertised myself so well that I find myself, whilst still in middle life, almost as legendary a person as the Flying Dutchman', he wrote in the preface to *Three Plays for Puritans* in 1900. But after he decided to give the house to the National Trust, he transferred all the 'Shaviana' from his White-hall Court flat (formerly the home of the novelist Elizabeth von Arnim) in order 'to titivate Shaw's Corner as a showplace', as he told James Lees-Milne of the National Trust. 'The Trust can sell what is surplus to pay for repairs', he added.

Shaw was aware that to leave the house furnished with his personal possessions would add to its attraction. 'He wanted it to be a living shrine, not a dead museum', noted Lees-Milne after visiting Shaw, by then aged eighty-seven, in 1944. So the hall-stand still holds his many and varied hats and walking-sticks. Handel's *Messiah* and the Italian operatic airs he loved to play and sing are still on the piano, and upstairs his much prized rational woollen underwear and even his neatly boxed dentures remain in the drawers.

George Bernard Shaw's
garden writing hut
could be revolved to
face the sun.

The drawing-room was very much Charlotte's preserve. A dynamic, independently wealthy woman, she was once a suffragette and could easily have had an exciting life of her own had she not chosen to mother Shaw and his muse. The dining-room was one of Shaw's favourite places – he used to listen to the wireless (still there) while he ate, and, if not in his summer-house, he took his afternoon nap on the sofa there.

The study is all Shaw. His spectacles, pens, inkwell and typewriter lie on the desk; pocket French, German and Italian dictionaries and a tiny biographical and historical dictionary stand at the ready. To the right, over a tall reading slope, hangs a photograph of William Morris, whom Shaw called 'four great men rolled into one'; on the left, over his secretary Miss Patch's desk, there is one of his friend Philip Wicksteed, whose economic ideas he admired. Perhaps the most surprising of the many photographs of mentors and friends is one of G. K. Chesterton, Lord Howard de Walden, Sidney Webb, William Archer and Shaw himself, who is dressed in a cowboy suit; all were acting in an (uncompleted) film by J. M. Barrie.

On the fur-covered sofa that flanks the fireplace is a worn green neck-rest. Well-filled bookcases reflect Shaw's interests, and the filing cabinets are labelled, sometimes cryptically, in his

handwriting: Self, Novo, Ayot, Keys and Contraptions, Touring, Russia. There are also two cameras. Shaw's enthusiastic but distinctly amateur photographs illustrate his light-hearted last published work, a *Rhyming Guide to Ayot St Lawrence* (1950). He had initially been as shy of the villagers as they were of him, but over the years mutual respect and affection were established. The *Guide* is for sale at Shaw's Corner, and is well worth acquiring for a succession of such gems as 'Here we go with gait elastic / In step to doggerel Hudibrastic'.

Shaw would rise early, and work intensively. He took two hours off for lunch and to deal with letters, then read a book, usually falling asleep over it. In the afternoon he took exercise. He and Charlotte measured out a mile-long walk within the boundaries of the garden, and lapped themselves by removing pebbles placed on the kitchen window-sill. Less creative work took place later. In the evening he played the piano to Charlotte, or they listened to the radio. He was last to go to bed, and liked to go out if the night was clear to look at the stars.

Charlotte died in 1943, aged eighty-six, after a long illness. Shaw grieved for her deeply, but rallied and lived on, as lively and wittily irascible as ever, until his ninety-fifth year. He died in 1950, on his much-loved dining-room couch.

In Search of Lyonesse

Medieval romancers, Victorian poets and twentieth-century novelists have all found inspiration in the places associated with King Arthur, Lancelot and Tristram and Iseult. Three are especially famous. Tintagel, Cornwall, was the scene of Arthur's conception. South Cadbury, near Yeovil, Somerset, is the most convincing contender for Camelot, head-quarters of Arthur's realm during its brief golden age. Finally, Glastonbury, Somerset, was the Isle of Avalon, the sanctuary to which he was taken after being mortally wounded at the battle of Camlann.

In the last few decades, archaeological findings have discovered evidence that historical realities lie behind the spoken and written legends. It seems that Tintagel and Cadbury were both occupied by remarkably substantial military forces in the sixth century, when tradition has it that Arthur flourished. Although Glastonbury only became an Abbey in the eighth century, it was a Celtic sanctuary in pre-Roman times, and a Christian hermitage staffed by Welsh missionaries in the sixth century.

THE ARTHUR OF THE CHRONICLES

The most substantial early record of the doings of Arthur was written by Geoffrey of Monmouth, an Oxford-based scholar whose *Historia Regum Britanniae* first appeared in about 1140. It was good timing. Henry I appreciated storytellers and poets, and after half a century's occupation of England the Norman conquerors were eager to find romance and inspiration in the past of their new country. An heroic defender of the nation on the scale of, but quite distinct from, Charlemagne was a highly desirable property.

Geoffrey made use of such earlier chroniclers as Gildas (born *c*.516), the Venerable Bede and Nennius of Brecon, but he claims that the bulk of his text was transcribed from a 'most ancient book' in Welsh that he was asked to translate into Latin by Walter, Archdeacon of Oxford. As the stories were 'of exceeding beauty', he agreed, 'albeit that never have I gathered gay flowers of speech in other men's little gardens, and am content with mine own rustic manner of speech and my own writing-reeds'.

La Morte d'Arthur by James Archer (1861) reflects the Victorian fascination with the Arthurian legends.

Geoffrey's *Historia* includes Uther's magical seduction of Ygerna at Tintagel. But he gives Arthur a sister, Anna, and Arthur lives with her and his parents instead of being kept a secret and growing up in the care of Sir Ector. He sets Camelot at Caerleon-on-Usk; he also mentions Arthur holding court at Winchester and refers to battles in Cornwall. In Arthur's final battle with Mordred, Mordred is killed in a hand-to-hand battle on the River Camlann at Slaughterbridge, near Camelford. In his later *Life of Merlin*, Geoffrey elaborates on how the poet Taliesin takes the wounded Arthur in a ship to Avalon (Glastonbury) and the beautiful lady Morgan receives them with honour.

Geoffrey's account of Arthur seemed endorsed when, following a tip from a Celtic bard he encountered in Wales, Henry II (1133-89) ordered excavations to be made at Glastonbury in order to scotch the rumours that Arthur was about to reappear. Nothing was found in Henry's life-time, but in 1191 a tomb was discovered buried, as the bard had promised, between two pillars in the cemetery. On it was a leaden cross on which was inscribed HIC IACET SEPULTUS INCLITUS REX ARTURIUS IN INSULA AVALONIA – 'here lies buried the renowned King Arthur in the Isle of Avalon'. Inside, it is said, was a great oak coffin containing the bones of a huge man and those of two women, one still with golden hair which fell away into dust the minute it was touched. In the same year, King Richard I presented a sword described as Arthur's Excalibur to King Tancred of Sicily; it too was said to have been found in the coffin.

In 1278, the coffin was opened again by Edward I, and the bones declared relics. They were reinterred in a black marble tomb which was placed before the high altar of Glastonbury Abbey. This is where the Tudor antiquarian John Leland saw the coffin in the 1530s, engraved with the famous words REX QUONDAM REXQUE FUTURUS – 'The Once and Future King'. Although some historians have regarded the much-publicised discovery in 1191 as bogus, more recent scholarship suggests that it is probably genuine. In 1607 William Camden made a drawing of the cross, which looks convincingly ancient, and excavations in 1962

The Knights of the Round Table about to depart on the Quest for the Holy Grail by William Dyce (1849).

The King Arthur Cross, said to be found on King Arthur's coffin at Glastonbury Abbey.

revealed that there was indeed a stone-lined grave at the Glastonbury site.

THE ARTHUR OF ROMANCE

Behind the historical Arthur established by Geoffrey of Monmouth there was an Arthur of pure romance. Welsh poems, preserved in thirteenth-century manuscripts, although of much older origin, are full of Arthurian references, and the setting is usually the sixth century. He is frequently mentioned in the 'Triads', verses spun around three names, as a great hero constantly embarking on ambitious quests. The most romantic elements in the Arthurian legends – Lancelot's love for Guinevere, the story of Tristram and Iseult, the quest for the Holy Grail – were first collected together by the French poet Chrétien de Troyes. Born in 1159, he spent most of his life at the court of Henri the Liberal

of Champagne, but specific references in his romances to English topography and cities suggest that he had spent time in England.

Wace, another French poet, translated Monmouth's history into octosyllabic verse, as *Le Roman de Brut*, and added an account of the Round Table to the Arthurian part of the history. The concept of the round table – an egalitarian group in which the king is merely the first among equals – has remained popular.

But it is, above all, Sir Thomas Malory who is responsible for the form in which Arthur came down the centuries to modern readers. Oddly, we know little about Malory's life. The only exact information about his identity is towards the end of his famous collection of Arthurian tales, when the author asks his readers 'to pray for me while I am alive, that God send me good deliverance, and when I am dead, I pray you all pray for my soul. For this book endeth the ninth year of the reign of King Edward the Fourth, by Sir Thomas Maleore, Knight.'

There were several Thomas Malorys flourishing, as the saying goes, at the time, but the consensus today is that the author of the *Morte* was Sir Thomas Malory of Newbold Revel in Warwickshire, who died in 1471, and was buried in the fashionable London church of Greyfriars. He was married, with at least two children, and probably spent some time overseas in Burgundy, Italy and France. We can guess at his birth being around the time of Agincourt (1415) and, as a squire in the retinue of the Earl of Warwick, he could have been both at the trial of Joan of Arc in Rouen in 1431 and at the siege of Calais in 1436. In 1445 he was elected MP for Warwickshire.

In the 1450s Malory was the subject of a succession of criminal charges, including wounding, theft, burglary, stealing cattle, abducting and twice 'lying carnally with' a certain Joan Smith, and extortion. He was even accused of laying an ambush for the Duke of Buckingham and breaking into the Duke's deer park – acting, in short, exactly as Sir Perys de Forest Savage does in Book VI of the *Morte*: 'What? ... is he a thief and a knight? And a ravisher of women? He doth shame unto the Order

An anonymous woodcut from Sir Thomas Malory's *Morte d'Arthur* (1498).

of Knighthood, and contrary to his oath. It is pity that he liveth!' He was arrested in 1451, but escaped by swimming the moat of the castle where he was being held. He then robbed an abbey before being recaptured. His case never came to trial, and he spent much of the next eight years in prison; perhaps this was when he settled down to reading early English chroniclers and medieval French romances and transforming them into his own unique account 'of the birth, life, and acts of the said King Arthur, of his noble knights of the Round Table, their marvellous enquests and adventures, the achieving of the Sangreal, and in the end the dolorous death and departing out of this world of them all'.

Malory was evidently well-read – he knew the French prose romances *Suite de Merlin*, *Tristram* and *Lancelot*, and two English poems – the alliterative *Morte Arthure* and the stanzaic *Morte Arthur*. He uses episodes from all of these, but also omits and inserts material. Like Geoffrey of Monmouth, Malory was writing the right story at the right time. The Welsh House of Tudor triumphed over the Yorkists in 1485, and were eager to establish their personal royal credentials by tracing their ancestry back to Arthur.

But Malory died too soon to enjoy any personal kudos for his work. It was William Caxton, who edited and printed Malory's masterpiece in 1485, who benefited from Tudor enthusiasm for the Welsh associations of the *Morte*. Henry VII named his oldest son Arthur, and when he was ceremoniously christened in Winchester Cathedral it seems likely that the great church was decorated in spectacular Arthurian style. The re-maining fragments of a tapestry woven for the occasion show the arms of King Arthur and his mythical ancestors, and it is probable that this was when the great Round Table which can be seen in the Great Hall was made. Although Arthur died young, in 1502, and it was his younger brother who succeeded to the throne as Henry VIII, the Tudors con-tinued to boast of their Arthurian connections. The famous magus Dr Dee reported in 1580 that Elizabeth I could claim royal title over half of Europe on the authority of Geoffrey of Monmouth's history, and Richard

Hakluyt's *Principal Navigations, Voyages and Discoveries of the English Nation* (1589) begins with an account of Arthur's northern conquests.

Malory's *Morte d'Arthur* is studded with real place-names. He certainly knew the Northumberland castles which inspired Lancelot's Joyous Garde. We don't know whether he visited Tintagel and Glastonbury, but Newbold Revel is close to the Fosse Way, which would have led him straight down to the West Country, and (as the A37) runs very close indeed to Cadbury Camp, the traditional site of Camelot. It may be just as relevant to ask whether the printer William Caxton ever made a pilgrimage to the traditional Arthurian locations. Comparisons of his printed version of Malory with the only surviving manuscript of the *Morte* (the three-volume Winchester Malory, edited by Eugène Vinaver in 1947) show more place-names than in the manuscript. Gawain's skull is said to be at Dover Castle, Lancelot's Joyous Garde was perhaps Bamburgh, Arthur and Guinevere are buried at Glastonbury, he tells the reader in his preface. The Arthurian scholar Stephen Knight believes that these specifics were deliberately inserted, and that Tudor readers would regard such places as shrines to be visited.

The next most famous rendering of Arthurian myth, Spenser's *The Faerie Queene*, was written in 1590 and dedicated to Gloriana, Queen Elizabeth I. It was the first – but not the last – to take the theme of the education of Arthur, depicted as Gloriana's most dedicated knight. An allegorical epic in the same vein as Tasso and Ariosto, it was dedicated to courtly themes and Aristotelian virtues. More pageant than history, it is nonetheless splendidly vivid in its imagery of the legendary king.

> His haughtie helmet, horrid all with gold,
> Both glorious brightnesse, and great terror bred;
> For all the crest a Dragon did enfold
> With greedie paws, and over all did spred
> His golden wings; his dreadfull hideous head,
> Close couched on the bever, seem'd to throw

Illustration by Walter Crane from the 1896 edition of Spenser's *Faerie Queene*.

They saw a Knight in dangerous distresse
Of a rude rout him chasing to and fro,
That sought with lawlesse powre him to oppresse
They spide a Lady left all succourlesse,

V. XI.

XL. IV.

One of Veronica Whall's seventy-two stained-glass windows from King Arthur's Great Halls in Tintagel, depicting events from the Arthurian legends. Here, the Holy Grail descends on Sir Galahad, who devoted his life to the virtuous quest.

From flaming mouth bright sparkles fierie red,
That sudden horror to faint hearts did show,
And scaly tail was stretched adowne his back full low.

Not unnaturally, it won the approval of the heir apparent James VI of Scotland, who was, according to his contemporary William Camden, flattered by the discovery that one anagram of Charles Iames Steuart was Claimes Arthures Seat – an appropriate coincidence for a Scot, as Arthur's Seat was the name of the prominent rock above Edinburgh, long associated with Arthur's Scottish manifestations. When James succeeded to the English throne, Ben Jonson wrote several masques in which Arthur made appearances, blessing the house of Stuart and paying homage to James.

Although the exploits of Arthur remained the stuff of vulgar folklore and were frequently referred to in popular broadsheets, romances and ballads, there was a distinct lull of interest in them in polite society over the next few centuries. Mercantile and manufacturing enterprise were replacing the old settled feudal hierarchies, and the ideal of the chivalric knight was being supplanted by that of the humanist gentleman. In his famous manual *The Scholemaster* (1570), Roger Ascham, one of the most prominent Protestant scholars of the day, criticised 'books of chivalry made for pastime and pleasure by certain idle monks and wanton canons', and singled out Malory's 'bold bawdry and open manslaughter' for special criticism.

Having been frequently reprinted between 1485 and 1634, Malory's *Morte d'Arthur* remained out of print until 1816. Its appeal to Renaissance classicism, seventeenth-century puritanism and eighteenth-century rationalism was distinctly limited, and pro-monarchic sentiment was out of fashion. Although Arthur received recognition from Edward Gibbon, greatest of British historians, in his *Decline and Fall of the Roman Empire* (1776-88), the mainstream of historical scholarship concentrated on realities rather than legends.

All these things considered, can no man reasonably gainsay but there was a king of this land named Arthur...You may see his sepulchre in the monastery of Glastonbury.

William Caxton, preface to Malory's *Morte d'Arthur*

Glastonbury Tor in the evening light.

TRAIL **The Isle of Avalon**

1

Glastonbury was once in truth an island, with a port: a Roman wharf has been unearthed close to Wearyall Hill. The Tor is the highest and most remarkable of the unusually shaped cluster of hills which embrace the town. It is terraced, which has led to speculation that it was once laid out as a ritual maze; there are also theories that the whole local landscape is marked out into figures from the zodiac, with the Tor itself as part of Sagittarius, the great warrior – perhaps even Arthur. Early Welsh legends state that the Tor is one of the few entrance points to the Otherworld of Annwn, which makes it a natural place for Arthur to be spirited away underground to await his second coming.

Before you reach Glastonbury, it is worth taking a look at the Tor from a distance – something that is easy enough to do. From almost every approach road its 525ft-high summit stands out clearly – the artificially drained Somerset Levels around it are still only a few feet above sea level. If you are coming via the M5, you might consider making a short detour at exit 22 and walking up 450ft Brent Knoll, another remarkably prominent summit. Together with Dinas Powys, across the Bristol Channel, Glastonbury and Cadbury Castle, it forms part of a chain of hills that were all fortified in or before the sixth century and are likely to have been linked by beacons.

Glastonbury Abbey was one of only three early sixth-century communities which, according to the Welsh Triads, had a perpetual choir (*laus perennis*), where the Holy Office was chanted in relays by a hundred men every hour. Glastonbury was far enough west to be protected by Ambrosius and Arthur from the first attacks of the Saxons. By the time the Saxons did reach it, in 658, they themselves had converted to Christianity, and became generous benefactors to the community there. It grew into an important symbolic bridge between the Celts and the Saxons, a national shrine to which pilgrimages were made.

MAP

OS Landranger 183:
Glastonbury

OS Explorer 141: Cheddar Gorge,
Mendips, Wells and Glastonbury

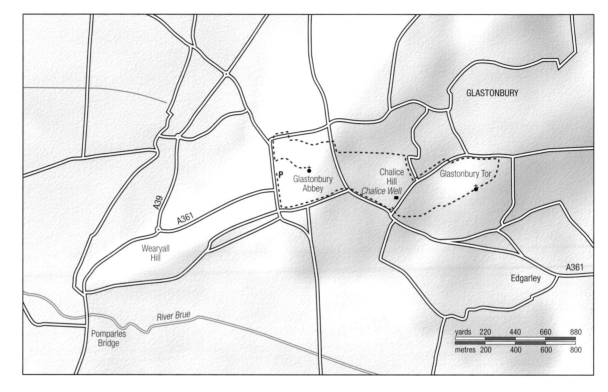

On Foot (2–3 miles)

To climb the Tor, park in one of the central Glastonbury car-parks and look for signs to the A361 Edgarley/ Shepton Mallet road. Follow this for about half a mile until you get to a turning off to the left called Well House Lane. The public footpath signposted to the Tor is now immediately on your right, but before you head uphill it is worth visiting the Chalice Well, which is a few yards further on along Well House Lane. Medieval stonework encloses the garden around it. Iron in the depths of the hill gives the spring that feeds the well a reddish tinge, and it is known as Blood Spring. The well is described in the early romance *Perlesvaus*, known in English as *The High History of the Holy Grail*. It was to the little Christian community around this well that Malory seems to have intended Lancelot to retreat after the death of Arthur.

Head uphill along the spine of the ridge to the

church tower on the top of the Tor. This is all that remains of the church of St Michael the Archangel, famed as the conqueror of hell. 'The powers of hell were perhaps incompletely conquered', writes Geoffrey Ashe dryly in *The Traveller's Guide to Arthurian Britain* (1997), 'because it fell down in an earthquake.'

Take the steep steps down the north-eastern side of the Tor to a lane. Turn left along it to find your way back to Glastonbury town. Take the second turning on the right to walk around Chalice Hill, then turn left on a footpath which brings you out in a small housing estate at the back of the town. The Abbey ruins are directly in front of you. To find their entrance gateway (just beside the Town Hall) turn right and then left into the town centre. The most ancient part of the site is at its western end, where the Old Church dedicated to the Virgin Mary once stood: it was said to have been built by Joseph of

Arimathea to house the Holy Grail. Its crypt was dedicated to him. A small sign about 50ft from the south door of the Lady Chapel shows the actual site of Arthur's grave. In the centre of the ruined transept of the Abbey you will see a much larger sign which shows where the disinterred remains were entombed in 1278.

You could complete your trail around Arthurian Glastonbury as you leave the town by visiting the Pomparles Bridge – the *pont périlleux*, or perilous bridge – which crosses the River Brue on the A39 road to Street. This is where one legend has it that Bedivere cast Excalibur into the magical mere, to be claimed by one of the Ladies of the Lake. At that time all the land here would of course have been under water. If you have time, a visit to the town's Rural Life Museum provides a good extension of one's understanding of the area's ancient atmosphere.

IDYLLS OF THE KING

The beginning of the nineteenth century witnessed an extraordinary resurgence of interest in matters Arthurian. It was poets and artists who began the rediscovery. In 1809 William Blake exhibited his paintings with a descriptive catalogue; the gloss on his painting *The Ancient Britons* (now lost) explained that 'The giant Albion was the Patriarch of the Atlantic; he is the Atlas of the Greeks, one of those the Greeks called Titans. The stories of Arthur are the acts of Albion, applied to a Prince of the fifth century.'

Robert Southey's eponymous hero of *Madoc* (1805) was of 'immortal Arthur's line' and early learned 'to lisp the fame of Arthur'. Malory, out of print for nearly two hundred years, appeared in six different editions in the first two decades of the century, and was read by both Wordsworth and Keats. And travellers in search of the picturesque, palpitating with emotions unacceptable in the cold rational days of the Enlightenment, were only too eager to lap up local legends of Merlin and magic, terrible mountains and giants Sans Pitié, Lancelot and Guinevere, chivalry and charlatans. But Arthur's time had not quite come. Wordsworth considered writing about him, but Coleridge dissuaded him: 'As to Arthur, you could not by any means make a poem on him national to Englishmen. What have we to do with him?'

Thomas Love Peacock (1785-1866) was one of the first nineteenth-century authors to make use of the Arthurian legend. Besides using it (in remarkably modern fashion) as a device for teaching children grammar and history ('Sir Hornbook, or Childe Launcelot's Expedition', 1814, and 'The Round Table; or, King Arthur's Feast', 1817), he began a verse satire called 'Caldiore', in which Arthur, rollicking in Bacchanalian jollities on the Isles of the Blessed, sends a youth to nineteenth-century Wales to see if the time is ripe for his return.

His most ambitious treatment of the story was *The Misfortunes of Elphin* (1829). This is derived from early Welsh romances and Peacock's own familiarity with the Welsh countryside. The hero is Taliesin, a

The Winter Smoking Room at Cardiff Castle by the Gothic architect William Burges, who was commissioned by Lord Bute to remodel the Welsh castle in 1865 and embellished it with his most extravagant interiors.

magically gifted child found in Elphin's salmon nets, who plays a critical role in saving Elphin and restoring Guinevere to Arthur. A contemporary critic called it 'the most entertaining book, if not the best, that has yet been published on the ancient customs and traditions of Wales'. Peacock's treatment was more akin to Monty Python than Milton, a ribald tale of rough tribal chieftains who grabbed each other's wives and sang exuberantly in medieval halls. He makes a running joke of the significant Triads – when Guinevere slaps the face of Mordred's wife, 'this slap is recorded in the Bardic Triads as one of the Three Fatal Slaps of the Island of Britain … it is said to have been the basis of that enmity between Arthur and Mordred which terminated in the Battle of Camlann, wherein all the flower of Britain perished on both sides.'

The Eglinton Tournament as commemorated by Edward Corbauld. Above: Archibald Montgomery, 13th Earl of Eglinton, who staged the spectacle. Below: Viscount Alford and the Marquess of Waterford join battle, forgetting the rules of chivalry.

But the typical Victorian treatment of the tales was very different from either Peacock or the romantic but sexually robust version offered by Malory. The recovery of Arthur was the literary aspect of a far-reaching revulsion against industrialisation and reversion to medievalism that affected art, architecture and music alike.

By 1850 the reprints of Malory had been joined by editions of Geoffrey of Monmouth, Nennius, Layamon, *The Mabinogion* and more than twenty medieval Arthurian romances. Just as the Normans had wanted to look beyond the Saxons to such ancient British ancestors as Fleance and Brut, and the Tudors had wanted to look back before the houses of York and Lancaster in order to root their legitimacy in their Celtic forebears, so the Victorians were concerned to look for something specifically British rather than of classical inspiration.

The Victorians' love of the Arthurian legends led to a move to update knightly chivalry to meet the requirements of the age. A comprehensive sourcebook of all things medieval was provided by Kenelm Digby's *The Broad Stone of Honour: or, The True Sense and Practice of Chivalry* (1822). Much reprinted and enlarged in the next five decades, it was subtitled 'The Rules of the Gentlemen of England'. The full-scale tournament mounted in the grand medieval manner in his Gothic Ayrshire castle by

Alfred, Lord Tennyson, painted by Samuel Laurence in 1840.

Lord Eglinton in 1839 was probably the most famous example of a self-conscious return to knightly values. Not everyone kept to the rules of chivalry, however. In the final 'grand equestrian mêlée', the Knight of the Dragon (Lord Waterford) distinguished himself by genuinely coming to blows with the Knight of the Black Lion (John, Viscount Alford, of Belton House in Lincolnshire).

It was Alfred, Lord Tennyson (1809-92) who did most of all to re-establish medieval chivalric traditions and to perpetuate Arthur's status and dignity in the popular imagination. As a boy, he was captivated by Malory's *Morte d'Arthur*, the 1817 edition with an introduction by the poet laureate Robert Southey. He also read Sir Walter Scott's *Marmion* (1808) and his *The Lady of the Lake* (1810). Tennyson's earliest Arthurian poem, 'The Lady of Shalott', was only Arthurian in its mention of Camelot and the almost incidental part in it played by Lancelot. It was derived from an Italian novelette, *Donna di Scalotta*, which was itself borrowed from an early fourteenth-century tale in the *Cento Novelle Antiche*. Tennyson added the island (in terms more evocative of the Lincolnshire wolds than the West Country), the weaving and singing, the magic curse and the falling in love with Lancelot.

Tennyson published his 'Morte d'Arthur' in 1842, but it would be decades before he completed his *Idylls of the King*. Originally, he planned a vast Arthurian epic, but then decided that 'a small vessel built on fine lines, is likely to float further down the stream of time than a big raft'. But the popularity of his dramatic narrative poem *The Princess* (1847) encouraged him to think on a grander scale. He compromised. Instead of a continuous narrative, he decided to emulate the form of a sequence of tales adopted by Malory and to continue the story as he had begun it, as a series of vignettes. The landscapes in which he set them constituted an important element, and it was with the idea of getting inspiration that he first visited Devon and Cornwall, including Tintagel, in 1848. It wasn't until 1855 that he settled down to the project in earnest. He visited Glastonbury, Cadbury, Salisbury, Amesbury and the New Forest and made notes of settings and impressions. Besides Malory, he read and reread Geoffrey of Monmouth, Wace, Nennius, Layamon and Lady Charlotte Guest's translation of the Welsh epic, *The Mabinogion*.

The first four poems of the *Idylls*, 'Enid', 'Vivien', 'Elaine' and 'Guinevere', were published in 1859. Their theme was the 'shadowing Sense at war with Soul', and their success was immediate – 10,000 copies sold in the first week. But the *Idylls* were not finally completed until 1885. 'I tried in my *Idylls* to teach men … the need of the Ideal', Tennyson wrote as he looked back over his fifty years of grappling with Arthurian themes. The final form of the *Idylls* was dedicated to Prince Albert and set in a high-Victorian frame. The dignified owner of an old country house is reading the salvaged fragment of an Arthurian epic which had been thrown into the fireplace. Stirred by reading it, he dreams of Arthur returning to Britain as 'a modern gentleman / Of stateliest port'. The contemporary world is described by an old parson as being in decline – 'all the old honour is from Christmas gone' and there is a 'general decay of faith / Right through the world.'

The Great Parlour at Wightwick Manor in the West Midlands, sumptuously decorated in glorious Pre-Raphaelite style.

The Lady of Shalott by
John Waterhouse (1888).

Tennyson's *Idylls* became enormously popular. They were lapped up
with especial enthusiasm and given vivid visual imagery by William
Morris, Dante Gabriel Rossetti and Holman Hunt. Rossetti frescoes
based on Arthurian themes can still be seen in the Oxford Union.
William Morris and Edward Burne-Jones planned to found an Order of
Sir Galahad to perform charitable works in the East End of London.
'Learn Sir Galahad by heart', Burne-Jones told would-be candidates.
It was this foundation which diversified into the Pre-Raphaelite
Brotherhood. At Wightwick Manor, just west of Wolverhampton, their
work can be seen in all its glory, with Morris wallpapers, textiles and
carpets, William de Morgan tiles, W. A. S. Benson metalwork, books
from Morris's Kelmscott Press, and paintings and drawings by Ford
Madox Ford, Hunt, John Millais, Burne-Jones and John Ruskin.

TRAIL **With Tennyson to Tintagel**

2

After the sunset down the coast, he heard
Strange music, and he paused and turning – there,
All down the lonely coast of Lyonesse,
Each with a beacon-star upon his head,
And with a wild sea-light about his feet,
He saw them – headland after headland flame
Far into the rich heart of the west.

Alfred Tennyson, 'Guinevere'

Tennyson's interest in Arthur was more firmly rooted in place than that of anyone before him. It was his descriptions of the rugged coast of north Cornwall ('the thundering shores of Bude and Bos') which set the fashion for pilgrimages west in search of Arthur, but it was the far-reaching network of Brunel's Great Western Railway that made them popular pastimes.

Tennyson visited Robert Hawker (1803-74), Vicar of Morwenstow, in 1848, ten years before he published the first of his Arthurian poems. He had come to see the waves at Bude, reputedly the biggest in Britain, and to visit Arthurian sites, and he had heard that the Parson Hawker was a great Arthurian expert. Hawker was also famously eccentric. On vacation as an undergraduate, he once made a merman's tail out of oilskin and a wig out of seaweed and spent several evenings sitting all but naked on the rocks at low tide, singing wailing songs.

He was a devout and generous vicar, steeped in medieval and saintly lore; he also believed in witchcraft and the evil eye. As a salute to Herne the Huntsman, he kept a stag in his paddock and encouraged his nine cats to attend church services. His dress was idiosyncratic, to say the least. He avoided black, except for his socks, which were knitted from the wool of his pet black sheep. He usually wore a claret-coloured coat with long tails over a dark blue guernsey which had a red cross embroidered on its side, a symbol of the piercing of Jesus's side by a spear when he hung on the cross. More often than not he wore knee-high wading boots and a

Left: Parson Hawker sketched in 1863 by George Howard, Earl of Carlisle, and (above) his writing hut, perched on the cliffs at Morwenstow in Cornwall.

brimless beige hat similar to those of priests of the Orthodox Church.

Hawker can fairly lay claim to having been one of the earliest Victorian poets to write of the Grail legend, although he didn't publish his *Quest of the Sangraal*, with its arresting opening line 'Ho! for the Sangraal! Vanished vase of Heaven!', until 1863. A rousing piece of versifying, it concludes with Merlin summoning up three visions of Britain's future for Arthur's benefit. The visions are obscure enough for Hawker to add a gloss for the benefit of his readers: they signify, respectively, Arthur's wars, the Saxon and Norman conquests and, finally, the period 'from 1536 to 1863, with my notions of the Battle of Waterloo and the Armstrong Gun – Gas, Steam, Electric Telegraph'.

Tennyson arrived at Morwenstow incognito. He was, Hawker wrote later, 'a tall swarthy man with an eye like a sword, a long black cloak and elflocks hanging around his face'. They talked of Arthur's Cornish connections, and Hawker quoted from *The Lady of the Lake*. Later, he quoted from 'Locksley Hall', and said that Tennyson was 'not only his favourite poet but that of all England'. Tennyson couldn't resist revealing himself and Hawker was delighted.

Hawker then offered to take Tennyson along the edge of the cliff to visit Morwenna's Well, and to admire his own little retreat, a hut made out of driftwood built right into the cliff face. Tennyson, who was something of a toper, may well have brought a bottle along. He certainly told Hawker over dinner that night that his 'chief reliance for bodily force was on wine'. Hawker noted this fondness for Bacchus in typically roundabout terms: 'I should conceive he yielded to the conqueror of Ariadne ever and anon'. When Tennyson left, Hawker lent him a large bundle of Arthurian books and manuscripts. History does not relate whether or not they were returned.

Tennyson went next to Tintagel, some twenty miles to the south. Its remote coastal position is perfect for the advent of a king whose origins are shrouded in magic and mystery. According to the French romance *La Suite du Merlin*, it was one of the strongest fortresses of Gorlois, Duke of Cornwall. When Uther Pendragon fell in love with Gorlois' wife, the fair Igraine, Gorlois withdrew in fury and ensconced her there, taking up a protective position at Dimilioc, a fortified camp nearby. This may have been a defensive hillfort on which is built the church of St Dennis, a village twenty-five miles away, between St Austell and Newquay.

Today Tintagel is a straggling and not especially attractive village, but there are two remarkable places in it. One is the Old Post Office, now owned by the National Trust. Further down the High Street are King Arthur's Great Halls, created by custard-powder millionaire Frederick Glasscock. He founded a modern Order of Knights of the Round Table, which generously included women, and reached considerable strength in the early 1930s. What looks like a large double-fronted Victorian villa turns out, once you are inside, to be a medieval-style hall, full of huge paintings on Arthurian themes, thrones and other medieval paraphernalia. Even more impressive is the much bigger hall built behind the first one, which uses a variety of different granites from all over Cornwall and has spectacular stained-glass windows on Arthurian themes by Veronica Whall (1887-1967).

The dramatic ruins on the promontory of Tintagel are those of an early thirteenth-century castle built by Richard, Earl of Cornwall, quite possibly because of the cachet of the place's traditional Arthurian connections. Beyond these ruins, on the windswept top of the promontory, some 250ft above sea level, there are traces of much earlier buildings. They were once thought to be monastic in origin, but excavations in 1994 revealed them as the remains of a late fifth-century stronghold, a far more substantial citadel than previously imagined. The likelihood is that a substantial bank and ditch defended the landward site. Very large quantities of fifth- and sixth-century Mediterranean pottery have been found at the site, substantially more than anywhere else in Cornwall, and identical to that found at Cadbury/Camelot.

The most recent confirmation of Tintagel's importance in post-Roman times, though not proving Arthurian connections, was the discovery, in August 1998, of a sixth-century slate plaque with a Latin inscription. It was found during excavations by the University of Glasgow under Professor Christopher Morris, and can be read as 'The mark of Paternius; the mark of Coliarus, he

Park House
Maidstone

My dear Mr Hawker,
            I have just received
your kind present. many Thanks.
I sent you my book, but that is, I
told my Publisher to send it you: had
it past thro' my hands I would have
written in it —
    I did not know that Bos was
only one — s^d

            Yours ever
                T. Tennyson

P.S. The verses are too complimentary
for me to put faith in

Above: The Old Post Office, on the left of this view of the main street at Tintagel, photographed in 1894 by Francis Frith.

Top: Letter from Tennyson to Hawker.

TRAIL
2
made it; the mark of Artognous'. Three at least of Tintagel's then occupants could still read Latin.

After visiting Tintagel, Tennyson continued south-westward. He visited Camelford, Zennor (where Arthur is said to have come to the rescue against invading Danes), St Ives, Land's End, Kynance and the Lizard. There he is likely to have visited Loe Pool, a lagoon in Mount's Bay, one of the most romantic and remote of Arthurian sites. His description of the 'great water' into which Sir Bedivere throws Excalibur in 'Morte d'Arthur' closely resembles Loe Pool, 'a dark strait of barren land: / On one side lay the Ocean, and on one / Lay a great water, and the moon was full'. Bedivere approaches the pool 'By zig-zag paths and juts of pointed rock / Came on the shining levels of the lake'. At Arthur's second command he went 'Across the ridge and paced beside the mere / Counting the dewy pebbles, fixed in thought', before eventually flinging in the sword.

Finally, Tennyson returned to Plymouth and took a Great Western locomotive back to London. In 1860 he made another tour of Cornwall, this time walking a good deal, with his friends Francis Palgrave, Thomas Woolner and Holman Hunt. They visited Tintagel and Boscastle again, then went down to the Lizard and Penzance. From there they crossed to the Scilly Isles. The trip did not only inspire Tennyson; it led Palgrave to embark on what was to become one of the most popular anthologies of all time, his *Golden Treasury of Songs and Lyrics* (1861). Tennyson played an important part in determining the contents, but refused to allow any of his own works to be included. As a result, Palgrave decided to exclude all authors still living.

Tennyson's last visit to Tintagel was by sea. In 1888 he charted Sir Allen Young's yacht *Stella* for a cruise around the coasts of Devon, Cornwall and Wales. When they visited Tintagel, an old lady recognised him, rushed out of her cottage and began reciting from the *Idylls*.

Loe Pool.

…ere he dipt the surface,

rose an arm

Clothed in white samite,

mystic, wonderful,

And caught him by the hilt,

and brandish'd him

Three times, and drew him

under in the mere.

Alfred Tennyson, 'Morte d'Arthur'

MAP
OS Explorer 111: Bude, Boscastle, Tintagel
OS Landranger 190: Bude, Clovelly

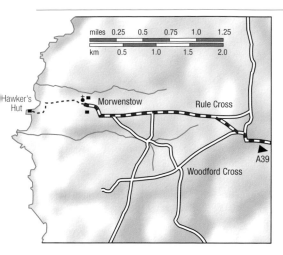

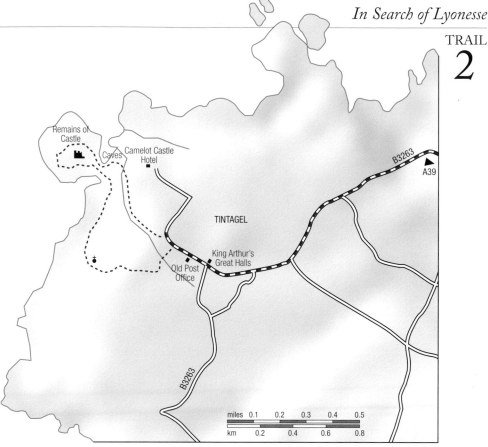

By Car and on Foot (*c*.30 miles)

A car is necessary to reach the first point on our
Tennyson Trail, the remote little seaside combe of
Morwenstow on the ruggedly romantic north Devon
coast, just north of Bude, two miles west of the A39.
When you reach the village, park in the car-park
opposite the church. Look down at the grey stone
rectory just below the church. Its chimneys are in the
form of church towers, each one a memento of previous
livings of Robert Hawker, the eccentric Vicar of
Morwenstow.

To follow in the footsteps of Hawker and Tennyson's cliff-top walk, take the well-marked track on the
left-hand side of the field seaward of the vicarage and
head southwards along the coast path. After a mile you
will see a discreet little sign down to Hawker's Hut.
Here, Hawker told Tennyson tales of the ghastly wrecks
and battered corpses washed up by the tide, which
were a recurring feature of the coast. Tennyson later
used the descriptions in 'The Passing of Arthur',
describing the 'wan wave' breaking:

> … in among the dead faces, to and fro
> Swaying the helpless hands, and up and down
> Tumbling the hollow helmets of the fallen.

Return to Morwenstow, and drive south
down the A39 until you see a turning (B3263) to
Boscastle and Tintagel. Drive through the gauntlet of
Arthurian themed cafés, pubs and shops to the car-park
just below the Tintagel Bookshop, a mecca for serious
researchers. From here you will see high on the cliff to
the north a great Victorian folly, once the King Arthur

Hotel, now lavishly restored as the Camelot Castle Hotel
and offering its fortunate guests an unparalleled
romantic vista.

Walk down the track to the cove just below the
rugged peninsula of Tintagel. This is where Tennyson
described Merlin receiving the baby Arthur from the sea,
washed or cast away from a 'dragon wing'd' ship, 'from
stem to stern / Bright with a shining people on the
decks'. (Uther Pendragon's rape of Igraine was not for
Victorian sensibilities.) The great cave on the left of the
little bay, known as Merlin's Cave, is worth climbing into;
at low tide intrepid and web-footed explorers can
scramble or swim right through to the other side.

After acquiring your entry ticket (on sale both at
the bookshop above or down at the shore), climb up
the steep steps and across the wooden bridge, once a
drawbridge, that is the only way to the famous fortress
from the mainland. It is easy to see what a formidable
defensive position it was. Supplies could be landed there
by small boats from the seaward side, so residents could
not even be starved out.

Go through the ruined fortifications to the top of
the promontory, and you will find a small ruined chapel
and a curious tunnel in the rock, the purpose of which
is still anybody's guess. It's a wonderful, wild and
windswept spot; don't be surprised if the odd Druid
passes by. When we were there, a latter-day Merlin
with cloak and crook strode past towards Arthur's
Seat, a strange chink in the rock that looks out
southwards along the dramatic craggy coastline.

Walk back over the wooden bridge and take the
steep stair straight ahead rather than circling back to
the track from the cove. The ruins here are of the
medieval fortifications on the mainland that defended
the entrance to Tintagel itself. Walk right through them
and take the footpath across Glebe Cliff (NT) to Tintagel
Church, which stands high above the village and looks
straight out across to Tintagel itself. The churchyard has
several unexcavated barrows in it. Take the lane eastwards from the church; you will pass a holy well as
you return to the village.

ARTHUR FOR MODERN TIMES

Early twentieth-century tellings of the Arthurian legends specialised in psychological sophistication and poetical obscurity. Ill-made knights became of more interest than heroic kings to such authors as Charles Williams and Edwin Arlington Robertson. The best and easily the most popular twentieth-century retelling is T. H. White's *The Sword in the Stone* (1937). White first became interested in Malory while he was at Cambridge, but he was then distracted by a convalescence from tuberculosis in Italy and a growing interest in late eighteenth-century history and literature. When he left Cambridge, aware that he wanted to write but needing to earn money, he became a schoolmaster, first in a prep school and then at Stowe, Buckinghamshire. The school there was only ten years old but was already renowned for being different and exciting in its approach to education under its innovative headmaster J. F. Roxburgh.

T. H. White (1906–64). The wild geese that he studied on his visits to the Norfolk salt-marshes, like those at Stiffkey (right) in the 1930s, later provided inspiration for scenes in *The Sword in the Stone*.

The building and grounds helped to make an education at Stowe a memorable experience. One of the great show houses of the eighteenth century, its grounds (now owned by the National Trust) were laid out in glorious vistas, lakes and avenues, and everywhere architectural conceits in the shape of pavilions, temples and obelisks attracted the eye. Statues and inscriptions spelt out in monuments the literary and political glories of the Augustan age (see Stowe Trail, p. 110). The setting inspired White's later book *Mistress Masham's Repose* (1947), in which descendants of the Lilliputians brought back by Gulliver are found by a little girl in the island temple on one of the lakes.

White arrived at Stowe in style, roaring up the great avenue in a (second-hand) black Bentley; a horse-box containing his hunter arrived shortly afterwards. A compulsive learner of skills as well as a dashing and unconventional teacher, White took flying lessons, studied bird song and collected snakes while he was at Stowe. He kept journals labelled 'Hunting', 'Flying', 'Fishing', 'Shooting' (though not 'Teaching'). After four years, which are still a legend in the annals of the school, White gave

up teaching and moved into a gamekeeper's cottage on the Stowe estate at Stowe Ridings. Records of pheasants killed were still marked on the door of its barn; there was a badger's set nearby and a fishpond stocked with carp. He soon acquired a goshawk, the first of many hawks, and set out to train it in the medieval fashion which he would describe in detail in *The Sword in the Stone*. He lost it, but promptly replaced it with another called Cully, and a pair of merlins called Balin and Balan. He cared for a dying young owl, which he called Archimedes, and another, which survived, which he called Sylvia Daisy Pouncer, a tribute to John Masefield's *The Midnight Folk* (1927), one of his favourite books. He went to stay in Wells-next-the-Sea in Norfolk to admire – and shoot – wild geese in the nearby marshes at Stiffkey and Morston. The cast of the book for which he is now most famous was steadily accumulating.

In 1938 he wrote a letter to L. J. Potts from Norfolk, explaining the genesis of *The Sword in the Stone*:

> It is a preface to Malory. Do you remember I once wrote a thesis on the Morte d'Arthur? Naturally I did not read Malory while I was writing a thesis on him, but one night last autumn I got desperate among my books and picked him up in lack of anything else. Then I was thrilled and astonished to find (a) that the thing was a perfect tragedy, with a beginning, a middle and an end implicit in its beginning, and (b) that the characters were real people with recognizable reactions that could be forecast. Anyway, I somehow started writing a book. It is not a satire. Indeed, I am afraid it is rather warm-hearted – mainly about birds and beasts. It seems impossible to determine whether it is for grown-ups or children. It is more or less a kind of wish-fulfilment of the things I should like to have happened to me when I was a boy.

The Sword in the Stone became hugely popular as a children's story. White did not only give himself an ideal childhood via young Wart – who grows up to be Arthur himself as an older and wiser man – but had a close identification with Merlyn, a schoolmaster with total freedom to teach his pupil Wart really important things about life ('The best thing for being sad is learning something'). The Stowe Ridings cottage, 'snug as a badger's set', is recognisably Merlyn's lair in the woods, right down to the well in front of it. An average day's questin' took Sir Grummore Grummursum across terrain well known to White's local hunt, the Grafton: 'Found a chap called Sir Bruce Saunce Pitié choppin' off a maiden's head in Weedon Bushes, ran him to Mixbury Plantation in the Bicester, where he doubled back, and lost him in Wicken Wood.'

The Sword in the Stone inspired a score by Benjamin Britten for a radio serialisation and a Disney film. Its sequels, written in a very different, much more adult vein, were *The Witch in the Wood*, which focuses on Morgan le Fay, *The Ill-made Knight*, the story of Lancelot, and *The Candle in the Wind*, the story of Arthur's last years. Together, as *The Once and Future King* (1958), they inspired the musical *Camelot*, which starred Julie Andrews and Richard Burton in the original Broadway production.

There was a sequel to the story, though it was not published until after his death. In an experimental fifth book, *The Book of Merlyn* (1977), Arthur is taken away by Merlyn just before the last battle of Camlann to a badger's set, where the various merits and demerits of humans and animals are debated. Wart's adventures in *The Sword in the Stone* come full circle when the aged King visits the worlds of the ants and of the geese – political slaves and freemen respectively. The setting of the episode of the wild geese (added to *The Sword in the Stone* in a later re-vision of the story) is unmistakably the Norfolk marshes – 'illimitable, flat, wet mud, as featureless as dark junket' in which lives 'only one element, the wind'. When light dawns, Arthur sees that 'a thousand geese were on the wing about him … wavering like smoke upon the sky as they breasted the sunrise'.

At the end of *The Book of Merlyn*, White gives a brief account of 'the beautiful, strange and positive' legends of the common people as

Merlin, the epitome of wisdom, presiding over good (the Lady of the Lake) and evil (Morgawse, Arthur's half sister). Stained-glass window at King Arthur's Great Halls, Tintagel, by Veronica Whall.

to the ultimate fate of Arthur – buried at Glastonbury, floating away to Lyonesse, waiting underground at Arthur's Seat in Edinburgh. He must also have known of the 60ft long stone enclosure on Bodmin Moor known as Arthur's Hall when he adds:

> As for myself, I cannot forget the hedgehog's last farewell, coupled with Don Quixote's hint about the animals and Milton's subterranean dream. It is little more than a theory, but perhaps the inhabitants of Bodmin will look at their tumulus, and, if it is like an enormous mole-hill with a dark opening in its side, particularly if there are some badger tracks in the vicinity, we can draw our own conclusion. For I am inclined to believe that my beloved Arthur of the future is sitting at this very moment among his learned friends, in the Combination Room of the College of Life, and that they are thinking away in there for all they are worth, about the best means to help our curious species.

JOHN STEINBECK'S ACTS OF KING ARTHUR

It is an extraordinary literary coincidence that in the very summer of the publication of T. H. White's *The Once and Future King* in America – it was in the top ten bestseller list for three weeks running in the summer of 1958, and the musical *Camelot* appeared on Broadway in December 1959 – the American novelist John Steinbeck was also at work on a personal version of the Arthurian legends. He had long been fascinated by the tales, having been introduced to them by a cut version of Caxton's Malory, which was given to him by his Aunt Molly in 1912. He later recalled sitting under a tree 'dazzled and swept up' by them. It felt, he wrote in his introduction to his own telling of the tales, peculiarly his own book:

> In that scene were all the vices that ever were – and courage and sadness and frustration, but particularly gallantry, perhaps the only

quality of man the West has invented. I think my sense of right and wrong, my feeling of noblesse oblige, and any thought I may have against the oppressor and for the oppressed, came from this secret book.

The Malorian quest for the 'good man' was crucial to his fiction. Sir Lancelot's betrayal of his king was a pivotal image in Steinbeck's mind, and it informed a good deal of his work and, perhaps, his life. Versions of Malory's idealised women also crop up regularly.

It was Eugène Vinaver's three-volume edition of the Winchester Malory which set Steinbeck on fire with a desire to write his own version. Early in 1956, he wrote his second wife Elaine a light-hearted poem:

> Old style Elaine in a time gone by,
> Got a red hot yen for a lukewarm guy,
> She sit up river in Astolat
> Singing the blues for Sir Launcelot.
> She love him good and she love him here,
> But he buzzing the Queen Bee Guinevere.

By late 1956, Steinbeck had begun intensive research on Malory, reading both the Welsh and French sources, and especially delighting in an eleventh-century Lancelot which he discovered in the Pierpont Morgan Library in New York. From what was known about Malory, Steinbeck surmised that he might have spent time in Italy as a mercenary soldier, and decided to go and follow in his footsteps in April 1957; while there he read Arthurian manuscripts in the Vatican. Like T. H. White, he came to the conclusion that Malory's talent as a novelist had been underestimated:

> Only a novelist could think it. A novelist not only puts down a story, he is the story. He is each one of the characters in a greater

or lesser degree…Now it seems to me that Malory's self-character would be Launcelot. All of the perfections he knew went into this character, all the things of which he thought himself capable.

Steinbeck came to England in the summer of 1957. He and Elaine 'rented a Humber Hawk and a driver called Jack' and toured Britain in search of Arthurian sites. Their itinerary took them to Warwickshire, Malory's home county, then to Manchester, where he met Professor Vinaver. From there it was north to Hadrian's Wall and the Northumberland castles associated with Malory. They came back through Wales and then ducked down to Cornwall, staying at St Mawes, near Falmouth. Finally they visited Winchester to see the Vinaver manuscript.

Autumn was spent poring over a facsimile of Caxton's Malory at home in Sag Harbor, Long Island, NY. Steinbeck built a six-sided light-house-like study overlooking the sea, with just room for a table and a chair and a place for manuscripts, and called it Joyous Garde, after the castle where Lancelot and Guinevere had their happiest times.

Dunstanburgh Castle in Northumberland. In the 1460s, during the Wars of the Roses, Sir Thomas Malory supported the Yorkist king Edward IV's sieges of Dunstanburgh, Alnwick and Bamburgh castles – hence the fascination of John Steinbeck.

In June 1958, he decided to visit England again. He spent more time with Vinaver, and met the playwright Robert Bolt. In March 1959 he and Elaine came over again. Robert Bolt had found them a little stone house in Somerset called Discove Cottage at Bruton (where the National Trust owns a medieval dovecote, part of the former abbey). Steinbeck described the cottage in a letter to his editor, Pat Covici:

> It is probable that it was the hut of a religious hermit. It's something to live in a house that has sheltered 60 generations. My little work room on the second floor overlooks hills and meadows and an old manor house. If ever there was a place to write the Morte, this is it. Ten miles away is the Roman fort which is the traditional Camelot.

Steinbeck spent happy days draught-proofing and improving the cottage. He chopped wood and began to lay out a garden. He visited Glastonbury, 'a holy place since people first came to it'. He explored Cadbury Castle time and again, frequently alone. 'I know a lot about Camelot since wandering there by myself. It's a matter of sensing "how it was".' On Midsummer Eve he climbed Cadbury because of the local tradition that Arthur and his knights could be seen riding out, their horses shod with silver, to water their steeds at the Sutton Montis well.

He spent a steady five to eight hours a day on the Malory book, using home-made goose-quill pens. Although his enthusiasm for the project never flagged, progress was slow, and his agent and publisher were disappointed with the sample chapter he sent them. They had been hoping for something with the instant appeal of White's *Once and Future King*, only to find that Steinbeck was merely translating into contemporary English – and losing much of the poetry of the original in the process.

Although Steinbeck fought their criticism gamely, it is easy to understand it on reading what he completed of his *Acts of Arthur*. It is as staid and pedestrian in comparison to Malory as the Good News Bible

John and Elaine Steinbeck at Wells Cathedral, Somerset, in 1959.

is to the King James Version. The book that Steinbeck envisaged might have been a wonderful thing – a translation bordered and embroidered with his own feelings about Malory, the discoveries he had made in exploring the real places in which the stories were set, and in immersing himself in parallel literature, scholarly studies, history and archaeology. But he might have been better advised just to have published the story of his personal quest for Malory. Certainly the letters to Chase Horton and Elizabeth Otis which Horton shrewdly adds to his 1976 posthumous edition of Steinbeck's *Acts of Arthur* are more exciting and illuminating than the translation.

In August 1959, the writing was creeping along at a snail's pace. Steinbeck decided to do some more exploring of Arthurian settings, travelling to Wales, the Wye Valley and Berkeley Castle, Gloucester-shire, scene of the murder of Edward II. 'I saw most of the things I wanted,' he wrote to Chase Horton, 'largely having to do with water-ways, topography, colors, etc. Caerleon was fine and Usk even better.' Seeing Caerleon made him understand why it was there. 'If in a boat, you catch an incoming tide at the mouth of the Usk, it will take you to Caerleon on one tide. And the same is true coming back.'

But the writing still hung fire. 'The work doesn't jell', mourned Steinbeck in a letter to Elizabeth Otis on 22 August. 'I am going to spend my last time seeing rather than writing, storing things up … I am much better when I have seen a place … I want to know the whole coastline from the Bristol Channel to Land's End. I learned so much from seeing the lake and noting the tides … We'll do the adjacent areas until September and when the traffic thins we'll go farther afield.' He and Elaine visited Amesbury Abbey, where Guinevere died, Stonehenge, where the Ministry of Works was in the process of raising the fallen stones, and Glastonbury, where more excavations were in progress. But things went no better: 'As to my own work I am completely dissatisfied with it … Maybe the flame has gone out.'

It was not until 1966 that Steinbeck proudly published an article on the great discovery he had made on his last trip to Northumberland in September 1961 – a forty-eight-page manuscript that began with a list of legendary kings and ended with the death of King Arthur. But it turned out that the manuscript was by no means unknown. Microfilms of it were lodged in both the Library of Congress and the British Museum. Abject, Steinbeck apologised and backed down.

He never returned to the Arthurian material. Perhaps too much modern footwork destroyed the dreamlike world of Arthur. Perhaps Steinbeck was more at home in the myths and dreams of the American people which he captured so exactly in both *Travels with Charley* (1962) and its pictorial sequel *America and the Americans* (1966). And besides, there was Vietnam. Offered an assignment as a special correspondent for Newsway in South-east Asia for three months in 1966/7, Steinbeck travelled extensively in and around the war zone, sending back columns from Vietnam, Bangkok, Penang and the Malay Peninsula. 'In many ways the Vietnam war sank Steinbeck as a writer', wrote his biographer, Jay Parini. 'It had sucked him into a vortex and would not free him'. On his return in 1968 he had to undergo an operation on his back from which he was slow to recover. A heart attack followed and he realised he was close to death. He called Elaine to his side and asked her what the best time they had had together had been. She hesitated. 'You say first.'

'No,' he answered. 'I'm dying and you'll just agree with me.'
'Then I'll write it down.' She scribbled something on a note pad and put it in his hand. 'Now tell me,' she said.
'The time in Somerset,' he answered.
'Open your hand,' she told him. Written on the piece of paper in capital letters was the one word SOMERSET.

They lay down together and reminisced. Later that afternoon, says Elaine, 'he slowly slipped into a coma…very peacefully and slowly. Then he just stopped breathing.' He was buried on Christmas Eve.

Camelot

The literary siting of Camelot has been very varied. Caerleon-on-Usk was Geoffrey of Monmouth's choice. Malory's was Winchester; Caxton claimed it was in Wales. In an early sketch, written in 1833 for *The Idylls of the King*, Tennyson opted for a lost citadel in Lyonesse – the land now sunk beneath the seas off the south-western tip of Britain, of which only its mountain peaks – the Scilly Isles – remain.

But oldest, most logical and most popular in folklore is Camelot's identification with Cadbury Castle, an enormous hillfort near Yeovil in Somerset. In a twelfth-century tale called *Palamedes*, Camelot is described as being desolate and derelict, razed to the ground after Arthur's passing by King Mark of Cornwall, a statement that suggests it must have been within reach of Mark's forces. A fourteenth-century Italian poet, Fazli degli Uberto, claimed to have seen 'wasted, ruined Camelotto' with his own eyes. The first printed edition of Ptolemy's geography mentions a place called Camudulanum in the area. But the earliest explicit siting of it at Cadbury is probably that by John Leland in 1542:

> At the very south end of the church of South Cadbury stands Camelot, sometime a famous town or castle, upon a very Hill or Tor, wonderfully enstrengthened by nature …In the upper part of the cup of the hill be four ditches or trenches, and a bulky wall of earth betwixt every one of them. In the very top of the hill above all the trenches is magna area or campus of twenty acres or more by estimation where in diverse places men may see foundations and rudera of walls. There was much dusky blue stone that people of the villages thereby have carried

Yesterday I climbed Camelot on a golden day. The orchards are in flower and we could see the Bristol Channel and Glastonbury too, and King Alfred's tower and all below. And that wonderful place and structure with layer on layer of work and feeling. I found myself weeping.

John Steinbeck, letter to Eugène Vinaver, 1959

Prospect of Camalet Castle by the antiquary William Stukeley. He visited Cadbury Camp in August 1723 and, like many, believed this was the site of Arthur's castle.

away … Much gold, silver and copper of the Romans' coins has been found there in ploughing; and likewise in the roots of this hill, with many other antique things, and especially by east. There was found in hominum memoria a horseshoe of silver at Camelot.

In 1586 Camden wrote of 'Camelat, a steep mountain of very difficult ascent. The inhabitants call it Arthur's Palace, and Cadbury the adjoining little village may by conjecture be that Cathbregion where Arthur (as Nennius has it) routed the Saxons in a memorable engagement.' Elizabethan maps write the word 'Camellick' at Cadbury, and in *King Lear* Shakespeare makes the Earl of Kent exclaim: 'Goose, if I had you upon Sarum Plain / I'd drive you cackling home to Camelot.' The nearby villages of Queen's Camel and West Camel add further endorsement of the site. On his way to Cornwall in search of Arthurian sites, Tennyson visited Cadbury, and its topography certainly fits the Camelot of the later *Idylls* well enough. Tennyson then made Lyonesse and the lost land off the Scillies the home of Mark of Cornwall and the star-crossed lovers Tristram and Iseult.

In the 1960s, archaeological digs led by Leslie Alcock revealed that Cadbury boasts the most important and massive sixth-century fortifications in Britain, and that pottery found there is identical to the Mediterranean sixth-century ware that has been found in such enormous quantities at Tintagel. It is a reflection of how modern fictions adapt to new discoveries that although White's *Once and Future King* follows Caxton's Malory in setting Camelot in Wales, in the 1967 film version of *Camelot*, Arthur is seen looking at a map which marks Camelot as being in Somerset.

Local legends had repeated for hundreds of years that Arthur's Palace had stood on the flattened plateau to the northwest of the site. Leslie Alcock's excavations uncovered the foundations of a massive timber hall there, 63ft long and 34ft wide, with holes for its posts cut deep into the bedrock. In outline, it was very like the hall at Castle Dore. Alcock also discovered that the 16ft-wide stone and timber ramparts around the site had been formidably reinforced in Arthur's time. Massive posts had upheld a high timber breastwork. Beams had run across this, supporting a platform, perhaps with wooden watch-towers at intervals. A 10ft-wide cobbled road ascended from below and into the enclosure by way of the towered and double-doored gateway to the south-west. According to Geoffrey Ashe:

What the project did prove was that Cadbury was occupied by the right sort of person at approximately the right time. A leader with uncommon resources took possession of this vacant hillfort and refortified it on a colossal scale … When they were at Cadbury, their encampment held fully 1,000 men, plus ancillary staff, followers and families. During the campaign season, the base may have been looked after by a garrison only. But it may have been a regional centre of government with a permanent civilian establishment.

Even more conclusive evidence of the site's importance is the fact that nothing remotely approaching the Cadbury fortifications in size has been found anywhere else in post-Roman Britain.

The archaeologists also made one gruesome discovery. At the south-east corner of the wall, the skeleton of a young man was found. He had been rammed head first into a pit, his knees tucked up to his chin, and the rampart continued above him. Was he a druidical sacrifice for the divine strengthening of the wall? In Bernard Cornwell's new Arthurian trilogy, *The Warlord Chronicles* (*The Winter King*, *Enemy of God* and *Excalibur*), a Druid Merlyn performs a very similar sacrificial act on Maiden Castle. Cornwell did detailed research into the social, religious and military realities of sixth-century Britain, and his trilogy is a brilliant integration of legend and history. He remembers Cadbury as the most unspoilt and evocative of all the Arthurian sites he visited.

I've been walking South Cadbury's hilltop for thirty years, and I rarely see another person inside its grass ramparts. No ticket-booth at the entrance, no entrance fee, no plaques up on the hilltop…

I like it because it doesn't dominate the landscape like Maiden Castle or Glastonbury Tor. From its ramparts the views are stunning; all across green Wessex, with only the scar of the newly widened A303 spoiling the view. But walk west from South Cadbury and it melds into the hills behind. It is, to this exile, the most English place I know, yielding its secrets grudgingly, and utterly peaceful. The peace, of course, is misleading. This was once a fortress. It bristled with spears and clamped its power on the surrounding country. Men feasted here and hung their banners from the wall, and now it is nothing but a lumpy hilltop where cattle graze. And I think Arthur ruled here. He was never at Tintagel – it is too far from where his Saxon enemies threatened.

On Foot (3 miles)

Cadbury Castle, which is privately owned but open to the public, can be seen on the south side of the road from cars travelling westward on the A303. Leave the road at Chapel Cross, a mile and a half before the village of Sparkford. Drive through the little village of South Cadbury to the church, and you will find a car-park on the left. But, as with Glastonbury, you might like to take a view of the site's splendours from the surrounding hills before ascending the main castle hill. Continue past the car-park and take the first lane on the left, a narrow track that winds past the back of the village. A bridlepath on the right leads up to Littleton Hill, once a quarry. To the west of the summit, you can appreciate the defensive strength of the little group of hills, which jut out of the ground with the same suddenness as the cluster around Glastonbury.

Return to the car-park near the church. From here, a steep high-sided bridlepath leads up to the summit of the hill, which is about 500ft above sea level. A well to the left of the path is known as King Arthur's Well. There are the remains of four lines of bank-and-ditch rampart defences around it. Where they are wooded, the ditches are much broken down, but towards the south their full scale can be appreciated.

The central area is about 18 acres in size. Glastonbury is clearly visible to the north-west, and beyond it, on a clear day, Brent Knoll can be seen.

To the north-west of the summit you can see the flattened plateau thought to be Arthur's Palace.

When you leave the car-park at Cadbury, turn left and follow the lane to Sutton Montis. Turn right towards Sparkford. The meadows between here and the River Cam, which you cross just after Mill Farm on the outskirts of Sparkford, could be where Arthur's last battle of Camlann took place, near as it is both to Cadbury/Camelot and Glastonbury/Avalon. Perhaps a sortie aggressively made from Camelot went badly wrong. Certainly something once happened there. According to Geoffrey Ashe, a local farmer reported digging up large numbers of ancient skeletons huddled together as if in a mass grave on the west side of the hill.

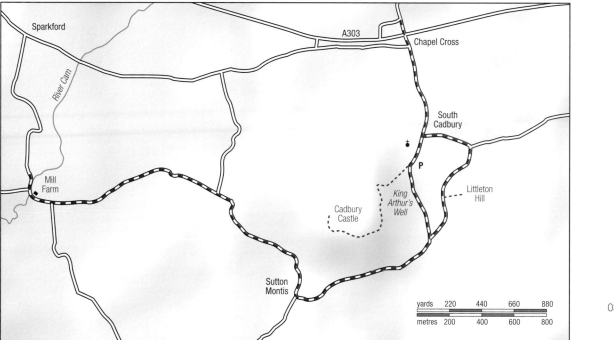

MAP
OS Explorer 129: Yeovil and Sherborne

It is evident that the famous 'Matter of Britain', as the Arthurian stories are traditionally known, is and will remain an inspiration for English-speaking writers. Their motives for returning to him are many and varied, sometimes highly personal, sometimes laudably idealistic. In light of the many archaeological endorsements of the ancient legends, writers have turned to spinning yarns about a far more real Arthur than that of Malory, Tennyson or White. But parallel to this, hundreds of fantasy novels, modern substitutes for the old morality tales, focus on Arthur. I asked Bernard Cornwell why he thought we were still so obsessed with this obscure sixth-century chieftain. 'Because of Camelot', he said. 'Arthur is depicted as establishing a country where justice prevails, where a farmer can sow a crop and expect to live to harvest it, where "right" wins! And isn't that what all of us want? To live in a fair, just world?'

PUCK OF POOK'S SUSSEX

I've seen Sir Huon and a troop of his people setting off from Tintagel Castle for Hy-Brasil in the teeth of a sou'-westerly gale, with the spray flying all over the castle, and the Horses of the Hill wild with fright. Out they'd go in a lull, screaming like gulls, and back they'd be driven five good miles inland before they could come head to wind … It was Magic – Magic as black as Merlin could make it, and the whole sea was green fire and white foam with singing mermaids in it. And the Horses of the Hill pick-ed their way from one wave to another by the lightning flashes! That was how it was in the old days!

Rudyard Kipling, *Puck of Pook's Hill*

Rudyard Kipling (1865-1936) and his wife Carrie fell in love with Bateman's the first time they saw it, in August 1900. It nestled in a natural bowl beneath wooded hills, grey-gold in the sunshine, an ancient, settled place that had been spared Victorian restoration. After they acquired the house in 1902, Kipling entered into the business of becoming an English squire with glee, and became as intensely interested in British folklore as he had been in that of India. He had a well dug by two local experts – 'dark and mysterious Primitives' who 'had the gift'. By the time they stopped at 25ft, they had found a Jacobean tobacco pipe, a Cromwellian latten spoon and the bronze cheek of a Roman horse-bit. In cleaning out an old marl-pit, they dredged up two intact Elizabethan sealed quart pots, 'all pearly with the patina of centuries', and 'a perfectly polished Neolithic axe-head with but one chip on its still venomous edge'.

The more Kipling explored, the more he understood that the valley and Pook's Hill above it were 'alive with ghosts and shadows':

Then it pleased our children to act for us, in the open, what they remembered of *A Midsummer Night's Dream*. Then a friend gave them a real birchbark canoe, drawing at least three inches, in which they went adventuring on the brook. And in a near pasture of the water-meadows lay out an old and unshifting Fairy Ring.

All this was to inspire Kipling's most mysterious and magical book, *Puck of Pook's Hill* (1906). In it, by acting scenes from the *Dream*, two children, recognisably the Kiplings' own John and Elsie, accidentally summon up Puck himself:

In the very spot where Dan had stood as Puck they saw a small, brown, broad-shouldered, pointy-eared person with a snub nose, slanting blue eyes, and a grin that ran right across his freckled face.

'What on Human Earth made you act *Midsummer Night's Dream* three times over, on Midsummer Eve, in the middle of a Ring, and under – right under – one of my oldest hills in Old England! Pook's Hill – Puck's Hill – Puck's Hill – Pook's Hill! It's as plain as the nose on my face.'

He pointed to the bare fern-covered slope of Pook's Hill that runs up from the far side of the millstream, to a dark wood. Beyond that wood the ground rises and rises for five hundred feet, till at last you climb out on the bare top of Beacon Hill, to look over the Pevensey Downs and the Channel and half the naked South Downs.

'By Oak, Ash and Thorn! If this had happened a few hundred years ago you'd have had the People of the Hills out like bees in June!'

The setting of the first scene of *Puck of Pook's Hill* is unchanged. Beyond the orchard at the end of the garden is 'the Little Mill that clacks, so busy by the brook' (it still grinds corn on summer Saturdays). Follow that brook, the Duddon river, with its glossy shingles and shallows. After crossing a stile, you will find on the left, exactly as described on the first page of *Puck*, the natural amphitheatre made by the mill-stream banks, 'overgrown with

Left: *Bateman's from the South West* by Sir Edward Poynter (1913).

Right: Rudyard Kipling's Nobel Prize medallion awarded in 1907.

Below: Detail of Puck from the frontispiece of *Puck of Pook's Hill*.

willow, hazel and guelder-rose' which 'make convenient places to wait in until your turn came'.

Through Puck's magic, Dan and Una half hear, half enter, a series of stories. The book, which is punctuated by some of Kipling's most famous poems, is a pageant of English history from Arthurian times onwards; it also teaches a profound respect for loyalty. Most of its settings are local – Burwash, nearby farms, the windy chalk Downs, Battle, Pevensey Castle.

In the sequel *Rewards and Fairies* (1910), written when John and Elsie were in their teens, the stories point up moral dilemmas. The phrase 'What else could I have done?' runs like a refrain through each one of them. But Kipling does not preach an ordinary moral code – the best known of the poems in *Rewards* is the interestingly amoral 'If'.

Hobden, the children's loyal ally in the stories, was based on a local countryman called Isden, who was seventy years old when the Kiplings arrived, 'a poacher by heredity and instinct [who] became our special stay and counsellor'. His cottage was on the site of the ancient forge, a field or two on from Puck's Theatre.

His sagas were lighted with pictures of Nature as he, indeed, knew her; night-pieces and dawn-breakings; stealthy returns and the thinking out of alibis, all naked by the fire while his clothes dried; and of the face and temper of the next twilight under which he stole forth to follow his passion.

Kipling admired any lawlessness that could be described as sporting. He was fascinated by Burwash's reputation as a haunt of smugglers ('watch the wall my darling, while the Gentlemen go by'). Its Bell Inn appears in the smuggling story 'Hal of the Draft' in *Puck*, and St Bartholomew's Church appears as St Barnabas. The clock and the ancient bells in 'The Conversion of St Wilfrid' are still there, and in the graveyard a worn tombstone sports a skull and crossbones. It is reputed to be not just a smuggler's grave but the way to a secret passage which led, some say to The Bell, some to Bateman's itself.

Leave Burwash by the little road beside the church that winds southwards down into the valley and then steeply uphill, and you come to a broad bare summit, with an obelisk and an observatory. A few steps to the south, and the Pevensey Levels are spread below you as if seen from an aeroplane, with the Channel a smudge of grey beyond them. A few yards to the north and you look down over the valley that holds Bateman's as if in the cupped palm of a hand. Oak, ash and thorn still cover the slopes below, though Forestry Commission woods have re-opened the lost road in 'The Way Through the Woods' with a vengeance.

She is not any common earth
Water or wood or air,
But Merlin's Isle of Gramarye
Where you and I will fare

Rudyard Kipling, 'Puck's Song'

Jane Austen in her Landscape

Jane Austen (1775-1817) spent the first twenty-five years of her life at Steventon in Hampshire, a rich, well-husbanded county which William Cobbett described in *Rural Rides* (1830) as 'the best of all landscapes for living in'. Her father held the livings of Deane and Steventon, and Jane, the seventh of his eight children, was born at Steventon Parsonage on 16 December 1775. The Austens were a happy, close-knit family, and five of Jane's brothers were suitable models for heroes: James and Henry ended up as clergymen, Charles and Frank became Admirals of the Fleet and Edward was adopted by wealthy relations. The sixth, George, was mentally disabled in some way, and lived with his similarly afflicted uncle in care in a nearby village.

Jane's natural childhood alliance with her only sister Cassandra lasted all through her life. Both had romances, both were disappointed and neither was prepared to marry just for the sake of it. Jane boasted more than once that her novels were substitute children. In 1813 she described the first published edition of *Pride and Prejudice* as 'my own darling child', and in 1815 she draws a parallel between her niece Anna's first child Jemima and her own *Emma*, both born that year. Her success as an author made it the easier to announce, as she did in 1813, that she 'must leave off being young', adding that she found 'many douceurs in being a sort of chaperone, for I am put on the sofa and can drink as much wine as I like'.

The social circle of which Steventon was the hub included Andover and Basingstoke, where the Assembly Rooms were the scene of many small triumphs and disasters. Like the Bennetts, the Austens socialised with a couple of dozen families, ranging from peers of the realm such as the Dorchesters at Kempshott Park to the widowed Mrs Lloyd at Deane Rectory. Mrs Austen was also a great one for visits to the 'cousinage', which meant excursions further afield, to Warwickshire, Bath, London, the south coast and Kent, where Edward lived in fine style with his rich relatives at Godmersham House, nine miles from Canterbury. These frequent removings valuably extended Jane's knowledge of all levels of

Jane Austen by her sister Cassandra (*c.*1810).

English society. They also furnished her eagerly acquisitive mind with characters and places which would in turn furnish her novels.

She believed that real knowledge of the places where novels were set was important. In a letter to her niece Anna, an aspiring novelist, she warned her against describing unknown scenes:

Silhouette showing
George Austen
presenting his son

Edward to the Knight
family for adoption.

> Let the Portmans go to Ireland, but as you know nothing of the Manners there, you had better not go with them. You will be in danger of giving false representations. Stick to Bath and the Foresters. There you will be quite at home.

Steventon Rectory by
Jane Austen's niece, Anna
Austen Lefroy (1820).

Jane took pains to make her settings realistic, studying guides, books of engravings, almanacs and road-books, and sending requests to friends for information about the places she used if she felt she did not know enough about them. Her place-names echo real ones (Cleveland for Clevedon Court in *Sense and Sensibility* (1811), for example), and distances from real to imaginary places are made consistent.

However, she deliberately kept her stories at a distance from Hampshire, in part to guard her anonymity, in part to disclaim copying from neighbours and neighbourhood. 'I am too proud of my gentlemen to admit they are only Mr A or Colonel B', she once wrote. *Sense and Sensibility* is set in the West Country, *Pride and Prejudice* in Hertfordshire and Derbyshire, *Mansfield Park* (1814) near Northampton (based perhaps in part on Cottesbrooke), *Persuasion* (1818) largely in Bath, and *Northanger Abbey* (1818) in the marches of Wales. Only *Emma* is set in anything like home territory, close to Box Hill in Surrey.

There is, however, no doubt that the Hampshire houses and families she knew so well were essential sources of inspiration for the settings, episodes and characters in her novels. Not all the houses still exist and only two are open to visitors, but evocative glimpses of most of them or their sites can be gained across fields or from churchyards.

To sit in the shade on a fine day and look upon verdure is the most perfect refreshment.

Jane Austen, *Mansfield Park*

Jane's Hampshire Homeland

All the houses in this tour are roughly contained in a triangle, of which Andover, Basingstoke and Winchester form the points. Steventon is a natural starting place. The tour's timing will vary, depending on how long you spend in churches and on extra strolls. But allow a good day, preferably a long fine one, to absorb the rhythms of this gentle, still marvellously peaceful landscape.

In early spring, the snowdrops that must once have grown in the garden of Steventon Rectory can still be seen there. You can judge its position, fairly close to the road, by the iron pump for the well which still remains, protected by a square of iron railings, and which would have been behind the house. There was apparently room in front of the site for 'a carriage-drive through turf and trees', James-Edward's memoir of his aunt Jane tells us. To the east of the house was 'one of the thatched mud walls common in that country … overshadowed by fine elms'.

High behind the house on the southern boundary of the home meadow a flattened terrace is visible. It is thought that Mrs Austen, an enthusiastic gardener, laid out a shrubbery above it, just the sort that occurs in *Persuasion* when Anne Elliot inadvertently hears Captain Wentworth and Louisa Musgrove talking about her. The Revd George Austen's study, lined with the books that were such an inspiration to Jane as a child, had a bow window which looked southwards towards it. There was a steep grassy bank between the shrubbery and the house – perhaps Jane, like Catherine Morland in *Northanger Abbey*, 'loved nothing so much in the world as rolling down the green slope' at the back of the rectory.

The glebe-land of the rectory included the meadows that flanked it and one opposite, so steep that it was called the Hanging Meadow. By its roadside gate was a large barn which the Austens used for their amateur theatricals. There was also a kitchen garden, a poultry-yard, and a 'nursery garden'. On the other side of the lane to the church, the edge of the Glebe's East Meadow was laid out as a Wood Walk. 'Our improvements have advanced very much', Jane wrote to Cassandra. 'The bank along the elm walk is sloped down for the reception of thorns and lilacs; and it is settled that the other side of the path is to continue turf'd and planted with beech, ash and larch.'

Jane's brother James succeeded her father as rector of Steventon in 1801, and when he died in 1819 his brother Henry succeeded him for three years. The next incumbent, Jane's nephew William Knight, was rector of the parish for the next fifty years, and it was he who had the old rectory house pulled down and a new one built on the hill to the north in 1826-7.

TRAIL 1 Steventon Church is a simple rectangular building not much changed from its twelfth-century structure. Here, first Jane's father George and later her brother James officiated at services. Jane was baptised in the church, and would have attended Sunday services regularly. Opposite the church in Jane's day there was an old manor house, which dated from the 1560s. It was the home of the Digweed family, whose memorials can be seen in the church. Jane records the fun she had dancing with the Digweed boys. Rebuilt and extended several times, it burnt down in 1970, and has been replaced by a new house in sixteenth-century style.

Another nearby family, the Terrys, lived at Dummer. Jane's contemporary Stephen Terry recorded in *Diaries of Dummer* many vivid details of his life there, and she herself records dancing five times with him at a local ball. It could have been held at Basingstoke's Angel Inn's Assembly Rooms, or at such nearby great houses as the Dorchesters' Kempshott Park or Hackwood, a substantial seventeenth-century house with Curzon family connections just three miles north-west of Dummer at Winslade. Hackwood was the grandest of all the houses Jane visited. Its owner after 1795 was Lord Bolton, a man in the mould of P. G. Wodehouse's Lord Emsworth, who designed pigsties in the grand manner for his much-beloved boars and sows, and, Jane told Cassandra in a letter, visited them every morning.

Even closer to home was Ashe Park. In Jane Austen's day it was let by the Portals, originally a Huguenot family who were substantial Hampshire landowners, to a West Indian nabob called James Holder and his family. They used to pass their newspaper on to the Austens. James also seems to have made the odd pass at Jane. In January 1801, she wrote to Cassandra that, having arrived ahead of the main party, she

> was shut up in the drawing room with Mr Holder alone for ten minutes. I had some thoughts of insisting on the housekeeper or Mary Corbett [a maid] being sent for, and nothing could prevail on me to move two steps from the door, on the lock of which I kept one hand constantly fixed.

North of Ashe Park is the still flourishing Deane Gate Inn. In the Austens' time it was a posting-inn to which the children used to walk over to collect letters left by the mailcoach. It was also a halt for the Exeter Telegraph, the coach between London and the West of England in which the family would have ridden to Bath. And it was a meeting spot for the local hunt, in which

Manydown House was at the hub of Jane's social circle in the 1790s – it was there that she danced with Tom Lefroy (above, left). Dances were also held at The Vyne, home of William Chute (above, right).

Jane's father and brothers regularly took part.

Just beyond the inn is Deane House, where Jane enjoyed balls given by the Harwood family. Deane House is reminiscent of the Westons' home as described in *Emma*. Is it coincidence or confusion, asks Anne-Marie Edwards, that an earlier novelist, Henry Fielding, based another family of Westons, the blustering Squire Weston and his lovely daughter Sophie in his novel *Tom Jones* (1749), on the Harwood family?

To the east, but on the north side of the B3400, is the site of Manydown House. Sadly, since it was closely connected with two of Jane Austen's most interesting romantic attachments, it was demolished in 1965. In 1796, Jane flirted and danced there with Tom Lefroy of Ashe Rectory. She was also very friendly with the three daughters of the house, Alethea, Catherine and Elizabeth Bigg. It was probably that friendship, as well as the temptation of a socially and materially excellent match, that, in 1804, while she and Cassandra were there on a visit from Bath, led her to accept the hand of their brother Harris Bigg-Wither, the heir to the property, when he shyly proposed to her one evening. But after a night of agonising – perhaps also remembering very different sensations for Tom Lefroy in the same house six years earlier – she told him she had changed her mind, rushed weeping to her brother James's rectory, and begged him to take her back to Bath post-haste.

North of Basingstoke, but still part of the Austens' social landscape, is The Vyne. Essentially a Tudor house, it was 'improved' with a classical portico and Strawberry Hill Gothick trimmings. In 1776, it was inherited by a Norfolk branch of the Chute family. Their youngest son Tom, born in 1772, was of an age to play with the Austen children. When older, he hunted with James and Frank, and he also danced and played cards with Cassandra and Jane.

The Vyne was inherited by Tom's much older brother William in 1790. It made the thirty-three-year-old bachelor, educated at Harrow and Cambridge, one of the most eligible matches in the district, and the fourteen-year-old Jane must have been aware of the flutters in neighbouring dovecotes when he took up residence after some years of absence. Did his return have a hint of the highly eligible Charles Bingley's arrival in *Pride and Prejudice*? William became MP for Hampshire, and had the reputation of being an Independent. Lord Palmerston referred to him as 'a hospitable squire' who 'preferred entertaining his neighbours at the Vyne to mixing with much zeal in parliamentary disputes'.

In matters matrimonial William Chute disappointed the local maidens by marrying Eliza Smith, daughter of Joshua

TRAIL 1

Smith, a hunting crony and MP for Devizes. Eliza arrived at The Vyne on 15 October 1793, and three days later she records in her diary that the Austins (*sic*: she never managed to master the spelling of their name) called on her. In November, a month before Jane was eighteen, Eliza met her new neighbours at the Basingstoke Ball – Frank Austen, then nineteen and just back from five years in the Far East, may well have been among them. He was certainly invited to dine at The Vyne not long after – but not with his sisters. Nor did they go to a dance given by the Chutes a few weeks later.

Eliza evidently also enjoyed Henry Austen's company – 'I danced six dances with Mr H Austin', she recorded of the Basingstoke Ball in 1794. James too was popular. He hunted with William and, as vicar of Sherborne St John, he was a regular visitor to the house and often took supper, Mr Collins-style, after the Sunday evening service. Perhaps he also called when visiting his brother George in nearby Monk Sherborne.

Eliza came from a family of girls, and was both musical and literary-minded, but she never became a close confidante of Jane or her sisters, even though she was only a few years older than they were. In her biography of Jane Austen, Claire Tomalin speculates that Jane and her sister may have felt a degree of condescension in the Chutes' approach; perhaps they resented Eliza muscling in on their local established friendships and found the grand lifestyle at The Vyne ostentatious. Or could it have been Eliza's persistent favouring of the men in the family that grated?

There were also practical difficulties to regular social interchange. At four miles away, The Vyne was too far for the ladies of Steventon to visit on foot, and would have required special carriage arrangements of the sort that are often intrinsic parts of the plots in Jane's novels. Perhaps this is why Jane's brothers, who would have ridden there, were more frequent visitors to the house than Jane herself.

The Chutes were childless, and in 1803, when the wife of a cousin of William's died, they adopted one of her children, a three-year-old girl called Caroline Wiggett. The position Caroline occupied in the family was similar to that of Fanny Price in *Mansfield Park*, albeit starting much earlier in the child's life.

The local house most dear to Jane Austen's heart was Ashe Rectory, home of the Lefroys. Tom Lefroy, Jane's dancing partner at Manydown, was a cousin, who visited from Ireland in 1796. 'A very gentlemanlike, good-looking, pleasant young man, I assure you', Jane wrote of him to Cassandra, perhaps in answer to an anxious enquiry as to rumours of a liaison that had reached as far as Kent. There is some suggestion that the family packed Tom hastily back to Ireland before what would have been a financially most undesirable connection was established. There are some ambiguous nuances in Jane's next letter to Cassandra – 'I can expose myself, however, only once more, because he leaves the country soon after next Friday, on which day we are to have a dance at Ashe after all.'

It seems that on that occasion Mrs Lefroy provided a compensatory suitor for Jane – the Revd Samuel Blackall. But Jane did not rise to the bait. Instead she poked fun at his pomposities; perhaps he helped to inspire Mr Collins, who also took the advice of a rich patroness in his choice of a suitable wife.

What was much more long lasting than such sentimental attachments was her easy and affectionate friendship with Mrs Lefroy. 'We had a very pleasant day on Monday at Ashe', Jane wrote to Cassandra in November 1800:

we sat down fourteen at dinner in the study, the dining room not being habitable from the storm's having blown down its chimney…there was whist and a casino table… Rice and Lucy made love, Mat Robinson fell asleep, James and Mrs Augusta alternately read Dr Jenner's pamphlet on the cow pox, and I bestowed my company by turns on all.

Tragically, Mrs Lefroy was killed in a riding accident in 1804.

In 1789 James Austen became vicar of Overton, two miles west of Ashe, where he successfully courted Anne Mathew of nearby Freefolk Priors. She was the daughter of an irascible but wealthy ex-Governor of Granada, General Edward Mathew, who rented the house from Joseph Portal. James cultivated good company and Anne was the daughter of a general and granddaughter of a duke. She was also thirty-two, perhaps more than ready to settle for a respectable rather than a grand marriage. The wedding was in 1792, and General Mathew provided them with a respectable rather than grand income of £100 a year. When James became vicar of Deane and he and Anne moved into Deane Rectory, Jane's close friends Martha and Mary Lloyd and their widowed mother moved fifteen miles away to Ibthorpe, near Hurstbourne Tarrant.

One of the grandest houses that featured on Jane's social calendar was Hurstbourne Park, a few miles west of Steventon, on the other side of Whitchurch. Built by James Wyatt, it was a vast mansion, set high on a hill in a landscaped park with service wings as large as the central building. As a child, its owner the Earl of Portsmouth had briefly been a pupil of Jane's father, and the Austens were regularly invited to the annual Hurstbourne

Ball. 'I believe I drank too much wine last night at Hurstbourne', Jane wrote to Cassandra on 20 November 1800. 'I know not how else to acount for the shaking of my hand today…It was a pleasant evening…There were only twelve dances, of which I danced nine, and was merely prevented from dancing the rest by the want of a partner.'

She also reported that the Earl spoke kindly to her, and asked to be remembered to Cassandra. It was just as well that neither of them attracted closer attentions from him, for he was far from normal. His life could easily have formed the subject for one of the Gothic novels Jane parodied in *Northanger Abbey*. He had a bizarre taste for staging funerals, was notoriously brutal with servants and, having been lured into marriage with the daughter of his outrageously corrupt steward, lived under the protection of trustees.

After the Lloyds moved to Ibthorpe, Jane used to make long visits to their house. She first came in 1792 when she was seventeen, and often stayed for weeks at a time – the twelve-mile distance to Steventon precluded daily visits for all but carriage folk. The closest town was Hurstbourne Tarrant, where the Revd Peter Debary was vicar. Jane evidently found his three daughters tedious company. 'It is a not uncommon circumstance in this parish to have the road from Ibthrop [*sic*] to the parsonage much dirtier and more impracticable for walking than the road from the parsonage to Ibthrop', she wrote dryly to Cassandra. Mrs Lloyd's mother, a noted society beauty called Mrs Craven, who was extremely unkind to her daughters, could have been the model for the outrageous Lady Susan, the eponymous heroine of what may well have been Jane Austen's first attempt at a novel.

The Lloyds shared Ibthorpe with an old lady full of inconsequential chatter called Mrs Stent, who had an evident kinship to Mrs Allen in *Northanger Abbey*, who 'as she never talked a great deal could never be entirely silent; and therefore … if she lost her needle or broke her thread, if she heard a carriage in the street, or saw a speck on her gown, she must observe it aloud'.

A year after James Austen's wife Anne died in childbirth in 1795, James came courting to Ibthorpe. In 1797 he and Mary Lloyd were married in Hurstbourne Tarrant Church, and she returned to her childhood home of Deane as his wife. Their son James-Edward, Jane's favourite nephew, was born there in 1798.

It was on returning from a visit to Ibthorpe in December 1800 that Jane was told that her parents had decided to move to Bath. She fainted from the shock, but rallied bravely, although the next seven years of urban life in Bath, Clifton and Southampton were to prove disastrous in writing terms. It was not until 1809 that she once more found herself in an environment in which she could devote herself methodically to revising her earlier writings and beginning new books.

TRAIL

1

The south front of The Vyne in the mid-nineteenth century.

TRAIL 1 By Car (*c*.60 miles)

Steventon is six miles south-west of Basingstoke. To reach it, turn off the M3 at exit 7 and head west on the A30. After a mile take the right-hand turning to North Waltham and Steventon. Keep left in North Waltham and turn right to Steventon at Hatch Gate. Steventon is only a tiny hamlet, perhaps even smaller than it was in the Austens' day. Stocks stood on the triangle of grass where the lane to the church turns right. Jane's wet-nurse Nanny Littlewort lived in a cottage, now demolished, a little east along this lane. Follow it for half a mile or so; at the point where you turn right down a lane signed to the church you will see the sloping field where Steventon Rectory, the Austens' home, once stood. High behind the house on the southern boundary of the home meadow a flattened terrace is still visible.

Continue along the lane to Steventon Church. The little spire post-dates the Austens. If you have time, take a stroll, one the Austens must often have enjoyed, along the footpaths and lanes that lead through North Waltham to Dummer; you could of course also drive. Dummer is much more built up than Steventon, but its twelfth-century church is gloriously unspoiled, with a musicians' gallery dating from the seventeenth century and a medieval rood canopy. The white manor house behind the church was once the home of the Terrys, a large and jolly family who may well have inspired the ebullient Musgroves of *Persuasion*.

Return to Steventon. Jane and Cassandra regularly walked across the fields to the nearby villages of Ashe and Deane, their father's second living, but if you are short of time, it would be better to drive there. Turn left past the site of the parsonage, then right through the tunnel under the railway and head northwards to Deane. High up on the left is Ashe Park, where James Holder and his family lived.

A little further on, look out on the left for Cheese-down Farm, which Jane's father farmed, grace of his cousins the Knights, who had also granted him the livings of Steventon and Deane. At the junction of the lane with the B3400 – once, as its milestones and fingerposts still show, the main London to Salisbury road – is the Deane Gate Inn.

Drive straight across the B3400 down the lane to Deane. On the right-hand side you will see a fine dower house, but the rectory in which George Austen lived before moving to Steventon was on the left-hand side of the lane and has been demolished. It became the home of Jane's close friends the Lloyds in 1790. Park by the gate to Deane Church. As you walk to it, you will get a fine view of the handsome settled façade of Deane House. When I visited, the church was locked, but a ramble around its churchyard gives fine views of the emparked landscape, with Ashe Park resplendent to the south. About a mile to the south-east is the great park of Hall Place at Oakley. The house, now a school,

was built in 1789 for Jane's friends the Bramstons.

From Deane, return to the B3400 and turn left. After about two miles, turn left to Wootton St Lawrence and Monk Sherborne, where Jane's brother George and her uncle lived in the care of the Culhams. Turn right just before the village to Sherborne St John. Drive straight through this village, following the brown National Trust oak-leaf signs to The Vyne, home of the Chutes, and a great haunt of Jane's brothers.

Return through Monk Sherborne to the B3400 and head westwards to Ashe, where a lane on the right leads down to the village. Close to the road on the left is the elegant, welcoming façade of Ashe Rectory (now Ashe House) a substantial four-square Georgian house that was once the home of the Lefroys. Follow the lane down the hill to Ashe Church (closed when I visited). It was rebuilt in 1877, but its graveyard is full of atmosphere. Over to the right as you approach are the Lefroy graves; Tom's of course is not there but in Ireland. Asked about Jane in his old age, he said that he had indeed loved her, 'but with a boy's love'.

Drive on through Overton, where James Austen was curate while courting Anne Mathew of Freefolk Priors. A lodge and a drive on the right will alert you to look out for Laverstoke House, well back from the road, but clearly visible. This was the ancestral home of the Portal family. In 1796 Portal's son Harry pulled the house down and rebuilt it to the designs of Joseph Bonomi, an architect whom Jane derides in *Sense and Sensibility*, when she has Robert Ferrars throw his plans for Lord Courtland's new house into the fire.

Continue through Whitchurch, its centre still dominated by the White Hart, once an important coaching inn, sited as it was on the crossing of the roads east–west London to Salisbury and north–south Oxford to Southampton. Duck under the A34, the new north–south arterial road, and almost immediately on your right you will see the main gates to Hurstbourne Park. The house burned down in 1870, and its replacement was

Hurstbourne Park, where Jane attended the Earl of Portsmouth's annual ball in November 1800.

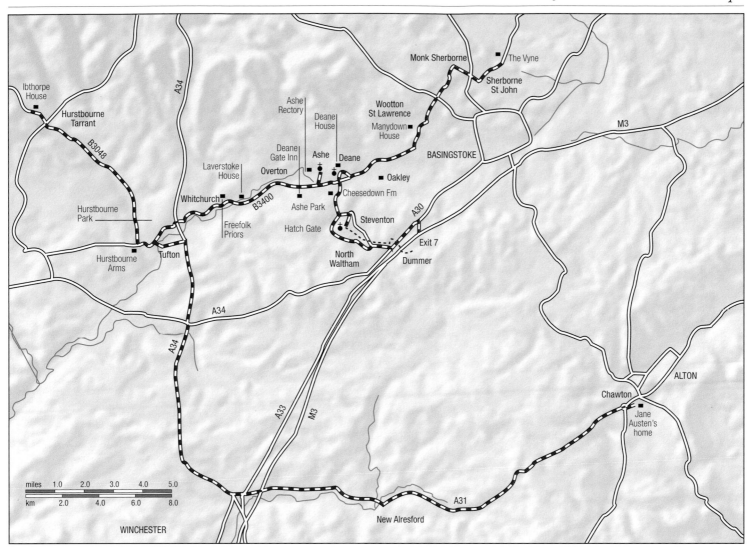

demolished in 1965. But there are still (private) buildings up there; chimneys can still be seen through the trees.

About a mile after passing the gates to Hurstbourne Park, turn right at the Hurstbourne Arms along the B3048 to Hurstbourne Tarrant. It's a beautiful drive, following the course of the River Bourne as it meanders through water meadows rich in cresses and buttercups. It is still very much as Jane must have seen it when she set out for one of her prolonged visits to Ibthorpe to stay with her friends the Lloyds. When you reach Hurstbourne Tarrant, you will see the church on your right. After joining the A343, turn right and then almost immediately left along a narrow lane signposted to Ibthorpe. Ibthorpe House (private property) is on the western edge of the village on the right, set in a walled garden behind a small triangle of grass where the western end of Horseshoe Lane meets the main lane. Built of mellow eighteenth-century brick, with two long windows on each side of the door, five above and three dormers in the roof, it was the kind of small but formal house that Jane liked best. If you have time, there are lovely walks around Ibthorpe, including a fine tramp up high to Windmill Hill, from where Jane could have seen the countryside around Steventon.

This trail ends at Chawton Cottage, Jane's last home. To reach it, return down the B3048 and the B3400, turning off to the right to Tufton just before Hurstbourne Park. Duck under the A34 again and turn sharp right to join its dual carriageway southwards. At the roundabout where the A34 joins the M3, go straight across on the A31 and follow it eastwards to Alton. Just before you reach Alton, you will see brown heritage signs to Chawton. The village was once on the main London to Winchester road but is now a peaceful little backwater of a place, even quieter than it was when the Austens lived there.

MAP
OS Hampshire Explorer 144: Basingstoke, Alton and Whitchurch

COUNTRYSIDE AS COUNTERPOINT

There was more to Austen's interest in landscape than a desire for verisimilitude. She repeatedly uses landscape and place in a skilfully constructed counterpoint which enriches both character and plot. The grounds and gardens around the houses she describes are as significant indicators of taste and character as the clothes people wear and the food they eat. Conservatives stick to walled gardens and dovecotes; dedicated followers of fashion create sublime artificialities; confident individuals follow their own horticultural inclination.

In this, her technique echoes that of Samuel Richardson, who wrote in *Sir Charles Grandison* (1754), one of the Austen family's favourite books, that the views from the windows of Grandison's spacious house were 'as boundless as the mind of the owner and as free and open as his countenance'. Similarly, when Elizabeth Bennett sees Darcy's great Derbyshire estate Pemberley, she understands 'where he came from' as she never did before. Moreover, it is not his material wealth, but his creation of natural beauty that converts her pique into admiration. 'She had never seen a place for which nature had done more, or where natural beauty had been so little counteracted by an awkward taste.'

Caroline Austen wrote that Jane 'had such a love of natural scenery that she would sometimes say that she thought it must form one of the delights of heaven'. In this, Jane was typical of an age poised between rural and industrial society. Although there were no dark satanic mills in Hampshire, it was impossible not to know that they existed.

It was that knowledge that lay behind the escapism of William Gilpin's *Tours in Search of Picturesque Beauty* (1782), the Gothic horrors of Ann Radcliffe's *Mysteries of Udolpho* (1794), and Capability Brown and Humphry Repton's deliberate romanticising of landscape with awful cells, mouldering towers, darksome pines, caverns, grots and twilight groves. The famous Ladies of Llangollen lived in a Gothick house with ruins and arches in the garden and a hermitage. Jane would also have known the hermitage halfway up Gilbert White's zigzag at Selborne.

'Picturesque' was an eighteenth-century coinage that described a newly artistic appreciation of nature, a seeking after views that were in themselves like pictures. It was made famous by William Gilpin (1724-1804), whose theories put several old words to new uses: 'scenery' had hitherto been limited to theatres, and 'landscape' applied to pictures rather than places. The first edition of Gilpin's *Tour of the Lakes* (1786) was sold out in a few days, and hundreds of 'tourists' (the word itself was in the first place derived from those who followed in Gilpin's footsteps) set out on the new turn-pike roads to see for themselves the beauties he described.

Seeking out the picturesque was an elegant and aloof occupation, very different from the palpitating involvement with sensibility demanded by either Jean Jacques Rousseau's *La Nouvelle Heloïse* (1760) or Ann Radcliffe's novels. Jane read Gilpin with close interest. Her brother Henry said that she was 'from a very early age enamoured of the picturesque' and that 'she evinced great power in the management of a pencil'. But she also read and laughed at *The Adventures of Dr Syntax in Search of the Picturesque*, the famous spoof of Gilpin written in 1812 by William Combe and illustrated by Thomas Rowlandson. 'I have seen nobody in London yet with such a long chin as Dr Syntax', she wrote to Cassandra while she was staying with Henry.

Her novels frequently poked fun at the frantic improvements which James Lees-Milne memorably described in 1985 as the overnight transformation of 'the wild English shires into one enormous landscape park'. *Northanger Abbey* is the most obviously satirical. Catherine Morland's visit to Bath introduces her to the circulating libraries and the horrible delights of Gothic novels. The misunderstandings which make up the plot rely on her eagerness to find the world a 'horrid' place. But besides satirising the Gothic imagination, Jane also points a teasing finger at the current rage for all things picturesque. Henry Tilney and his sister view the country 'with the eyes of persons accustomed to drawing and decided on its capability of being formed into pictures with all the eagerness of real taste'. While Catherine wonders if the view from Bath's

In pursuit of the Picturesque: *Dr Syntax Sketching the Lake* by Thomas Rowlandson (1812).

Beechen Cliff is Italianate in the best tradition of Mrs Radcliffe, Tilney encourages her to look at it in Gilpin's picturesque manner:

> He talked of foregrounds and distances and second distances – sidescreens and perspectives – lights and shades; and Catherine was so hopeful a scholar that when they gained the top of Beechen Cliff, she voluntarily rejected the whole city of Bath as unworthy to make a landscape.

In *Pride and Prejudice*, Elizabeth Bennett enthuses to her aunt, Mrs Gardiner, in best Gilpin style at the prospect of a tour of the Lakes:

> 'My dear, dear Aunt,' she rapturously cried, 'what delight! what felicity! You give me fresh life and vigour. Adieu to disappointment and spleen. What are men to rocks and mountains? Oh! what hours of transport we shall spend!'

Although they do not get as far as the Lakes, their route northwards passes through Oxford, Blenheim, Warwick, Kenilworth and Birmingham, just as Gilpin's did when he set off to tour the Lakes. He returned via Matlock, Chatsworth and Dovedale, which is as far as the Gardiners go. And it is in Derbyshire that Elizabeth sees Pemberley, built 'on rising ground and backed with a ridge of high woods'.

Jane Austen, like Elizabeth, never visited the Lakes, but she could well have seen, as Elizabeth did, 'all the celebrated beauties of Matlock, Chatsworth, Dovedale, or the Peak' in 1806, when she stayed for five weeks with her cousins the Coopers at Hamstall Ridware, eight miles south of Dovedale. She endows Pemberley with a 'circuit walk', a gardening fashion approved by Gilpin, who believed foreground planting encouraged a hide-and-discover approach to views – 'such interruptions add the charm of renewal'. The Pemberley circuit is described in some detail:

They entered the woods, and bidding adieu to the river for a while, ascended some of the higher grounds; whence, in spots where the opening of the trees gave the eye power to wander, were many

A Prospect in Dove-Dale by Antoine Benoist (1721–70), after Thomas Smith.

charming views of the valley, the opposite hills, with the long range of woods overspreading many, and occasionally part of the stream …they pursued the accustomed circuit which brought them again, after some time, in a descent among hanging woods, to the edge of the water, in one of its narrowest parts. They crossed it by a simple bridge, in character with the general air of the scene; it was a spot less adorned than any they had yet visited; and the valley, here contracted into a glen, allowed room only for the stream, and a narrow walk amidst the rough coppice wood, which bordered it.

Just such a walk exists along the River Manifold at Ilam, near Dovedale, and Mavis Batey has suggested that Ilam House, now destroyed, might well have been the original inspiration for Pemberley. Gilpin describes its setting admiringly: a house on a hill 'which slopes gently in front but is abrupt and broken behind'. Izaak Walton fished in the Manifold, and the scenery was also praised by Dr Johnson. The National Trust owns 900 acres at Ilam and 1,400 at Dovedale. However, the television version of *Pride and Prejudice* used the exterior of Lyme Park, a National Trust house in Cheshire, for Pemberley.

Humphry Repton was the most fashionable landscape gardener of the age, and in *Mansfield Park* there is some gentle satire at his expense – inspired no doubt by the experiences of Jane's cousin the Revd Thomas Leigh, who invited Repton to improve first the hundred acres of Adlestrop (Gloucestershire), and then the 700 of Stoneleigh Abbey (Warwickshire), which Leigh unexpectedly inherited a few years later. 'Smith has not much above a 100 acres altogether in his grounds, which is little enough, and it makes it more surprising that the place can have been so improved', says Mr Rushworth in *Mansfield Park*. 'Now, at Sotherton, we have a good 700, without reckoning the water meadows; so that I think if so much could be done at Compton, we need not despair.'

Jane Austen herself was more in tune with an older and more conservative appreciation of the beauties of nature than what Dr Johnson

Humphry Repton's proposal for the landscaping of Uppark in Sussex from his *Red Book* of 1810.

called 'the fashionable whine of sensibility'. 'God made the country and man the town', wrote her favourite poet William Cowper in *The Task* (1785). She loved walking in the countryside for the sake of it, covering six miles a day as a matter of course, and her letters are full of references to the changing seasons. In *Mansfield Park*, Fanny shows herself to be a devotee of Cowper, who argued for the preservation of avenues and against 'improvements'. In *Sense and Sensibility*, for all Marianne's hankering after romantic bowers and sentimental vistas, she ends up with the thoroughly sensible Colonel Brandon at Delaford, an old-fashioned house with walled gardens, canal and fishponds, and a dovecote.

The house which Jane described with more affection than any other is Donwell Abbey, the home of Mr Knightley in *Emma*. It was set close to Box Hill, one of Jane's favourite jaunts.

The considerable slope, at nearly the foot of which the Abbey stood, gradually acquired a steeper form beyond its grounds; and at half a mile distant was a bank of considerable abruptness and grandeur, well clothed with wood; and at the bottom of this bank, favourably placed and sheltered, rose the Abbey-Mill Farm, with meadows in front and the river making a close and handsome curve around it.

It was a sweet view – sweet to the eye and the mind. English verdure, English culture, English comfort, seen under a sun bright without being offensive.

The house is as unpretentiously attractive as Mr Knightley, 'rambling and irregular, with many comfortable and one or two handsome rooms … just what it ought to be, and looking what it was'. Although he is not averse to sensible improvements, Mr Knightley has a deeply conservative attitude to his estates. The old fishponds are left in place, and 'ample gardens [stretched] down to meadows washed by a stream of which the Abbey, with all the old neglect of prospect, had scarcely a sight'.

TRAIL **A Promenade in Jane Austen's Bath**

2

Bath was built to be walked in, a city of promenades and wide pavements, vistas and gardens. A walk round Bath today will of course be a very different experience from the sort of strolls that Jane and her characters took, but much of the spirit of the eighteenth-century city remains. Moreover, actually seeing the homes in which she chose to locate her fictional creations reveals the pinpoint accuracy with which she defined status and character by choice of lodgings.

Why did Jane write so little in Bath? Was she preoccupied with her own increasingly remote marital prospects or her parents' health? Or was she discouraged by the rejection of *First Impressions*, later *Pride and Prejudice*? In 1803, perhaps fired by the fiasco of Harris Bigg-Wither's proposals, Jane did return to her writing, revising and copying out *Susan* (later *Northanger Abbey*). Her brother Henry arranged for it to be offered to a publisher, Richard Crosby, who paid £10 for it and promised to publish it speedily. It was even advertised as 'in Press' but time passed and nothing happened. Meanwhile, Jane had started *The Watsons*, a tale with obvious personal resonances of a family of four unmarried sisters without much money who are desperately contriving to improve their circumstances by marriages before their invalid father dies, when they will lose their home, his rectory. But after the death of her own father, or perhaps because nothing had come of *Susan*, she seems to have given the story up.

Although Bath proved less than conducive to writing, it was full of characters and settings which would be employed to good effect later on. All her novels except *Pride and Prejudice* make some use of Bath, and to two, *Northanger Abbey* and *Persuasion*, it is of central importance.

The Austens' first home after they moved to the city in 1801 was a charming town house at 4 Sydney Place, overlooking Sydney Gardens. This quarter of the town had recently been made accessible by Robert Adam's shop-lined Pulteney Bridge, and Sydney Gardens, modelled on the famous London South Bank pleasure garden of Vauxhall, was full of novel delights, as an 1800 Bath Guide reveals:

Sydney-Garden Vauxhall is situated at the termination of Great Pulteney Street. It was opened for publick entertainment on the 11th May 1795. This pleasure-ground was designed by Mr Harcourt Masters, Architect, in which he has displayed much taste and judgement. The style is quite new, and exhibits the most pleasing variety. There is also an elegant and spacious

Left: Sydney House from the Gardens, Bath by G. Wise (*c.*1815).

Right: The Pump Room by J. C. Nattes, *c.*1804 and (above) the magnificent eighteenth-century chandeliers in the ballroom of the Assembly Rooms today.

Morland is introduced to Henry Tilney by the Master of Ceremonies (*Northanger Abbey*), were demolished in 1933, but the Pump Room just behind the Abbey can still be visited.

In the Octagon Room, gambling took place; it was also used as a tea-room on concert nights. Here, in *Persuasion*, Anne Elliot bravely makes an advance towards Captain Wentworth. In May 1801 Jane described a soirée there to Cassandra:

> Before tea, it was rather a dull affair … think of four couples, surrounded by about an hundred people, dancing in the Upper Rooms at Bath! After tea we *cheered up*, the breaking up of private parties sent some scores more to the Ball … I am proud to say that I have a very good eye for an adulteress, for tho' repeatedly assured that another in the same party was the she, I fixed on the right one from the first … she was highly rouged and looked rather quietly and contentedly silly than anything else …

Just a few hundred yards from the Assembly Rooms is Royal Crescent, which was completed in 1774. Its thirty houses were for decades the most fashionable of all Bath residences. This was an elegant area in which to promenade of an afternoon, seeing and being seen. Catherine Morland hurries through the genteel Sunday throng in the Crescent in search of the Tilneys; Anne Elliot and Captain Wentworth, having appropriately met in Union Street, resolve their misunderstandings as they 'slowly paced the gradual ascent' up to it along 'the comparatively quiet and retired' Gravel Walk, 'heedless of every group around them, seeing neither sauntering politicians, bustling housekeepers, flirting girls, nor nursery maids and children'.

On a visit to Bath in 1799, the Austens stayed downhill of Gravel Walk, in Queen Square. With that famous unfairness with which the humbler side of a street always has a more elegant view than the grander side, they could look from their house at number 13 to the handsome north side of the square, designed to look like a single mansion. 'We are exceedingly pleased with the house', Jane wrote to Cassandra. 'The rooms are quite as large as we expected. Mrs Bromley [the landlady] is a fat woman in mourning, and a little black kitten runs about … I like our situation very much; it is far more cheerful than the Paragon, and the prospect from the drawing-room window, at which I now write, is rather picturesque.' In 1799, the square was a fashionable quarter; by 1814, when mentioned in *Persuasion*, it was not. 'We must be in a good situation', insist the Misses Musgrove. 'None of your Queen Squares for us.'

Hotel. [The Garden] is let to Mr Holloway, who conducts it with great spirit and liberality … there are swings, bowling greens and a Merlin's swing in the labyrinth; a plan of which is sold at the bar at 6d each.

An earth track around the perimeter gave ladies and gentlemen an opportunity for horseback exercise, and in the summer public breakfasts were served and there were gala nights with 'music, fireworks and superb illuminations'. The hotel (now the Holburne of Menstrie Museum) had a ballroom, tea- and coffee-rooms and a card-room.

The Upper Assembly Rooms are now looked after by the National Trust. Finished in 1771, they were the newest and most popular of the three main centres of social intercourse in Bath. In the 1790s Jane much enjoyed dancing there in the great green and gold ballroom. The Lower Rooms, where Catherine

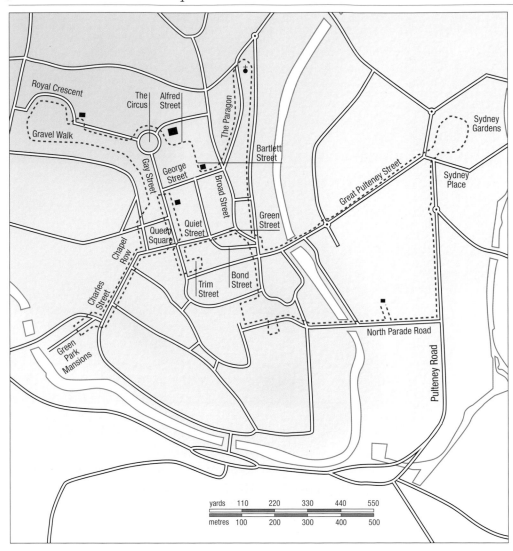

architectural features of the city. Walk halfway round the Circus and then along Brock Street to Royal Crescent. Number 1, the home of the Woods, builders of the Crescent, is now owned by the Bath Preservation Trust and can be visited. It provides a splendid example of the layout of a Georgian house of the first rank (the Duke of York was one of its many distinguished tenants). The dining-room is on the ground floor; the drawing-room upstairs.

Walk down Gravel Walk to Queen Square, where Jane lodged with her mother and Edward's family at number 13 in 1799. Leaving Queen Square by Chapel Row, walk down Charles Street to Green Park Mansions, a quiet dignified terrace facing over Kingsmead Fields, a notorious spot for duels. The Austens moved to number 27 in 1804, perhaps so Mr Austen, who was becoming frailer, could be nearer the Pump Room, perhaps because of expense. Walk back to Queen Square and along Gay Street, where Jane and her mother lived at number 25 for a few months after George Austen's death in 1805; she tells us in *Persuasion* that 'the Crofts had placed themselves in lodgings in Gay Street, perfectly to Sir Walter's satisfaction'. There is now a shop devoted to Jane Austen books and memorabilia in Gay Street. Head south of Queen Square to find a left-hand turn to Trim Street, once the home of Sheridan, but also where the Austens took their humblest and final lodging in Bath, in 1806.

From the south-east corner of Queen Square follow Quiet Street eastwards to Bond Street (where Sir Walter Elliot 'watched 87 women go by without there being a tolerable face among them'). It continues northwards as Milsom Street (number 2 was Mollands the pastrycooks, where Anne sheltered from the rain and Captain Wentworth found her). Cross Milsom Street and continue east on Green Street until you join Walcot Street again at Northgate. Turn right and walk along High Street to the Abbey, behind which is the Pump Room. This is featured time and again in Jane's writings. Cross the bridge and follow North Parade to the car-park.

TRAIL 2 On Foot (*c.*4 miles)

Park in North Parade Road and walk northwards along Pulteney Road to reach Sydney Gardens. The Austens' house, 4 Sydney Place, is on the west side. Walk down Great Pulteney Street (where the Allens in *Northanger Abbey* settled into comfortable lodgings with Catherine Morland), across Laura Place, where *Persuasion's* Lady Dalrymple 'lived in style', and over Pulteney Bridge. Turn up hill along Walcot Street; at the junction where it joins The Paragon you will find St Swithin's Church, where Jane's parents, then George Austen and Cassandra Leigh, were married in 1764, and where George Austen was buried in 1805.

Turn left and walk along The Paragon, a curved terrace of tall, handsome balconied houses built by Thomas Atwood in 1770; number 1 was the house where Jane stayed when she first visited Bath at the age of nineteen as the guest of the Leigh Perrots, her mother's brother and his wife. When The Paragon joins Broad Street, cross over into George Street. On the right are Edgar's Buildings, much less grand than Camden Place where the elegant Elliots park themselves in *Persuasion*, but appropriately central lodgings for *Northanger Abbey's* Isabella, eager to make the most of Bath's delights. Turn right up Bartlett Street to Alfred Street and the Upper Assembly Rooms.

Opposite the entrance to the Assembly Rooms there is a lane into the Circus, one of the best

MAP

Bath A–Z Street Plan

The Palladian Bridge
at Prior Park, looking
towards Bath.

Escapes from the City

In *Persuasion* Anne Elliot has a sense of being hemmed in. Deafened by 'bawlings of newsmen, muffin-men and milkmen, and the ceaseless clink of pattens', she 'disliked Bath and did not think it agreed with her'. For her and Jane alike, relief could be found in walking out of the city. In 1799, while staying at Queen Square, Jane describes 'a very charming walk from 6 to 8 up Beacon Hill, and across some fields to the village of Charlcombe, which is sweetly situated in a little green valley, as a village with such a name ought to be'.

Lyncombe and Widcombe, little villages just to the east of the city, were easily accessible on foot when the Austens moved to Sydney Gardens. They lie in the same valley as Prior Park, a great Palladian mansion built by Ralph Allen, the architect of much of fashionable Bath, high on the ridge of the valley, 'for all of Bath to see, and to see all of Bath'. The grounds, one of the most important survivals of eighteenth-century landscape art, are now looked after by the National Trust. Its woody wilderness was laid out with the help of the poet Alexander Pope, who had just such a feature in the grounds of his villa on the Thames at Twickenham.

And all, impatient of dry land, agree

With one consent to rush into the sea

William Cowper, *The Task*

Mr Austen took his daughters on more substantial excursions. Seaside holidays were a new fashion, made possible by the improvement in roads and the development of seaside towns as resorts for the leisured middle classes, and half the point of moving to Bath had been to be closer to the health-giving climate of the south-west coast. 'The prospect of spending future summers by the sea or in Wales is very delightful', Jane wrote to Cassandra when trying to reconcile herself to leaving Steventon.

In 1801 the Austens holidayed at Sidmouth because one of George's pupils, Richard Buller, was vicar of Colyton, a few miles away. It may have been at Sidmouth – it was certainly on one of the Austens' four Devon seaside holidays – that, Cassandra revealed in old age, Jane met a young clergyman who was on a visit to his brother, a local doctor. Cassandra described him as a man 'whose charm of person, mind and manners was such that she thought him worthy to possess and likely to win her sister's love'. He asked if they could meet again, and Jane said yes. But before a second meeting could take place, he fell ill and died, very suddenly. It seems likely that the wistfulness of *Persuasion*, which is set in part in Somerset and Lyme Regis in Dorset, has echoes of this incident. Sidmouth's landscape is protected by the National Trust holdings on each side of it. The Trust also owns a small Regency villa on the seafront.

In 1802 the Austens ventured a bit further west to Dawlish. It was then little more than a 'bathing-village', three days' journey by coach from Bath, but it was nonetheless regarded as fashionable. Robert Ferrars remarks in *Sense and Sensibility* that 'it seemed rather surprising to him that anybody could live in Devonshire without living near Dawlish'.

Jane's favourite seaside resort was Lyme Regis. The Austens first stayed there in 1803, probably in a little cottage overlooking the Cobb

Early nineteenth-century aquatint of Lyme Regis. The sweeping route around the bay to the Cobb (right) is immortalised in *Persuasion*.

called Wings – a garden is named for her there. They visited again in 1804, this time staying in a lodging-house at the foot of the High Street. John Fowles, who set his famous novel *The French Lieutenant's Woman* (1969) in Lyme, believes they stayed at Pyne House, in Broad Street. Jane bathed every day, went to dances in the Assembly Room, and walked on the Cobb (off which Lydia tumbles in *Persuasion*, jumping from 'Granny's Teeth', the protruding blocks of stone that form a perilous stair up to the top of the breakwater). She also enjoyed the coastal walk past The Spittles and Black Venn Cliff to Charmouth. Her description of Lyme and the walks around it in *Persuasion* is so enthusiastic that it would sit as well in a guidebook as in a novel.

As there is nothing to admire in the buildings themselves, the re-markable situation of the town, the principal street almost hurrying into the water, the walk to the Cobb, skirting round the pleasant little bay, which in the season is animated with bathing machines and company, the Cobb itself, its old wonders and new im-provements, with the very beautiful line of cliffs stretching out to the east of the town, are what the stranger's eye will seek; and a very strange stranger it must be who does not see charms in the immediate environs of Lyme, to make him wish to know it better.

AN EXPLORING PARTY TO BOX HILL

Box Hill has been a wonder to travellers and an inspiration to writers for centuries. John Evelyn mentions walking in its 'rare natural bowers' in 1655. 'It's a greate heighte and shows you a vast precipice down on the farther side', wrote Celia Fiennes in 1694. According to Daniel Defoe, in the 1720s 'an abundance of ladies and gentlemen from Epsom used to take the air, and walk in the boxwoods; and in a word, divert or debauch, or perhaps both'.

Such a reputation adds an extra piquancy to the proposed 'exploring party' to Box Hill which is a pivotal scene in Jane Austen's *Emma*. 'We are going to Box Hill tomorrow', says Emma gaily to the unaccountably fractious Frank Churchill. 'It is not Swisserland, but it will be something for a young man so in want of a change.' Emma had never been to Box Hill, and 'she wished to see what everybody found so much worth seeing'.

The name Box Hill is so well known that it is easy to assume that it is merely an overtrampled back garden to Dorking. In fact, it is a startlingly unspoilt place. Hilaire Belloc christened it 'the strongest and most simple of our southern hills', and at its 634ft summit it still boasts what Sarah, Duchess of Marlborough, called in 1732, 'the best air in England'. All in all, well worth packing up your own pigeon pies and cold lamb for, and approaching for a literary ramble and picnic.

To get the full effect of Surrey's chalk alp, leave the A24 at the car-park just south of the Burford Bridge Hotel. From here a footpath takes you to some picturesque stepping stones across the River Mole where kingfishers and a colony of rose-winged parakeets have become established. The path then rises in a steepish slant across the south face of the hill, through slopes spangled with an astonishing variety of wild flowers and butterflies (of which Box Hill boasts forty of the fifty-eight British species).

A little below the summit on the precipitous south-west slope is just the spot for an Austen-style picnic 'in tranquil observation of the beautiful views beneath'. I like to think that this is where Emma flirted with Frank and carelessly insulted Miss Bates, but it is more likely that they climbed the gentler slopes on the north-west side, and ate there. 'Let my accents swell to Mickleham on one side and Dorking on the other', carolled Frank to Emma, 'with very lively impudence' as they tucked into

Left: Fanny Burney (1752–1840) in an engraving by Charles Turner.

Below: Stepping stones over the River Mole.

their cold collation before a silent, disapproving audience.

From the summit at Donkey Green a footpath eastwards (close to the road to Headley) leads through the shady glades of box round Flint Hill down the Happy Valley to Juniper Bottom. Take a footpath to the left just before the road (Headley Lane), and below to the north-west, you will see Juniper Hall, a red-brick eighteenth-century house. In 1792 it became the home of such distinguished refugees from the Terror as Madame de Staël and Talleyrand. The novelist Fanny Burney, author of *Evelina* (1778) visited them there in 1793, while on a visit to her sister in Mickleham. 'There can be nothing more charming, more fascinating than this colony', she wrote. 'They are a marvellous set

Box Hill, Surrey

Above: Flint Cottage,
home of George Meredith
between 1867 and 1909.

Left: View over vineyards
to the westward slopes
of Box Hill.

for excess of agreeability.' Six months later she married one of the exiles, the Comte d'Arblay, and they moved into a small house in Great Bookham. There she wrote *Camilla* (1796), and with the profits from it built Camilla Cottage, now part of Camilla Lacey, in West Humble, just west of Box Hill.

Wander on, turning left when the footpath joins the road, for an opportunity to admire Flint Cottage, home of George Meredith (1828–1909) for more than thirty years. 'I am every morning at the top of Box Hill – as its flower, its bird, its prophet', he wrote. 'I drop down the moon on one side, I draw up the sun on t'other. I breathe fine air. I shout "ha ha" to the gates of the world. Then I descend and know myself a donkey for doing it.' A little further on you will see his writing-hut, a picturesque gabled chalet:

Anything grander than the days and nights in my porch you will not find away from the Alps: for the dark line of my hill runs up to the stars, the valley below is a soundless gulf. There I pace like a shipman before turning in. In the day with the south west blowing I have a brilliant universe rolling up to me.

The Egoist (1879) was written in that chalet, but the Meredith novel most closely connected with Box Hill is *Diana of the Crossways* (1885). Diana's close friend is another Emma, and her estate lay approximately at Box Hill. 'Seven counties rolled their backs under this commanding height ... Sunrise to right, sunset leftward, the borders of the grounds held both flaming horizons. So much of heaven and earth is rarely granted to a dwelling.'

The road (A24) will take you back to the Burford Bridge Hotel, where John Keats lingered in November 1817 to finish *Endymion* in a small back room. 'I went up Box Hill this evening after the moon', he wrote. 'I like this place very much.' Robert Louis Stevenson stayed there while visiting Meredith and enjoyed 'its arbours and green gardens and silent eddying river'. (Gower Woodseer, in Meredith's *The Amazing Marriage* (1895), is a portrait of RLS.) Other vistors were Henry James, Alice Meynell and J. M. Barrie. The hotel's finest literary hour, however, was the meeting there in July 1895 of the Omar Khayyám Club. Besides the editors of most of the London papers, the guests included Edmund Gosse, George Gissing and Thomas Hardy. Meredith, though frail, came down to join them after dinner.

'OUR CHAWTON HOME'

Our Chawton home, how much we find

Already in it, to our mind;

And how convinced that when complete

It will all other Houses beat

That ever have been made or mended,

With rooms concise; or rooms distended

Jane, to Frank, July 1809

View of Chawton village
from the pond, *c.*1910.
Jane Austen's house is
on the left.

Chawton, owned by the Jane Austen Memorial Trust, is the only one of Jane's many homes that both survives and is open to the public. It is an unostentatious little seventeenth-century town-house with about six bedrooms, some very small. After Mr Austen died in 1805, his widow and daughters spent some time in Clifton, then made a tour of relatives, and ended up in Southampton. But in 1808 Edward's wife Elizabeth died following the birth of their eleventh child. In 1809, perhaps not least because of the support that he knew they would give him with the children, Edward offered his mother and sisters the choice of two houses. One was a cottage near his great estate at Godmersham in Kent, the other the former bailiff's house on his Hampshire estate at Chawton, close to Alton and only seventeen miles from Steventon, the old family home where James and Mary were now settled.

They opted for Chawton, a wise decision. Gilbert White of nearby Selborne praised its happy 'assemblage of hill, dale, woodlands, heath and water'. In *Mansfield Park*, the first novel Jane wrote entirely at Chawton, much is made of the contrast between Portsmouth, where Fanny Price came from, and the delightful countryside around Mansfield Park. When Fanny returns to Mansfield, 'liberty, freshness, fragrance and verdure' came back into her life.

In this tranquil, settled little house, Cassandra, Jane and Martha Lloyd shared the housekeeping tasks and Mrs Austen concentrated on the garden and needlework. Jane, whose main domestic commitment was to get breakfast ready, almost instantly refound her ability to write – by now the love-lives of her nieces and nephews were providing her with much useful material. All six of her novels date in their finished forms from the eight years she lived at Chawton. In the version of *Sense and Sensibility* revised after the move there, the circumstances of the widowed Mrs Dashwood, living in a cottage on the estate of a rich relative, echoed Jane's situation, and Barton Cottage, though said to be in Devon, closely resembled their Chawton house:

As a house, Barton Cottage, though small, was comfortable and compact; but as a cottage it was defective, for the building was regular, the roof was tiled, the window shutters were not painted green, nor were the walls covered with honeysuckles.

Originally built as an inn at the turn of the seventeenth century, the house was very much in the mainstream of village life. A friend wrote to Edward's daughter Fanny: 'I hear of the Chawton party looking very comfortable at breakfast, from a gentleman who was travelling by their door in a post-chaise.'

Edward arranged numerous improvements. Though the dining-room remained open to passers-by, the drawing-room window looking on to the high street was closed off and converted into a bookcase, and a prettily gothicised window was put into its west wall, looking out over the garden. Jane once more had a piano, ostensibly so that country dances could 'provide some amusement for our nephew and nieces', but actually because Jane, although shy of performing in front of an audience, loved to play it. Her niece Caroline recorded memories of her aunt playing every morning before breakfast. Her neat transcriptions of favourite melodies are on view in the Chawton drawing-room today, on an 1810 piano. Among then is Caroline Austen's own favourite, a French song that begins 'Que j'aime voir les hirondelles / Volent ma fenêtre tous les jours'.

The garden had a shrubbery to stroll in, a flower garden, a vegetable garden, a poultry-yard and a donkey paddock. Mrs Austen was a keen gardener, and her efforts at Chawton are echoed in *Mansfield Park*. 'Every time I come into this shrubbery I am more struck with its growth and beauty', says Fanny to Dr Grant of Mansfield Parsonage.

Three years ago, this was nothing but a rough hedgerow along the upper side of the field, never thought of as anything, or capable of becoming anything; and now it is converted into a walk, and it would be difficult to say whether most valuable as a convenience or an ornament.

When Cassandra was away on visits, Jane wrote letters to her that provide vivid glimpses of the everyday delights of life at Chawton:

The chickens are all alive and fit for the table, but we save them up for something grand. Some of the flower seeds are coming up very well, but your mignonette makes a wretched appearance... Our young peony at the foot of the fir tree has just blown and looks very handsome and the whole of the shrubbery border will soon be very gay with pinks and sweet-williams, in addition to the columbines in full bloom. The syringas, too, are coming out. We are likely to get a good crop of Orleans plums, but not many greengages – on the standard scarcely any, three or four dozen perhaps, against the wall.

Detail of the patchwork quilt made by Jane Austen and her family.

Edward, who never remarried, allowed the tenancy of the rambling sixteenth-century Chawton manor house to lapse, and often stayed there himself. In 1813, while Godmersham was being repainted, he brought his entire family to live there for five months. 'We go about in the most comfortable way, often dining together and always meeting in some part of every day', Jane wrote to Frank, then away at sea. He and Jane's other brothers, Charles and Henry, could also now visit with ease, bringing their whole families. Between 1814 and 1816 Frank and Mary became Edward's tenants and their sixth child was born there in 1815.

Visitors to the cottage in Chawton today will find it overflowing with touching relics of Jane's occupancy. Everyone will have their own favourite among them: the faded lock of her hair, the generous flowing handwriting of her letters and manuscripts, the jewelled crosses that she and Cassandra were once given by their youngest sailor brother Charles to celebrate the prize he had captured in the Napoleonic War. To my mind, the most moving exhibit is a patchwork quilt which hangs on the wall of the little upstairs bedroom which Jane shared with Cassandra. 'Have you remembered to collect pieces for the patchwork?' Jane asks Cassandra in a letter to her on 31 May 1811; 'we are now at a standstill'. Made partly from pieces begged from other households and samples from shops, and partly from the remnants of their own dresses, the quilt perfectly reflects the unity and co-operation between the ladies of the house – Jane, Cassandra, Mrs Austen and Martha Lloyd (who came to live with the Austens when they moved from Bath to Southampton). Its design is as carefully contrived as the plots of Jane's novels; the placing of its contrasting colours and patterns is as effective as the social minuets between her various characters; and the immaculately neat stitching as exquisite as her choice of words and turns of phrase.

The first task that Jane set herself when she had settled into the even tenor of life at Chawton was to revise the three manuscripts she had written in her early twenties. *First Impressions* became *Pride and Prejudice*, perhaps inspired by the reiteration of that phrase in the last chapter of *Camilla* by Fanny Burney, whom Jane much admired. *Elinor and Marianne* became *Sense and Sensibility*, and *Susan* was given the ironically Gothick title of *Northanger Abbey*.

With her London-based brother Henry's help, Jane found a new publisher, and *Sense and Sensibility* appeared in print in 1811. When *Pride and Prejudice* followed in 1813, it received excellent reviews. *Mansfield Park* was published in May 1814 and had sold out by November. *Emma* was finished in March 1815, and was sent to a new publisher, John Murray. 'He is a rogue of course, but a civil one', Jane wrote to Cassandra.

In 1816, Jane finished the novel that would be *Persuasion*, but she was also suffering from the first symptoms of Addison's disease, the debilitating tuberculosis of the kidneys of which she would die within a year. Early in 1817 she began work on *Sanditon*, a gentle satire on the seaside resorts they used to visit while living in Bath, but she soon became too weak to continue. In May she moved to Winchester, to be nearer her physician, Mr Lyford, and on 18 July she died. 'I have lost a treasure', wrote Cassandra to their much-loved niece Fanny, 'such a sister, such a friend as never can have been surpassed. She was the sun of my life, the gilder of every pleasure, the soother of every sorrow; I had not a thought concealed from her, and it is as if I had lost a part of myself.'

Jane lies buried in the north aisle of Winchester Cathedral. The inscription on the black marble slab that marks her grave was composed by her brother Henry and is full of generous pieties. It is also oddly egocentric, dwelling at length on the grief of those she left behind and making no mention at all of her as an author.

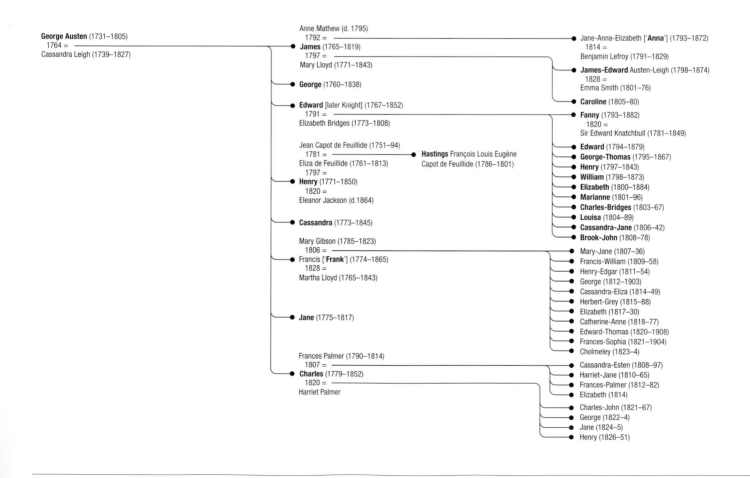

George Austen (1731–1805)
1764 =
Cassandra Leigh (1739–1827)

Anne Mathew (d. 1795)
1792 =
James (1765–1819)
1797 =
Mary Lloyd (1771–1843)

Jane-Anna-Elizabeth ['**Anna**'] (1793–1872)
1814 =
Benjamin Lefroy (1791–1829)

James-Edward Austen-Leigh (1798–1874)
1828 =
Emma Smith (1801–76)

Caroline (1805–80)

George (1760–1838)

Edward [later Knight] (1767–1852)
1791 =
Elizabeth Bridges (1773–1808)

Fanny (1793–1882)
1820 =
Sir Edward Knatchbull (1781–1849)

Edward (1794–1879)
George-Thomas (1795–1867)
Henry (1797–1843)
William (1798–1873)
Elizabeth (1800–1884)
Marianne (1801–96)
Charles-Bridges (1803–67)
Louisa (1804–89)
Cassandra-Jane (1806–42)
Brook-John (1808–78)

Jean Capot de Feuillide (1751–94)
1781 =
Eliza de Feuillide (1761–1813)
1797 =
Henry (1771–1850)
1820 =
Eleanor Jackson (d.1864)

Hastings François Louis Eugène Capot de Feuillide (1786–1801)

Cassandra (1773–1845)

Mary Gibson (1785–1823)
1806 =
Francis ['**Frank**'] (1774–1865)
1828 =
Martha Lloyd (1765–1843)

Mary-Jane (1807–36)
Francis-William (1809–58)
Henry-Edgar (1811–54)
George (1812–1903)
Cassandra-Eliza (1814–49)
Herbert-Grey (1815–88)
Elizabeth (1817–30)
Catherine-Anne (1818–77)
Edward-Thomas (1820–1908)
Frances-Sophia (1821–1904)
Cholmeley (1823–4)

Jane (1775–1817)

Frances Palmer (1790–1814)
1807 =
Charles (1779–1852)
1820 =
Harriet Palmer

Cassandra-Esten (1808–97)
Harriet-Jane (1810–65)
Frances-Palmer (1812–82)
Elizabeth (1814)

Charles-John (1821–67)
George (1822–4)
Jane (1824–5)
Henry (1826–51)

'A Rural, Shelter'd Unobserved Retreat'

Few places in Britain have remained more unspoilt and rich in flora and fauna than Selborne, the tiny Hampshire village where England's best-loved naturalist was born in 1722 and lived until his death in 1793. Gilbert White's *Natural History of Selborne* was first published in 1789 and is the fourth most published book in the English language. Coleridge called it 'a sweet delightful book', and Darwin praised it as one of the chief reasons for his interest in zoology. Its author was a modest, affable man, who was only persuaded to publish what were originally letters to two naturalist friends on the urgings of his family. In this lies the *History*'s charm: immediate, informal and unpretentious.

To walk in the footsteps of White is be taken back to his age of intelligent speculation into the workings of Providence. Now, as then, Selborne is 'a very abrupt, uneven country, full of hills and woods, and therefore full of birds', a rustic Arcadia full of variety and contrast.

A footpath from the car-park behind the Selborne Arms leads to the zigzag, or 'Zic-Zac' as White called it when he had it constructed in 1753 as part of an elaborate neo-classical landscaping scheme in the manner of William Kent. It looks dramatically steep; rising in hair-pin bends up the face of the hill, outlined with a low, neatly cropped hedge. The going is uneven, and slippery after rain, especially at the turns of the path but good views may be had of the shifting vistas of the horizon.

At the first iron bench, about a third of the way up, you can see the garden and south face of Gilbert White's house through the trees. Nostalgic for home while in Oxford at the age of twenty-five, he wrote:

Now climb the steep, drop now your eye below;
Where round the verdurous village orchards blow;
There, like a picture, lies my lowly seat
A rural, shelter'd unobserved retreat.

You can also see the woods and water meadows of the Short and Long Lythes, stretching away to the north.

Eighteenth-century engravings show a hermit's hut set off the path to the right two-thirds of the way up. Here, Gilbert White's brother used to lurk in homespun hermit garb for the benefit of visitors, and picnics were consumed.

Another iron bench and a rough boulder known as the Wishing Stone mark the top. A detour to the south-east edges of the hill will provide views of what White called the 'vast range of mountains called the Sussex Downs', but it is rewarding to return by the Bostal Path – also made by White – which goes from the Wishing Stone along the lip of the hill, through mossy glades of ancient beeches. Seen from a distance the beeches clothe the hanger like a thick pelt. Seen from below, their silvered trunks soar up 100ft or more, their layered canopies of leaves caverns of translucent green light.

The gentle descent to join Love Lane provides a shady route along the base of the hill. The remains of an old hollow lane may be seen at this point, carved deeply into the earth by centuries of use. White refers to the 'grotesque and wild appearance' of such lanes, often up to 18 or 20ft deep: 'These rugged gloomy scenes affright the ladies when they peep down into them from the paths above, and make timid horsemen shudder while they ride along them, but delight the naturalist with their various botany.'

The Wakes, where White lived except when at Oriel College, Oxford, is in the centre of Selborne. At the heart of the rambling building is the old cottage bought by White's grandfather in 1700. White added a Grand Parlour in 1776, and transformed the garden with statues, a ha-ha and a hide for

Selborne, Hampshire

Far left: *The Hermitage at Selborne with Henry White as the Hermit,* by S. H. Grimm (1777).

Left: The Long Lythe at Selborne with *Cardamine pratensis* or cuckoo flowers growing in the grass.

Below: St Mary's church-yard, Selborne, with Gilbert White's typically modest tombstone.

observing birds. The naturalist Thomas Bell bought the house in 1844 and added a bay-windowed library. In 1954, thanks to the generosity of R. W. Oates, it became a shrine both to Gilbert White and to Oates's cousins, the naturalist Frank Oates, who died in Africa in 1873, and Captain Lawrence ('I may be some time') Oates of Scott's ill-fated 1912 Antarctic expedition.

It is now a beautifully run place, full of White mementoes, including the four-poster bed-curtains embroidered with flowers for him by his four aunts, books and furniture, and busy with gardening, cookery and field studies courses. Leave time to explore the garden, now in the process of restoration to Gilbert White's plan.

Inside the church across the square opposite his house are two stained-glass windows erected in White's memory. Even more touching is his 18in-high gravestone, modest at his own request, which lies in the churchyard just north of the chancel. A path through the churchyard runs down to a stream and the oaks of the Short Lythe, then across a steep pasture to the Long Lythe, giving fine views back of the zigzag. To return to the village, turn right after the ash grove at the far end through a field down to a bridge across the Oakhanger Stream and follow the path to Hucker's Lane, which enters the village just to the right of the Selborne Arms.

GILBERT WHITE
1720-93

Literature and the Country House

The country house has given inspiration to the poet, stage settings to the dramatist, properties of horror to the Gothic novel, and countless victims to both the satirist and the purveyor of murder mysteries.

Richard Gill, *Happy Rural Seat*

Hardwick Hall in Derbyshire, where the philosopher Thomas Hobbes (above) lived and worked for much of his life, under the protection of the Earls of Devonshire.

Country houses – self-sufficient, wealthy little states within the state – have supported and inspired writers in very different ways across the centuries. London, with its growing trade in the printing and selling of books and periodicals, was always the centre of literary culture, but, unlike their European counterparts, the English aristocracy liked to spend substantial parts of the year at their country seats. This meant that great patrons often invited poets, essayists and satirists to spend long periods with them in the country. In the seventeenth and early eighteenth centuries, the reliance of writers on such patronage ensured that the keynote of literary reference to the great houses and their owners was adulation. 'Be pimp to some worthless man of quality', advises Henry Fielding. 'Write panegyrics on him, flatter him with as many virtues as he has vices' (*The Author's Farce*, 1730).

However, there were also examples of disinterested support. After he left Oxford at the age of twenty, the philosopher Thomas Hobbes (1588-1679) came to Hardwick Hall in Derbyshire as tutor and companion to Bess of Hardwick's grandson, William Cavendish, 2nd Earl of Devonshire. The family was a pillar of support to him all through his life, despite the hostility of the Establishment to his political ideas. From 1675, he was cared for at Hardwick, writing right up until his death. A touching portrait in the Long Gallery shows him still wise, but aged and toothless, shortly before he died in his room in the house at the age of ninety-one.

There was also a marked tendency for literature, liberality and liberalism to run together. The great Whig aristocrats promoted freedom in the face of Tory repression and censure by bankrolling satirists, poets and dramatists who were the publicists and spin-doctors of the day. Then, as now, it seems to have been either temporary exile in the political wilderness or permanent opposition to those in government which encouraged the most exciting cultural energy.

PRINCE OF PATRONS

> Dorset, the grace of Courts, the Muses' pride.
> Patron of Arts, and judge of nature, died.
> The scourge of pride, tho' sanctify'd or great,
> Of fops in learning or of knaves in state.
> Yet soft his nature, tho' severe his lays
> His anger moral and his wisdom gay

Alexander Pope, *Epitaph*

Among the most famously generous of seventeenth-century aristocratic patrons was Charles Sackville (1638-1706), 6th Earl of Dorset. His rambling great house at Knole, Kent, with its legendary 365 rooms, 52 staircases and 7 courtyards, offered plenty of space to lodge artists and writers on a semi-permanent basis. Sackville's plump, lascivious-lipped face gazes out of the frame of his life-sized portrait at Knole with a quizzical and alert expression. He had a remarkable life to look back on. In the early 1660s, as Lord Buckhurst, he was a renowned libertine. Pepys mentions him as a close friend of Charles II, and tells us that Buckhurst kept 'merry house at Epsom' with a charming young orange-seller called Nell Gwynn. Two years later, she became the King's mistress.

When he came into his inheritance in 1677, Sackville took to touring Europe, and embarked on the collecting that provided Knole with its magnificent furnishings. In 1685, he married a seventeen-year-old heiress, Lady Mary Compton, by whom he had a son and a daughter. It was while he was out of favour with the Catholic James II that he first made Knole a notable literary centre. A 'Poets' Parlour', decorated with

Charles Sackville, 6th Earl of Dorset by Sir Godfrey Kneller.

portraits of famous writers past and present, was created as a setting for literary evenings with a distinctly racy character.

The poets and dramatists who enjoyed Dorset's liberal hospitality included Matthew Prior, John Dryden, Thomas Otway, William Congreve, William Wycherley and Thomas Shadwell (whom Dorset would make Poet Laureate when he was back in favour at the court of William and Mary). The dramatist Thomas d'Urfey was something of a house pet, a kind of resident court jester. He lived in rooms over the dairy, and rattled off second-rate couplets exaggerating the house's glories:

Knole most famous in Kent still appears,
Where mansions surveyed for a thousand long years,
In whose domes mighty monarchs might dwell,
Where five hundred rooms are, as Boswell [the butler] can tell.

A striking portrait of him in profile hangs in Lady Betty Germain's room at Knole; another, a conversation piece, shows him in the Steward's Room with the senior servants.

The most famous of Dorset's protégés was Matthew Prior. The Earl noticed him as a boy reading Horace in a Westminster tavern, and was so struck by his intelligence that he paid for his schooling. Many of Prior's late poems were dedicated to his patron, and several were addressed to members of the Sackville family. 'A freedom reigned at his table which made every one of his guests think himself at home. His good nature was supreme', he wrote of Dorset.

Other famous faces on the walls of the Poets' Parlour include those of Thomas Hobbes, John Locke, Samuel Butler, Abraham Cowley, Nicholas Rowe, Sir Kenelm Digby, Edmund Waller and Thomas Flatman. Horace Walpole later described the room as 'a chamber of parts and players, which is proper enough in that house'. Sackville evidently had a well-developed sense of humour. One evening he suggested a poetry competition, to be judged by Dryden. He watched while the others scribbled, then tossed two short lines into the ring. Dryden read them, and announced that after careful consideration he had decided that his Lordship's verses were the best of all the entries. They ran: 'I promise to pay Mr John Dryden or order five hundred pounds on demand. DORSET'.

After the Glorious Revolution of 1688, Dorset was restored to favour at court, and became an even more influential patron of literature. He was a founder member of the Kit-Cat Club, which flourished between 1696 and 1720. Named after the mutton pies served by Christopher Cat, proprietor of the Cat and Fiddle in Gray's Inn Lane, London, the club was a talking-shop with a purpose: the creation of a network of patronage and influence for the writers and artists whom it favoured. Members subscribed to finance editions of books, especially from the publisher and bookseller Jacob Tonson, who was the club's original convener. They set up the Queen's Theatre in the Haymarket in 1704, and provided pensions and sinecures in government bureaucracy for needy writers. The aims of the club were political as well as cultural, and its members were almost exclusively Whig and aristocratic – it numbered no fewer than ten dukes among its members.

Dorset himself was no mean versifier. In his *History of England* (1849-55), Macaulay said that Dorset's songs 'have the easy vigour of Suckling', and that his satires 'sparkle with wit as splendid as those of Butler'. Dorset could also be cruel. When he was young, his friend the Earl of Rochester wrote: 'For pointed satire I would Buckhurst chuse; / The best good man, with the worst-natured muse.' The most notorious lines of Dorset's poetry were those on James II's mistress, Lady Dorchester:

Tell me, Dorinda, why so gay,
Why such embroidery, fringe and lace?
Can any dresses find a way
To stop th'approaches of decay,
And mend a ruined face?

Wilt thou still sparkle in the box,
Still ogle in the ring?
Can'st thou forget thy age and pox?
Can all that shines on shells and rocks
Make thee a fine young thing?

Dorset's literary interests were diverse. Vita Sackville-West reproduces in *Knole and the Sackvilles* half an alphabet of thieves' cant which she found in the Knole papers of his day. It includes such words as 'autem mort' (a married woman), 'Abram' (naked) and 'abramcour' (a tatterdemalion), 'tomager prater' (a hen), 'muffling-cheat' (a napkin) and 'mumpers' (gentile [i.e. not Romany] beggars). 'During the whole of his life', wrote his grandson George Sackville, 'he was the patron of men of genius and the dupe of women, and bountiful beyond measure to both.' In 1704 he married a former housekeeper, 'a Woman named Roche, of very obscure Connexions, who held him in a Sort of Captivity down in Bath, where he expired at about sixty-nine'. His family, as families will in such circumstances, thought he must have become senile, but Matthew Prior, loyal to the end, demurred: 'Lord Dorset is certainly greatly declined in his understanding, but he *drivels* so much better sense even now than any other man can *talk*, that you must not call me into court as a witness to prove him an idiot'.

TRAIL **An Education in Stone**

1

Consult the Genius of the Place in all;
That tells the Waters or to rise or fall,
Or helps th'ambitious Hill the heav'ns to scale,
Or scoops in circling theatres the Vale…
Nature shall join you; Time shall make it grow
A Work to Wonder at – perhaps a STOW

Alexander Pope, *Of Taste*

In the eighteenth century, the most powerful great house in the country was Stowe, Buckinghamshire, seat of the prominent Whig family of Temple-Grenville. The Tories had become tarred by their association with Jacobitism, and for the first half of the century Whig values of parliamentary supremacy and international commercial dominance prevailed. Thanks to shrewd political manoeuvrings and a series of marriages to heiresses (involving an accumulation of surnames that bordered on the absurd), the Temple-Grenville family grew steadily in financial and political prominence. Their ultimate ambition, a dukedom (of Buckingham) for Richard Temple-Nugent-Brydges-Chandos-Grenville (1776-1839) was won in 1822.

Stowe remains a monument to their beliefs and achievements, a three-dimensional architectural and horticultural catechism. To tour the gardens today is an exhilarating experi-ence; they are, in the words of John Martin Robinson, the 'equivalent of the landscape paintings of Claude and Poussin or the poetry of Milton and Pope'. The numerous follies and monuments, of which thirty-two still survive, were built by such great architects as Sir John Vanbrugh, James Gibbs, Willliam Kent and Robert Adam. Charles Bridgeman and Capability Brown laid out the gardens; prominent contemporary sculptors and painters added further embellishments.

The landscape illustrates three great traditions of English gardens: heroic formality, represented by the magnificent vista from the Corinthian Arch to the south front of the house, class-ical allegory (the Elysian Fields) and naturalism (the Grecian Valley). Walking in the footsteps of its patrician eighteenth-century ghosts, you can experience both the deeply felt principles and the buoyant confidence of the 'Grand Whiggery'.

The most literarily inclined of the creators of Stowe was the first. Richard Temple, Viscount Cobham (1669-1749), was a military hero of Marlborough's wars against the French. He in-herited the estate in 1697 and began his improvements to its gardens while out of favour in 1713. But he backed the right horse in supporting the Hanoverian succession of George I, and from 1714 he became increasingly powerful and prominent. However, in 1733 he fell out with the Prime Minister, Sir Robert Walpole, over his trade and foreign policy, and once more retired, like Voltaire's Pangloss, to cultivate his garden. But he was far from

Left: View of the house at Stowe across the lake.

Right: The Temple of British Worthies.

politically inactive. Stowe became the centre for opposition to Walpole, and several of its monuments are visual jokes at Walpole's expense.

Viscount Cobham was a friend to many of the leading poets and writers of his day. The satirical playwright and poet William Congreve (1670-1729) was an especial friend, and in his one of his last poems, 'Epistle to Viscount Cobham' (1729), described him as 'Sincerest Critick of my Prose and Rhime'. Better known are his quips that hell has no 'fury, like a woman scorned' and that courtship was to marriage 'as a very witty prologue to a very dull Play', as well as his famous play *The Way of the World* (1700). An affectionate monument to Congreve is a prominent part of the Elysian Fields.

James Thomson, author of 'Rule Britannia', and according to Michael Schmidt, 'one of the most successful poets of all time … in terms of unit sales and vast editions' (*Lives of the Poets*, 1999), is celebrated on a marble fountain bearing an inscription from his most famous poem, *The Seasons*. Over 5,000 lines long and frequently updated, *The Seasons* was an extraordinary mixture of scientific knowledge, political prejudice and sentimental reflections, and was once as omnipresent in cultured households as the works of Shakespeare. On publishing its fourth edition, Thomson added nearly fifty lines in praise of 'the Elysian vales' of Stowe. In them, he emphasised the seriousness of Stowe's educational purpose:

> While there with thee the enchanted round I walk –
> The regulated wild-gay fancy then
> Will tread in thought the groves of Attic land,
> Will from thy standard taste refine her own,
> Correct her pencil to the purest truth
> Of nature or, the unimpassioned shades
> Forsaking, raise it to the human mind
>
> 'Autumn', II

Alexander Pope stayed at Stowe for long periods, and he too wrote an 'Epistle to Lord Cobham' (1733). A bust of Pope, as well as those of Hobbes, Milton, Shakespeare and Locke, stands in the Temple of British Worthies. This temple was part of a conceit almost certainly inspired by an essay in *The Tatler* by Joseph Addison (1672-1719). In it he described an allegorical dream in which he found himself in a wood, full of paths and people. Its central focus was a Temple of Virtue and a Temple of Honour, and all around were 'marble trophies, carved pillars, and statues of law-givers and heroes, statesmen, philosophers and poets'. There was also a Temple of Vanity, 'filled with pedants, free-thinkers, and prating politicans'.

William Kent's version of the Elysian Fields at Stowe has most of these features. The semi-circular Temple of British Worthies is reflected in a little river, a symbolic Styx, the river of death across which the dead reach the Underworld. On the tip of the pediment there was once a statue of Mercury, the traditional guide across the Styx. Visible across the water is their destination: the Elysian Fields proper, and a Temple of Ancient Virtue, full of ancient worthies to keep them company. No longer visible is Cobham's caustically conceived equivalent of the Temple of Vanity, a Temple of Modern Virtue, constructed as a ruin, with a headless statue, recognisable by its robes as Sir Robert Walpole, inside it. The Prime Minister's son Horace Walpole (1717-97) was not amused when he saw it on a visit in 1753: 'I have no patience at building and planting a satire.'

When Cobham died in 1749, Stowe was inherited by his nephew, Earl Temple (1711-79). His additions to the Stowe landscape were largely patriotic celebrations of Britain's victory in the Seven Years War against France, and the expansion of the British Empire. In 1779, the estate was inherited by George Grenville (1753-1813), who became Marquess of Buckingham. He and his sons (the 1st and 2nd Dukes of Buckingham) made further additions to what was becoming an increasingly cluttered classical landscape, more Disneyland than Arcadia. The zenith of Stowe's glory was a visit in 1845 by Queen Victoria and Prince Albert, when, legend has it, the entire chorus of Covent Garden was scattered in concealed groups around the grounds, and 'sang like nightingales' as the royal party drove past. But nemesis was close at hand. In 1848, the spendthrift habits of the 2nd Duke of Buckingham almost brought bankruptcy to the estate. Everything moveable in the house, and 36,000 acres of the estate, were sold. The house remained in the Grenville family until 1921, when there was another great sale. In 1923, Stowe became a public school.

TRAIL
1

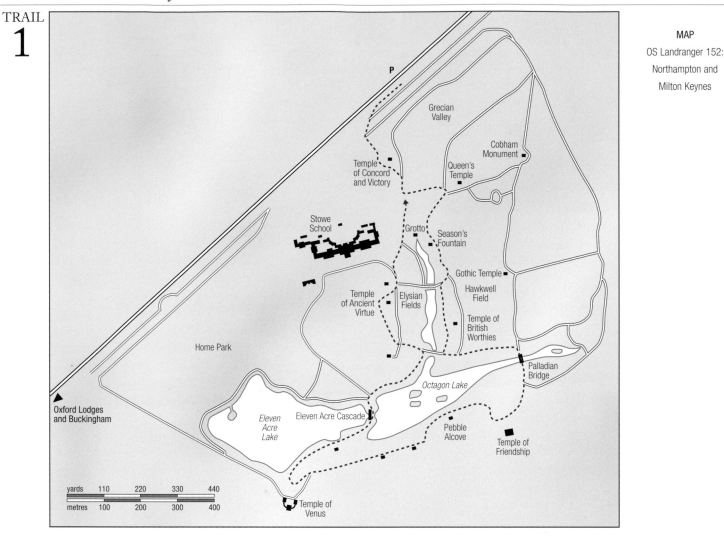

On Foot (2½ miles)

To appreciate Stowe's two great avenues, it is
worth approaching and leaving by different routes.
I suggest you arrive from Buckingham and leave on
the Bicester road. Leave Buckingham on the A422,
and take the very first turning on the right to Stowe.

You are now in the Great Avenue, which is
being replanted to restore it to its former glory.
Straight ahead of you is the great Corinthian Arch
which is one of the most important elements of
the Augustan, or heroic, sector of Stowe's
landscape. Through it, you will see the south façade
of the house, designed by Robert Adam. Turn left in
Chackmore, then turn right into the estate between
the Oxford Lodges. Here you join the second great

avenue, built beside the Roman road to Bicester, on
which you will leave.

Follow directions past the house (Stowe
School) to the National Trust car-park for the
gardens. After parking, you will enter the gardens
across the ha-ha, built in 1724, which surrounds
the whole of the garden. A 'sunken fence' of this
sort, which left the aspects beyond the boundaries
of the garden completely visible, was first described
in Dezallier d'Argenville's *Theory and Practice of
Gardening* (1712), and this was its first large-scale
appearance in England.

A full tour of the gardens would involve turning
left here and following the ha-ha to the (still
unrestored) Gibbs temple, the 'Fane of Pastoral

Poetry', and all round the perimeter of the grounds,
then criss-crossing to view the many follies and
features of the gardens. My tour focuses on the
Elysian Fields, the most literary element, and takes
1–2 hours.

The first building you come across is the
Temple of Concord and Victory, begun in 1745.
Plaques inside celebrate the 1763 British victory
over the French that ended the Seven Years War.
In front of it is Capability Brown's artfully casual
Grecian Valley. This pioneering example of informal
landscape gardening was in fact scooped out in
innumerable wheelbarrow loads by an army of
gardeners. A tall column to your right was once
topped by a statue of the 1st Viscount Cobham;

sadly, he lost this stupendous vantage point over his creation when it was struck by lightning in 1957.

Follow the gravel footpath eastwards as it winds through the trees until you reach the Seasons Fountain, and follow the instructions of its inscription from Thomson's famous poem:

Here pause in Silence, while beneath the Shade
Of solemn Oaks, that tuft the Swelling Mount,
You pensive listen to the Plaint of Rills
That Pushing down their dewy Murmurs shake
On the Sooth'd Ear...

Continuing on and looking to your left, you will see Hawkwell Field, once the setting for a *ferme ornée*, where gadding heifers, buxom milkmaids, beribboned sheep and carefully posed haymakers were once all bit-players in a permanent visual pageant. Across the field is James Gibbs's Gothic Temple (now maintained by the Landmark Trust). Intended to celebrate the values of Magna Carta, it is adorned inside with the invented heraldry of Cobham's Saxon ancestors. Over the door, Cobham had carved a defiantly anti-Roman line from Corneille's *Horace*: 'Je rends graces aux Dieux de nestre pas Romain.' In the distance to the north is the Queen's Temple, originally built for the ladies to spend time in while Cobham and his political and literary friends gathered in the Temple of Friendship which faces it from the southern boundary of the park.

You are now walking on the left-hand side of the literary showpiece and hub of the whole garden: the Elysian Fields. The inscriptions on the Temple of British Worthies are well worth reading; behind the building is the remains of another little joke by Cobham, a tribute to his favourite dog, Fido. Sir John Barnard, the last of the Worthies, will seem curiously obscure. He was one of the MPs who opposed Robert Walpole's Customs and Excise Bill, a measure which Cobham regarded as an outrageous infringement of British liberty.

Continue past the temple. You now have two options. A longer circuit through the gate on your left will take you past such beautiful though not especially literary monuments as the Palladian Bridge, the Chinese House, the (ruined) Temple of Friendship and the Pebble Alcove, and the Temple of Venus, originally decorated with some notoriously indecorous murals of scenes from Spenser's *Faerie Queene*, one of Lord Cobham's favourite books, to the Eleven Acre Cascade between the two great lakes to the south of the house, and so to the

Temple of Ancient Virtue. Alternatively, you can take a short cut to this temple by turning right and strolling back through the Elysian Fields on the other side of the little river.

After sitting in the temple contemplating ancient Greek virtue in the shape of the poet Homer, the philosopher Socrates, the law-giver Lycurgus and the military general Epaminondas, walk back towards the Temple of Concord. You will pass a somewhat shabby Grotto, built across the river. In July 1770 Horace Walpole witnessed a candle-lit 'Vauxhall' here, from a boat on the lake, laid on for the benefit of George III's aunt, the Princess Amelia Sophia. Venus arose from the cave and there was much merrymaking. But it was a cold night, and his fellow guest Lady Mary Coke recorded that he insisted on a glass of cherry brandy on his return to the house to ward off a chill.

Left: *The Temple of Concord and Victory* by Thomas Medland (1796/7).

Above: View of the Gothic Temple from the Elysian Fields.

A Somerset Salon

> As they came up to the house at Walcote, the windows from within were lighted up with friendly welcome; the supper-table was spread in the oak-parlour; it seemed as if forgiveness and love were awaiting the returning prodigal.
>
> William Makepeace Thackeray, *The History of Henry Esmond*

After the French Revolution, a conservative backlash in Britain meant that few great country houses had liberal, let alone radical, sympathies. Nor was patronage as the eighteenth century had known it deemed appropriate any longer. Depressingly often, such support required either slavering flattery or established fame. 'Is not a Patron, my Lord,' said Dr Johnson caustically to Lord Chesterfield, 'one who looks with unconcern on a man struggling for Life in the water, and when he has reached ground encumbers him with help?' The development of the periodical and the subscriber-financed publication of novels meant that writers could, if they were lucky, earn an independent living. But cultured families continued to enjoy their company.

Sir Charles Abraham Elton (1778-1853) made his family seat at Clevedon Court, Somerset, the hub of an influential literary circle. He was a classical scholar and a talented poet – the best known of his verses was 'The Brothers', written in memory of two of his sons, who drowned at Weston-super-Mare in 1819. His translation of Hesiod remained in print until the twentieth century. Through his connection with the *London Magazine*, to which he was a regular contributor from its launch in 1820, he came across such writers as John Clare, Charles Lamb, William Hazlitt, Robert Southey and Hartley Coleridge (son of the more famous Sam, who himself spent his early married life in a wooded 'Valley of Seclusion' a little west of the village of Clevedon, in a house called Myrtle Cottage).

Charles Lamb is thought to have had Clevedon in mind in an essay he wrote for the *London Magazine* on country houses in 1824. In it, he describes the pleasure garden of 'Blakesmore', 'rising backwards from the house in triple terraces … the verdant quarters backwarder still; and stretching still beyond, in old formality, the firry wilderness, the haunt of squirrel, and the day-long murmuring wood-pigeon with that antique image in the centre'.

Sir Charles's sister Julia married the historian Henry Hallam, whose son Arthur was a close friend of Alfred Tennyson. It was his death in Vienna in 1833 that would, much later, inspire *In Memoriam*, the poem

Clevedon Court in Somerset, home of the Elton family since 1709.

that earned Tennyson the poet laureateship. Tennyson stayed at Clevedon Court when he visited Hallam's tomb while on his honeymoon in 1850, the year *In Memoriam* was published.

   The next generation of Eltons at Clevedon continued its literary distinction. Sir Charles's daughter Jane Octavia (1821-96), who was married to William Brookfield, was at the centre of a brilliant literary world which included Thomas and Jane Carlyle, Samuel Rogers, Tennyson, Charles Dickens, and, to what became an embarrassing degree, William Makepeace Thackeray (1811-63). One of the most striking pictures at

The Travellers' Breakfast by Edward Villiers Rippingille shows Sir Charles Elton's literary circle. Charles Lamb is handing Rippingille the bill. Coleridge is holding out a boiled egg for Wordsworth to sniff, while Dorothy Wordsworth sits at the table with folded hands. Robert Southey eyes Lucy Caroline, Sir Charles's daughter, as she pours out the tea, while her father looks on. To the right, her twin Caroline Lucy laughs as an ostler tries to get a tip from a old lady; on the extreme left, another daughter, Julia Elizabeth, prods a porter with an umbrella; yet another stands close to the stairs. Sir Charles's wife Sarah is holding her sons Arthur and Edmund.

Clevedon is the almost life-size, full-length cartoon of Thackeray, which hangs at the head of the stairs up to a room which is now known as the Thackeray Room, but was once Jane Octavia's bedroom. There has been much speculation over the nature of the relationship between Jane Octavia and Thackeray. They were evidently kindred spirits from the first, and met in London, where Jane Octavia held regular literary salons at the Brookfields' house in Great Pulteney Street. Jane's relationship with her husband was amicable rather than passionate, and Thackeray, whose wife Isabella was mentally ill and lived separately from her husband in the care of a nurse, developed a deep affection for her. They corresponded regularly and openly, and Jane always passed his letters on to her husband. There were occasionally jealous rumbles, but Jane dispelled them with a light touch: 'I do think, at near 30, one may take up a line of one's own, and when one feels affectionately, one may venture to say so…It is not as if Mr Thack were some Adonis in the guards.'

But in October 1848, while Jane was staying with her family at Clevedon, Thackeray came for a visit, using the former chapel, just off the State Bedroom, as a study while he was working on *Pendennis* (1848-50). 'What took place [there] is beyond the range of forensic analysis', says D. J. Taylor, Thackeray's biographer:

Late one evening, something happened between Thackeray and Jane that took their relationship into a new orbit. Thackeray's re-capitulation of the incident, written in French – which he tended to adopt at moments of high emotion – talks about 'that clear voice which called me at night at Clevedon'. The same letter represents him as one of the damned and Jane as an 'angel full of pity'.

It seems likely that what happened was an intenser than usual exchange of confidences as to each other's emotional loneliness. Thackeray later said that Clevedon was the inspiration for Castlewood, the ancient house in *The History of Henry Esmond* (1852). Lady

William Makepeace
Thackeray by
Ernest Edwards (*c*.1863).

Castlewood certainly had elements of Jane Octavia, as seen through
Thackeray's increasingly adoring eyes:

> She stretched out her hand – indeed, when was it that that hand
> would not stretch out to do an act of kindness, or to protect grief
> and ill-fortune?…Her golden hair was shining in the sun; her
> complexion was of a dazzling bloom; her lips smiling, and her eyes
> beaming with a kindness which made Harry Esmond's heart beat
> with surprise.

The letters exchanged in the next few months show, Taylor says, 'a sharp rise in the emotional temperature'. 'I must say to someone that I love you', wrote Thackeray to Jane, after his visit. 'Why not? To you, to William [Jane's husband], to anyone who will listen to me.' Jane began to cut out sections of his letters, and scored out various passages. Her husband became a little jealous, but was confident enough of his wife's fidelity to believe her when she explained that the over-fondness was entirely on Thackeray's side.

Whatever had bubbled to the surface simmered down considerably when, in February 1850, Jane had her first child. Any illusions Thackeray might have privately entertained over her relationship with her husband were abruptly dispelled. 'I am an extinct crater and my volcano is poked out', he wrote sadly. His *Pendennis*, finished in November 1850, has veiled references to the relationship, as Thackeray saw it, in the love triangle between Pen, Laura and Warrington. In September 1851, he made a sad fool of himself by openly accusing Brookfield of neglecting Jane, and there was a complete breach between them. Thackeray went to Chatsworth in Derbyshire for an emotional convalescence, but wrote to friends that 'the Devil is with me still and making me miserable'. Soon after, the Brookfields went abroad to Madeira, and, though occasional letters were later exchanged, things were never the same. After Thackeray's death, Jane wrote several novels, in two of which, *Only George* (1866) and *Influence* (1871), there seem to be subtle parallels with their relationship.

Sir Charles's son, Sir Arthur Hallam Elton, continued the literary traditions of his father, but was more politically active and influential in a way that reflected the concerned Toryism of the nineteenth century. He was a great philanthropist, who parcelled off some of the Clevedon estate as allotments, established lending libraries, coffee-houses and lodging-houses for working-class men and did what he could to extend their education. His novel *Below the Surface* (1857) revealed his feelings about the divided state of the nation and the need to improve the lot of both the industrial and the agricultural poor.

BLISS IN BEACONSFIELD

The great statesmen of English history looked upon the nation as a family, and upon the country as a landed inheritance. Generation after generation were to succeed to it, with all its convenient buildings and all its choice cultivation, its parks and gardens, as well as its fields and meadows, its libraries and its collections of art, all its wealth, but all its encumbrances.

Benjamin Disraeli, *A Vindication of the English Constitution*

Memorabilia in the Disraeli Room at Hughenden Manor includes a miniature of his wife, Mary Anne, and examples of the paper on which he wrote his novels in longhand. The portrait of Disraeli in 1852 by Sir Francis Grant (right) hangs in the Library.

In the middle of the nineteenth century, the Englishman's home was becoming his castle, and the keeping of open house was beginning to die away. To the increasingly wealthy middle classes, the country house was a prize to be attained, a sign of having 'arrived' in society. It was a sign of the times that a self-made man like Benjamin Disraeli (1804-81) should be deeply conservative in his respect for all that the country house stood for. A sparklingly witty man, eventually much loved by Queen Victoria, he was also intensely ambitious and distinctly opportunist ('never complain and never explain' was his watchword). His enemies called him 'the sphinx without a riddle'. He became Tory leader in 1849, but remained in opposition for almost the whole of the next twenty-five years. It was only in 1874, aged seventy, that he came into power with a workable majority.

Hughenden, Disraeli's Beaconsfield house, is a monument to both his political success and his literary achievements. He was already an established novelist when he and his vivacious wife Mary Anne moved there in 1848 – his political trilogy *Coningsby, or The New Generation* (1844), *Sybil, or The Two Nations* (1845) and *Tancred, or The New Crusade* (1847) was the manifesto of the group of aristocratic young Tories known as Young England.

Mary Anne threw herself enthusiastically into furnishing the house, ordering crimson and yellow Aubusson carpets from Maples and shields from a Mr Lacey of High Wycombe to ornament the hall in baronial style. 'My Darling,' wrote 'Dizzy' to her, 'you have, I am sure, done at Hughenden what no other woman, or man either, could do. You have gained a year in our enjoyment of that place, where I trust every year we shall be happier and happier.' During the next eighteen years of their occupancy, Hughenden was substantially remodelled, incorporating a mishmash of architectural references: Moorish fretwork, Tudor arches, Gothic arches and Italian terraces. The alterations were in themselves a political statement. Disraeli wrote to his patroness Mrs Brydges Wilyams in September 1863: 'We have restored the house to what it was before the Civil War, and we have made a garden of terraces in which cavaliers may roam and saunter with their lady loves.'

Books were a central part of Disraeli's life. 'I have a passion for books and trees', he wrote. 'I like to look at them. When I come down to Hughenden, I pass the first week in sauntering about my park and examining all the trees, and then I saunter in the library and survey the books.' He inherited most of these from his father's vast library (of 25,000 volumes) at nearby Bradenham Manor. He himself collected history, theology and the classics, and was especially fond of early Italian books. In his time the library was the room now furnished as the drawing-room (and vice versa). Its twin arched openings decorated with the heads of bishops and green men were made in the 1840s, as, in all probability, was the diamond-patterned ceiling. It also had oak bookcases which Disraeli's nephew removed when he reorganised the house. A visitor in 1876 remembers it full of 'writing tables, couches covered with yellow satin and profusely gilt, oak cabinets ornamented with caryatids, columns and entablatures of Dresden china'. Dizzy enjoyed 'watching the sunlight sparkle on the gilt bindings of my books'.

During a visit to Hughenden, Sir Stafford Northcote noted in his diary in 1880:

> After dinner, we chiefly talked books; the Chief is always at his best in his library, and seemed to enjoy a good ramble over literature. He was contemptuous of Browning (of whom, however, he had read very little) and the other poetasters of the day, none of whom he thought would live except Tennyson.

Disraeli was contemptuous of most contemporary novelists. 'When I want to read a novel, I write one', he is famously quoted as saying. But his novels were not just highly readable amusements; they epitomised his social and political thinking. For though he was an able trimmer, Disraeli was far from lacking in principles. An outsider himself, he sympathised with others in the same position. 'Upon the education of the people of this country the fate of this country depends.' Although staunchly Tory, he was conscious of the evils of an irresponsible abuse of inherited wealth and power. He and his cronies looked back nostalgically to the past and bemoaned the loss of chivalry. 'Bores have succeeded dragons', complains May Dacre in Disraeli's *The Young Duke* (1831).

Many of the contemporary figures who were the originals of characters in Disraeli's novels can be seen in the portraits with which the house is lined. William Lowther, 2nd Earl of Lonsdale, of whom a sculpted bust stands in the Disraeli Room, was Lord President in Disraeli's first ministry and the original for Lord Eskdale in *Coningsby*: 'clear-sighted, unprejudiced, sagacious; the best judge in the world of a horse or a man; the universal referee'. In the Garden Hall is a portrait of Lord John Manners, one of the founders of the Young England Movement and a lifelong friend and political associate. He was the inspiration for Lord Henry Sidney in *Coningsby* and *Tancred*. Disraeli's houses were also usually modelled on real places – Coningsby Castle is an amalgam of Chatsworth and Welbeck Abbey; Beaumanoir, in *Sybil*, is Belvoir Castle.

The library at
Hughenden in 1881.

H. G. WELLS AND THE TIME MACHINE

> Within these households, behind their screen of deer park and park wall and sheltered service, men could talk, think, and write at their leisure, curious and interested to make, foster, and protect the accumulating science and literature of the seventeenth and eighteenth centuries. Their large rooms, their libraries, their collections of pictures and 'curios' retained in the nineteenth century an atmosphere of unhurried liberal inquiry, of serene and determined insubordination and personal dignity, of established aesthetic and intellectual standards.
>
> H. G. Wells, *Experiment in Autobiography*

At the end of the nineteenth century, literary references to the great country houses begin to have an elegiac feel. 'Bladesover is the clue to almost all that is distinctively British and perplexing to the foreign inquirer in England', writes H. G. Wells (1866-1946) in *Tono-Bungay* (1909). The book was conceived as a snapshot of upper-class English society in the autumn of its power, an account of its degeneration and decay in the face of the forceful, energetic and entrepreneurial middle classes.

> We have never broken with our tradition, never even symbolically hewed it to pieces, as the French did in quivering act after the Terror. But all the organising ideas have slackened, the old habitual bonds have relaxed or altogether come undone.

But Wells's portrayal of Bladesover as a symbol of the declining aristocracy is complicated by his very personal feelings about Uppark, the Sussex house on which it was based. His mother, Sarah Wells, was the housekeeper at Uppark, the ancestral home of the Fetherstonhaughs. Most of the house remained in a time-warp for almost a hundred years. The last in line of the family, the high-living regency rake Sir Harry

The south front of
Uppark in Sussex, where
H. G. Wells lived with his
mother in the servants'
quarters when she was
housekeeper between
1880 and 1892.

Fetherstonhaugh, married his dairymaid late in life and had no children. The house passed first to his wife, then to her sister, neither of whom made many changes anywhere except in the household offices.

His years there as a teenager left Wells with two legacies: a smarting sense of injustice at being treated as one of the lower orders, and a respect for the institution of the country house itself. He was given the run of the library, and was something of a pet among the servants. During a great snowstorm, when Uppark was cut off for a fortnight,

> I provided a daily newspaper of a facetious character, *The Uppark Alarmist* – on what was probably kitchen paper – and gave a shadow play to the maids and others, in a miniature theatre I made in the housekeeper's room …
>
> The place had a great effect on me; it retained a vitality that altogether overshadowed the insignificant ebbing trickle of up-stairs life, the two elderly ladies in the parlour following their shrunken routines.

There may well have been something heartfelt in George Ponderovo's words about Bladesover in *Tono-Bungay*: 'It was the first time I had knowingly met beauty.' He contrasts Bladesover's 'spacious hall and salon and galleries, its airy housekeeper's room and warren of offices with the meagre dignities of the vicar, and the stuffy rooms of even the post-office people and the grocer'. As the book continues, its hero George begins to perceive the hollowness and vulgarity of his uncle's flashy inventiveness and splashy use of his wealth. Crest Hill, the 'truly twentieth-century house' which Edward Ponderovo, 'the Napoleon of domestic con-veniences', builds on the proceeds of his miraculous medicine, is merely a wildly over-ambitiously conceived storehouse, filled with bought grandeur. It has no 'established aesthetic and intellectual standards'. Like grocer millionaire Julius Drewe's Castle Drogo in Devon, built a year after *Tono-Bungay* was published, it was never finished and hardly lived

The Housekeeper's Room at Uppark, preserved as it may have been during the time of Sarah Wells.

in. But the novel is not a simple antithesis between the merits of the past and the vulgarities of the present. The society of which Bladesover is a symbol is also in decay. George's insincere childhood sweetheart Beatrice turns up at the end of the book as 'a sick and tired woman': 'One gets bored, bored beyond redemption. One goes about to these huge expensive houses, I suppose – the scale's immense…They go about making love. Everybody's making love. I did.' At the end of the book, Bladesover itself is occupied by *nouveau riche* tenants. The old leather volumes in the library are replaced by 'new books in gaudy catchpenny "artistic" covers'; a hideous collection of china cats litter every surface. 'There was the trail of the Bond Street showroom over it all.'

Bridesheads Revisited

Old stone to new building, old timber to new fires . . .
Houses live and die: there is a time for building
And a time for living and for generation
And a time for the wind to break the loosened pane
And to shake the wainscot where the fieldmouse trots
And to shake the tattered arras woven with a silent motto

T. S. Eliot, *Four Quartets*

In the first half of the twentieth century, the decline of country houses
as seats of power and, by analogy, the decline in the power of the English
upper classes were mapped in many novels. Real houses often inspired
them. Aldous Huxley's *Crome Yellow* (1921) is a satirical portrait of both
Garsington Manor, near Oxford, and its eccentric hostess Lady Ottoline
Morrell. E. M. Forster's *Howards End* (1910) is a love song to Rooksnest,
Hertfordshire, his childhood home.

In D. H. Lawrence's *Lady Chatterley's Lover* (1928), Connie drives
through the Midlands and sees collieries invading the parks of the once
'proud and lordly county' and a thinly disguised Hardwick Hall:

Looming against and hanging on the brow of the skyline, was the
huge and splendid bulk of Chadwick Hall, more window than
wall, one of the most famous Elizabethan houses. Noble, it stood
alone above a great park, but out of date, passed over. It was still
kept up, but as a showplace. 'Look how our ancestors lorded it!'

Next, Connie sees Fritchley, a Georgian mansion in perfect repair which
was being demolished because it was 'too big, too expensive, and the
countryside had become too uncongenial. The gentry was departing to
pleasanter places, where they could spend their money without having
to see how it was made.'

In Evelyn Waugh's *Decline and Fall* (1928), Llanabba Castle has become a fifth-rate public school and the beautiful Tudor manor of King's Thursday is torn down to be replaced by 'something clean and square' designed by the architect of a chewing-gum factory. In *Vile Bodies* (1930), Doubting Hall, home of one of England's most notable Catholic families, is symbolically banished to the past by being made into a film set for a life of John Wesley. In *A Handful of Dust* (1934), Hetton Abbey is a sham, a mock-Gothic pile in which, as Richard Gill puts it, its hero Tony Last 'lives out a fantasy inherited from his Victorian forebears and their literature and so has lost touch with the realities of the contemporary society around him'. The house is a parody of Camelot, its bedrooms named after characters in the Arthurian legends. Tony still sleeps in his boyhood room 'Morgan le Fay'; his wife Brenda sleeps, ominously, alone in 'Guinevere'. Though 'madly feudal', Tony rejects the hospitable traditions of the past: 'I don't keep up the house to be a hostel for a lot of bores to come and gossip in'. But he will lose Brenda because she is bored by Hetton, preferring the excitements of the city and life in a thoroughly modern maisonette.

As well as satirising upper-class life, Evelyn Waugh (1906-66) repeatedly uses his novels to contrast the 'integrated and purposeful existence' on a nobleman's estate with the chaos of modern times. *Brideshead Revisited* (1945), written during the Second World War, portrays an 'enchanted palace', a living, formidable place, its great fountain symbolising the way it is bubbling with life. Even at the end of the novel, though it is deep in hibernation and occupied by the army, it is far from derelict. In Waugh's respect for the enduring power of the country house, he took another twentieth-century literary approach: to see the country house and its self-sufficient estate as an ark of tradition, a vital link with the past that can enrich both present and future and which embodies creative harmony. In *Knole and the Sackvilles*, Vita Sackville-West draws her ancestral home as a living thing, a place 'with the deep inward gaiety of some very old woman who has always been beautiful, who has had many lovers and seen generations come and go, smiled wisely over their sorrows and their joys, and learnt an imperishable secret of tolerance and humour'.

In the twentieth century, Knole could no longer afford to support aspiring artists and writers. Instead, the house itself became a symbol of changing times. Vita Sackville-West chronicled the contemporary shift in social values by using it as Chevron, the great house in her novel *The Edwardians*. The thoroughly modern Leonard Anquetil, a much-fêted explorer, dismisses Chevron as 'a dead thing, an anachronism, an exquisite survival', a prison of outdated responsibilities which he feels its heir, his friend Sebastian, should abandon to join his expedition to the Arctic. But Sebastian sees beyond the superficial life of his mother's parties to value 'the whole community of the great house', the 'carpenter's shop, and the forge, and the wood-cutters', which stood for 'warmth and security, leisure and continuity'. The novel's ending is ambivalent: Sebastian accepts Anquetil's invitation, but only, as Anquetil concedes, to 'be a better master to Chevron'. Virginia Woolf also painted a portrait of Knole in *Orlando*, her tribute to her friend and lover Vita Sackville-West. In it, she voices what is a recurring theme both of her novels and of the poetry of Thomas Hardy, the idea of something which lives on from one set of occupants to another and which imposes its own spirit:

> Better it was to go unknown and leave behind you an arch, a potting shed, a wall where peaches ripen, than to burn like a meteor and leave no dust. For, after all, [Orlando] said, kindling as he looked at the great house on the greensward below, the unknown lords and ladies who lived there never forgot to set something aside for them who come after.

Virginia Woolf's *Between the Acts* (1941) was the last book she wrote at Monk's House. The fictional house that is the symbol of local unity in the book is the Elizabethan manor of Pointz Hall. It is 'middle-sized and unpretentious', the kind of house that could and should survive as the

The ballroom at Knole in Kent, which is hung with Sackville family portraits.

centre of its surrounding community in a way that was now not possible for huge houses such as Knole. In its gardens all the village gathers for a pageant, a visual embodiment of traditional values. E. M. Forster described the book as an 'exquisite final tribute' to 'something more solid than patriotic history and something better worth dying for'.

Similarly, in Evelyn Waugh's *Sword of Honour* trilogy (1952-61) the country house Broome, seat of the significantly named Crouchbacks, is very much part of its village rather than being locked away in a distant park. The main house has found a new use as a convent school; the heir, Guy Crouchback, lives in the Lesser House. And though Broome will be inherited not by a Crouchback but by a distinctly unaristocratic Trimmer, what is important is not his (healthily) mongrel ancestry but the house's position in the local community.

The present role of the great country houses in literature is predominantly one of nostalgia. Rather than being the powerhouses of their age, the energisers of literary creation, the ultimate aspiration of Jane Austen's heroines, country houses are now merely monuments to past times. Historical novels are set in places like Ightham Mote, Kent (Anya Seton's *Green Darkness*) and Trerice, Cornwall (Winston Graham's Poldark series). Modern novels such as Ishiguro's *The Remains of the Day* and Penelope Lively's *Next to Nature, Art* use them as symbols half lovingly, half critically.

This attitude was prefigured by the American novelist Henry James (1843-1916), who lived so long and so happily in his adopted country. Although, or perhaps because, he was American, Henry James was unusually obsessed with English country houses, 'round which experience seems piled so thick' (*English Hours*, 1905). In this travel diary, he tells us how, weary with the vulgarity and ugliness of American cities, he set off for Europe 'in quest for the ancient':

> It was the old houses that fetched me – Montacute, the admirable; Barrington, that superb Forde Abbey, and several smaller ones … These delicious old houses … I thought of all the stories, of dramas, of all the life of the past – of things one can hardly speak of; speak of, I mean, at the time. Such a house as Montacute, so perfect, with its grey personality, its old-world gardens, its accumulation of expressions, of tone – such a house is really, au fond, an ineffaceable image; it can be trusted to rise before the eyes in the future.

'Every step you take in such a house', he writes of Stokesay Castle in Shropshire, a fortified manor house, 'confronts you in one way or another with the remote past. You devour the documentary, you inhale history… It is not too much to say that after spending twenty-four hours in a house that is six hundred years old you seem yourself to have lived in it six hundred years. You seem yourself to have hollowed the flags and to have polished the oak with your touch.' In *The Portrait of a Lady* (1881), Gardencourt (which was to some extent modelled on Cliveden, Buckinghamshire) is an important symbol for traditional English values, a 'modern Eden' that now has a serpent within.

Huge establishments and prodigious wealth were no longer necessary to the creation of a literary salon. In 1902, Henry James acquired his own little foothold in history by renting Lamb House, an early eighteenth-century town house in Rye, East Sussex. It became, while he lived there, a popular focus for well-known writers. The Kent and Sussex coast, cheap and picturesquely rural, but conveniently close to the capital, had become an acceptable London annexe. Visitors to Lamb House included G. K. Chesterton, Ottoline Morrell, Hilaire Belloc, H. G. Wells, Rupert Brooke, Logan Pearsall Smith, Edith Wharton, A. C. and E. F. Benson, Max Beerbohm, Ford Madox Ford, Stephen Crane, Joseph Conrad, Hugh Walpole, Violet Hunt and Rudyard Kipling – who wrote off £2,000 of new car on Rye's bumpy cobbles.

'A Charming, Braceful, Sturdy Little Habitation'

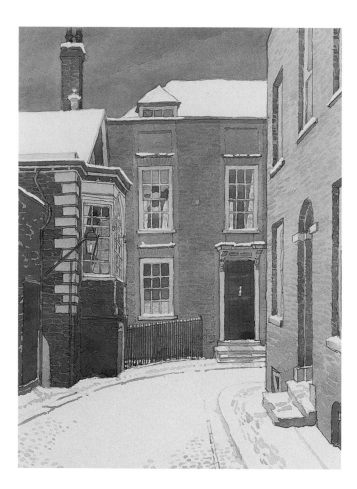

Originally built in about 1705, it was prettily provincial in appearance. Henry James first saw it in 1896, when he was in his early fifties and at the height of his fame. He lived in London and was on holiday in Rye. It was a sketch of the house, with its enchanting garden-room jutting out into the street, made by his architect friend Edward Warren, that brought him there. After a couple of summers in Rye, frequently 'casting sheep's eyes at Lamb House', he began to consider the idea of removing to the town altogether, confessing to a 'long-unassuaged desire for a calm retreat'. In 1900 he received a letter from the Rye ironmonger, 'to whom I had whispered my hopeless passion', telling him that the owner had died and it was available for rent. James leased it 'on quite deliciously moderate terms' and two years later bought the freehold. The novelist Edith Wharton wrote observantly of how 'he who thought himself so detached from material things tasted the simple joys of proprietorship when, with a deprecating air, he showed his fine Georgian panelling and his ancient brick walls to admiring visitors'. James himself described it lovingly:

> There are two rooms of complete old oak – one of them a delightful old parlour, opening by one side into the little vista, church-ward, of the small old-world street, where not one of the half-dozen wheeled vehicles of Rye ever passes; and on the other straight into the garden and the approach, from that quarter to the garden-house aforesaid, which is simply the making of a most commodious and picturesque detached study and workroom.

He worked in the garden-room in summer, dictating to a secretary as he roamed around the room. In the winter he moved to the cosiness of the Green Room, in the main house. Unfortunately, the garden-room was destroyed by a bomb in 1940.

French windows were added to the ground-floor rooms, and built-in bookcases for James's 5,000-volume library. He began to acquire furniture, developing 'the most avid and gluttonous eye and the most infernal watching patience in respect of lurking "occasions" in not-too-delusive Chippendale and Sheraton'. He did not acquire, though he lusted after, the golden bowl

The very calmest and yet cheerfullest [little old house] that I could have dreamed in the little old cobble-stoned, grass-grown, red-roofed town, on the summit of its mildly pyramidal hill and close to its noble old church – the chimes of which will sound sweet in my good old red-walled garden.

Henry James, *Letters*

Lamb House in Rye could not be in stronger contrast to the great country house salons where writers and poets once congregated. But when owned by Henry James, it became a Mecca for twentieth-century literati, many of whom lived locally.

which had been given to James Lamb by George I as a christening present for the son who was born while he was staying in the house; it was kept safely locked up in a local bank. But it gave him the title for his last novel. When he wrote to its owner expressing admiration, he added that he felt

> personally indebted to your peculiarly civilized ancestor who kindly conceived and put together to my benefit, so long ago, exactly the charming, braceful, sturdy little habitation (full of sense, discretion, taste) that suits alike my fancy and necessity, and in which I hope (DV) to end my days.

In 1910, heart trouble led James to change the pattern of his life, and he decided to spend only summers in Rye so that he could be near his doctor in the winter months. 'I have had to make a nest – a perch – for myself in London, which involves the desertion of Rye for the winter – only temporarily, hibernetically speaking.' He once more took up residence in the Reform Club in winter, visiting his secretary Miss Bosanquet's flat (women were not allowed to enter the Reform Club) to dictate every morning. In 1912 he acquired a London flat again: 21 Carlyle Mansions in Chelsea.

After Henry James's death, Lamb House was let to Fred (E. F.) and Arthur (A. C.) Benson, both prolific writers. Arthur, who was Master of Magdalene College, Cambridge, spent only the vacations in Rye, often bringing down literary-minded undergraduates. After his brother's death in 1925, Fred lived there alone until his own death in 1940. A delightfully clubbable man, he was mayor of Rye for three years running, and immortalised Lamb House as Mallards, home of the redoubtable Miss Mapp. In his autobiography, he explained how he

> outlined an elderly spinster and established her in Lamb House. She should be the centre of social life, abhorred and dominant, and she should sit there like a great spider behind the curtains in the garden room, spying on her friends, and I knew that her name must be Elizabeth Mapp.

It is not until the fourth novel, *Mapp and Lucia* (1931), that Miss Mapp's status as First Lady of Tilling (Rye) is challenged by the arrival of the exquisitely pretentious Lucia.

Lamb House also has a ghost: a man murdered in mistake for its original owner James Lamb, who incurred the wrath of a local butcher. When E. F. Benson held a séance there, the medium pointed to the chair he had died in and said she saw a man in a cloak. Benson told the vicar he had seen a ghost in the garden. In 1968, Lamb House became the home of the novelist Rumer Godden, who wrote in an article in 1990 that she always had the sense of a 'presence' there. Late one mild December night in 1973, she was taking a stroll in the garden when she smelt

the strong scent of nicotiana. Nicotiana do not bloom in December, but I smelled them, and with them another smell, a cigar, but James [her husband] had not smoked cigars, nor was there anyone near who did. The scent came with me as I walked, and I sensed a companionship.

Left: A Christmas card by Sir Brian Batsford showing Lamb House and the garden-room in the snow.

Above: E. F. Benson in the garden – his 'outdoor sitting room' – at Lamb House.

Muses and Mountains

Oh my God! what enormous Mountains these are close by me, and yet below the Hill I stand on … the Clouds are hast'ning hither from the Sea – and the whole air seaward has a lurid Look and we shall certainly have Thunder – yet here (but that I am hunger'd and provisionless) here I could lie warm, and wait methinks for tomorrow's Sun, and on a nice Stone Table am I now at this moment writing to you – between 2 and 3 o'Clock as I guess – surely the first Letter ever written from the Top of Sca'Fell!

Samuel Taylor Coleridge to Sarah Hutchinson, 5 August 1802

Few places in Britain are as rich in literary associations as the mountains, lakes, dales and fells which make up the English Lake District. Whole books have been written on the multifarious ways in which it has inspired poets and novelists – one of the earliest and best of them was written by a founder of the National Trust, Canon Hardwicke Drummond Rawnsley. It has, moreover, a splendid literature all its own – classics inspired by walking, climbing, sailing, geologising and botanising there, to say nothing of studies of its archaeology, history and folklore.

I'm going to concentrate on just one aspect: its capacity to inspire romance – literary, poetic and real. This is a relatively recent development. It is only in the last two hundred years that the rugged fell scenery has been considered sublime rather than horrific, and that visitors have gazed on the mighty works of nature and delighted, not despaired. Given half a chance, they have looked around a bit more and fallen in love. This chapter is the story of the women who inspired the height-intoxicated literati – either in the flesh or in the imagination.

Poetic evidence that men and women were made more susceptible to each other because of the drama of the setting is not hard to find. Mountain tops are apostrophised as looming or soaring male presences, lakes and streams as clusively or profoundly female. Freud would have loved these lines describing the rivers of south-west Furness by the poet topographer, Michael Drayton (1563-1631):

View of the Cumbrian Lake District towards Skiddaw, with Derwentwater to the right and Bassenthwaite in the distance.

As Eske her farth'st, so first, a coy Cumbrian Lasse,
Who cometh to her Road, renowned Ravenglasse,
By Devock driven along (which from a large-brim'd lake,
To hye her to the Sea, with greater haste doth make)
Meets Myte, a nimble Brooke, their Rendezvous that keepe
In Ravenglasse, when soone into the blewish Deepe
Comes Irt, of all the rest, though small, the richest Girle,
Her costly bosome strew'd with precious Orient Pearle,
Bred in her shining Shels, which to the deaw doth yawn,
Which deaw they sucking in, conceave that lusty Spawn,
Of which when they grow great, and to their fullnesse swell,
They cast, which those at hand there gathering, dearly sell.

Poly-Olbion, 1619

Drayton was unusual in finding the Lake District sexy. Much more typical of early attitudes was Daniel Defoe's (1660-1731) description of the 'unhospitable terror' of its 'unpassable mountains'; Westmorland was 'a country eminent only for being the wildest, most barren and frightful of any that I have passed over in England, or even in Wales itself' (*A Tour Through the Whole Island of Great Britain*, 1724-6). It was Thomas Gray (1716-71) who, after a tour of the Lakes in 1769, was the first to spell out the inspirational quality of the landscape in terms of a female muse:

In climes beyond the solar road
Where shaggy forms o'er ice-built mountains roam
The Muse has broke the twilight-gloom
To cheer the shivering native's dull abode

By the end of the eighteenth century improved roads and the difficulty of Continental travel caused by the war with France encouraged a national reassessment of the delights of Britain's own scenery. A new breed of travellers known as 'tourists' began to make their way

*Derwent Water with
Skiddaw in the Distance*
(*c*.1795–6) by Joseph
Wright of Derby
(1734-97).

along the new road (now A591) through Kendal and Ambleside to Keswick to view the landscape through a Claude glass picturesquely. 'Here is beauty indeed – Beauty lying in the lap of Horror!' exclaimed the eighteenth-century Newcastle composer Charles Avison on seeing Derwentwater. The theme of male mountains and female waters would recur, overtly and subliminally, across the centuries.

Samuel Taylor Coleridge (1772-1834) was undoubtedly the most extreme and extrovert of Lakeland romantics. In November 1799 he was visiting Eusemere House, home of the slavery abolitionist Thomas Clarkson, at Pooley Bridge, Ullswater, and the notes in his diary run:

> Monday Morning – sitting on a Tree Stump at the brink of the Lake by Mr Clarkson's – perfect serenity / that round fat backside of a Hill with its image in the water made together one absolutely undistinguishable Form – a kite or paddle or keel turned to you / the road appeared a sort of suture, in many places exactly as the weiblich tetragrammaton [i.e. female four-letter word] is painted in anatomical Books! I never saw so sweet an Image!!

In strong contrast to Coleridge's overheated imagination are Charles Lamb's healthily fraternal perceptions of Skiddaw and the surrounding hills as 'glorious creatures, fine old fellows … broad-breasted brethren'.

It was a short step from enjoying the beauties of nature to enjoying real local beauties. On his tour of the North in 1818, John Keats (1795-1821) happened on a county dancing-school held in the Tun Inn at Ireby, Cumberland's oldest market town 'There was as fine a row of boys and girls as you ever saw; some beautiful faces, and one exquisite mouth', he wrote to a friend.

> They kickit and jumpit with mettle extraordinary, and whiskit, and friskit, and toed it, and go'd it, and twirl'd it and whirl'd it,

and stamp't it, and sweated it, tattooing the floor like made. The difference between our country dances and these Scotch figures is about the same as leisurely stirring a cup o'Tea and beating up a batter pudding … I never felt so near the glory of Patriotism, the glory of making, by any means, a Country happier. This is what I like better than scenery.

The vigorous and bohemian essayist William Hazlitt (1778-1830) went even further in his admiration of local talent — with disastrous results. Touring the Lakes in 1803 as a painter (he sketched both Wordsworth and Coleridge, but both pictures have been lost), he spotted a beauty in Keswick and propositioned her. She called him a black-faced rascal, whereupon (according to a later account by Wordsworth) the enraged Hazlitt pushed her down, 'and because, Sir, she refused to gratify his abominable and devilish propensities, lifted up her petticoats and smote her on the bottom'. He was chased out of town by a mob of some two hundred local men, took refuge with Coleridge and Southey in Greta Hall and then slipped away across the fells to Grasmere and Dove Cottage, where the Wordsworths, unaware at the time of the full enormity of Hazlitt's behaviour, took him in and lent him the money for the mail-coach south. He never returned again.

TRAIL **The Fell-climbing Philosopheress**

1

> Miss Smith was really a most extraordinary person ...
> Had it been possible for the world to measure her by her
> powers, rather than her performances, she would have
> been placed, perhaps in the estimate of posterity, at the
> head of learned women.

Thomas de Quincey, 'Society of the Lakes'

History does not record whether either Coleridge or Hazlitt
made the acquaintance of Elizabeth Smith (1776-1806), a prod-
igiously talented young woman who was much admired – from
afar – by Thomas de Quincey. An avid reader from the age of
three, she taught herself twelve languages, including Welsh,
Erse, Hebrew, and African and Oriental dialects as well as the
more usual European ones. She also loved scrambling up and
down 'rude mountains, roaring torrents and rocky precipices'.
'We are going, to my great satisfaction, to settle somewhere in a
cheap and romantic country', she wrote cheerfully in 1800, after
financial disaster had struck her family and they decided to move
to the Lakes.

At first, her parents rented a cottage in Patterdale, and, while
living there, Elizabeth met the Wordsworths and many of their
friends. Dorothy records two visits from the family in her
journal; on another occasion Elizabeth kept Wordsworth and
Humphry Davy waiting impatiently for the upstairs room at
the Patterdale Hotel which they had booked for a night's rest
while on their walking tour. She was holding a jolly women's
evening, and had no intention of curtailing it, although William
and Humphry walked up and down under the windows impatiently, loudly calling out the hours in imitation of the
nightwatchman.

Her greatest admirer among the wordsmiths of Grasmere
was Thomas Wilkinson of Yanwith, an amiable dilettante with
a great love of gardening (his spade is apostrophised in what
is arguably Wordsworth's worst poem: 'Spade! with which
Wilkinson hath tilled his lands ...'). Wilkinson wrote poetry of
a sort, but his best claim to literary fame was his gossipy and
intensely personal *Tours to the British Mountains* (1824). In it
there are admiring accounts of the exploits of the three Smith
sisters on Helvellyn while they lived in Patterdale, and on the
Langdale Pikes when they moved, in 1801, to Coniston. They
climbed without guides and regardless of weather, using
ironshod staves when Helvellyn was covered with 'wreaths of
snow and sheets of ice'. When Wilkinson pleaded cold fingers
and frozen toes, 'they ridiculed my effeminacy'.

Elizabeth Smith, from
a drawing taken during
her last illness by
J. G. Wood.

At Coniston, the family lived at Townson Ground, on the
north-east shore of the lake. It had (and has) a boathouse, and
Elizabeth and her sisters took to rowing enthusiastically. 'She
and her sisters were so practised at the oars that they could show
the beauties of the scene from any point of the lake', recorded
Harriet Martineau. Perhaps the sight of the girls was a source of
inspiration for her enormously popular children's book *Feats on
the Fjord* (1841). Thomas Wilkinson, who helped them to landscape the Townson Ground gardens, became a frequent visitor.
Soon after the Smiths settled themselves at Townson Ground,
he accompanied the girls on an ascent of the Langdales, which
is still a wonderful walk today.

In between rambling over the fells, Elizabeth studied
assiduously. She loved languages and drew up complex tables
comparing and contrasting their structure. She translated the
odes of 'the German Milton' Frederick Klopstock (Coleridge,
who visited him on his tour of Germany in 1798, and hailed him
as 'the venerable father of German poetry', had meant to do this,
but never got round to it). She translated large chunks of the Old
Testament from Hebrew, winning especial praise from scholars
for her rendering of the Book of Job.

She wrote critically about Locke's *Essay on Human Understanding*, and composed music and some good but not great
poetry. Her most striking poem described how, losing her way
while climbing Aira Force, she despaired of getting down alive
and prayed to God for help. Suddenly she saw her sister opposite
looking terribly anxious and she had a vision of how, if she
tumbled down the fall, her sister would have 'to meet below my
mangled lifeless limbs and tattered garment'. She gathered her
forces and got safely back home – where she discovered that

her sister had never left the house; what she had seen was 'a vision sent / To save me from destruction'. De Quincey tells this story at length in his 'Society of the Lakes' and Wordsworth borrowed the incident for his own poem set on Aira Force, 'The Somnambulist'.

Elizabeth was only twenty-nine when, in 1805, she developed tuberculosis. London doctors advised her to go abroad, but money was short. She came back to Townson Ground in May, and spent most of her time in a tent pitched on the lawn. 'However languid she appeared, still the grandeur of the scenery never failed to call forth her admiration', recalled her mother.

Before she died, she pointed out a site closer to the lake than Townson Ground, saying that it would be a wonderful place for a new house. Her father took her advice, and named the new house Tent Lodge in memory of her sojourn under canvas. Townson Ground was renamed Tent Cottage. The Tennysons stayed at Tent Lodge on their honeymoon tour in 1850 and again in 1857.

Elizabeth was buried in St Michael's Church, Hawkshead.

View from Langdale Pikes by W. H. Kelsall (*c.*1835).

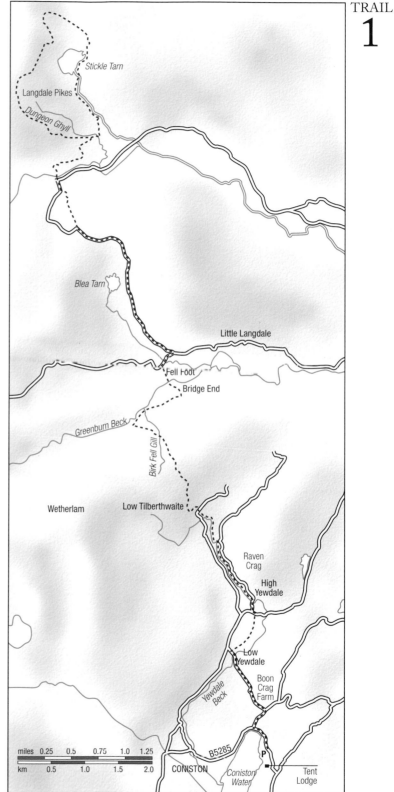

On Foot (*c.*25 miles)

This is a long trip, but if the three Smith mountain nymphs could do it, you can. Park in the car-park at the head of Coniston Water and imagine you have just walked from Townson Ground (now Tent Lodge). If you really want to emulate the Smith sisters and their admirer Thomas Wilkinson, you will have to get up at three in the morning and breakfast 'in Queen Elizabeth style on bread and beef', before setting off 'light-heeled and light-hearted as the roes of the mountains'.

Walk along the road to its junction with the B5285. Turn right, then take the footpath off to

TRAIL 1

the left at Boon Crag Farm. Follow this to Low Yewdale, and cross the Yewdale Beck. Turn right to High Yewdale, where you will cross the beck again and follow it up to Low Tilberthwaite.

Pause as the Smiths and Wilkinson did on the ridge between Wetherlam and Raven Crag to enjoy the view. This was one of the official 'stations', or viewpoints, listed by Thomas West in his 1778 *Guide to the Lakes*. Wilkinson thought it was wonderful:

> Few stations by turning on the heel, afforded so strong a contrast. If we looked back, we saw below us the Lake of Coniston, with its bays and woody points, stretching a long way: if we looked forward, we had Raven's Crag right before us; an immense assemblage of very lofty mountains – rather of clustering crags – rugged and broken in the finest manner. In the foreground, in solemn majesty, rose a stupendous mountain, that bore in its frowning forehead the Pikes of Langdale, which seemed like pillars to support the heavens.

At Low Tilberthwaite, take the footpath northwards which follows the Birk Fell Gill at first, then meets Greenburn Beck. Turn right without crossing the beck, and follow it down to Bridge End. Cross the beck here, and walk to the lane at Fell Foot. Follow the (unfenced) road up to Blea Tarn; if you prefer, there is a footpath on the west side of the tarn. As you descend the other side, look out for a footpath off to the right; it is a shortcut down to the valley bottom. Here there are clear signs to the now heavily eroded path up to the Langdale Pikes. Wilkinson records that he and Juliet 'followed the long zig-zags of the track slowly upwards', while Elizabeth and Kitty 'ascended in a straight direction'. When they reached 'the sublime and dreadful regions' around Stickle Tarn, he confessed himself afraid. Kitty, 'who feels a kindness for the whole creation', took his hand. Elizabeth announced that she was off to explore. In the poem he wrote in memory of her, Wilkinson recalled 'How scal'd the aerial cliffs th'adventurous maid, / Whilst far beneath, her foil'd companion stay'd.' She disappeared for a 'terribly extended' length of time, and Wilkinson shivered at the thought of her tumbling down precipices. But at last she reappeared, well above them, waving triumphantly, although admitting that she had got somewhat lost.

Climb as high as takes your fancy in memory of Elizabeth, and then descend as they did, looping around Stickle Tarn, and coming down via Dungeon Ghyll, and hoping that you will not emulate too exactly their return through Yewdale, with 'the skies now pouring down on us'. Wilkinson's three 'intrepid maids' were undeterred.

> Drenched as we were with rain, we were still pleased and interested. If hedges and rivulets crossed our way, and I lamented on our difficulties, there was never anything worse than a smile on the part of my female companions: the walls were climbed and the rivulets were waded; and after being eleven hours on our feet, and walking between 20 and 30 miles, we arrived in safety.

MAP
OS Outdoor Leisure 6: The English Lakes (South-West)

The fells of Langdale Pike, seen over Blea Tarn.

Fragment of a pencil
drawing of Dorothy
Wordsworth.

Handmaid to the Lord

She, in the midst of all, preserved me still
A Poet, made me seek beneath that name,
And that alone, my office upon earth

William Wordsworth, *The Prelude*, Book ix

The most influential of all Lakeland muses was undoubtedly William Wordsworth's sister Dorothy (1771-1855). Her journal, written 'to give Wm Pleasure by it', provided recollections, ideas and even adjectives and verbs used in his poems. One passage (15 April 1802), describing the daffodils they saw together at Gowbarrow Park on the shores of Ullswater, is eerily kin to his famous poem 'I Wandered Lonely as a Cloud':

When we were in the woods beyond Gowbarrow Park we saw a few daffodils close to the waterside. We fancied that the lake had floated the seeds ashore and the little colony had so sprung up. But as we went along there were more and yet more; and at last, under the boughs of the trees, we saw that there was a long belt of them along the shore, about the breadth of a country turnpike road. I never saw daffodils so beautiful. They grew among the mossy stones about and about them; some rested their heads upon these stones as on a pillow for weariness and the rest tossed and reeled and danced, and seemed as if they verily laughed with the wind, that blew upon them over the lake; they looked so gay, ever glancing, ever changing.

Several years later the vision of the flowers 'tossing their heads in sprightly dance' flashed upon the bard's inward eye and was written down – with such remarkably similar imagery that one can't help thinking William must have leafed through Dorothy's journal in search of inspiration just before writing it. But the poem itself erases Dorothy

Engraving of Wordsworth House in Cockermouth, birthplace of William and Dorothy Wordsworth.

entirely, opening with the line 'I wandered lonely as a cloud': poetic licence indeed.

In spring the daffodils are now at least as plentiful as they were in 1802, thanks to planting and protection by the National Trust. To see them, drive along the A592 and park in the car-park 100 yards north of Glencoyne Bridge. Cross the road and take the footpath to the lake shore and walk north-east along it. Gowbarrow Park was once a hunting ground; Celia Fiennes records setting her greyhound on a hare there, and Willliam Wordsworth commended its 'rich and happy intermixture of native wood' in his *Guide Through the Lakes* (1835).

William also composed poems around incidents that Dorothy had experienced, and people she had seen, without him. To be fair to him, he frequently expressed his appreciation of 'the Sister of my heart'. 'She gave me eyes, she gave me ears', he declared in 'The Sparrow's Nest'. She also softened the extremer aspects of his nature and reassured him when the black dogs of pessimism gnawed at his soul, 'whispering still that brightness would return' (*The Prelude*, Book XI). And she was a willing amanuensis, writing out his innumerable drafts and redrafts again and again.

The romance between brother and sister began in their first home, Wordsworth House in Cockermouth. 'Our native place', Dorothy called it, and in *The Prelude* William celebrates how 'the bright blue river passed /Along the margin of our terraced walk; a tempting playmate whom we dearly loved'. The house and garden running down to the River Derwent, a favourite haunt, now belong to the National Trust.

Built in 1745 by the High Sheriff of Cumberland, Joshua Lucock, Wordsworth House boasts seventeen long windows in its two-storey façade and a porch approached by six steps and flanked by two Doric columns. 'Quite a swagger house for such a town', comments Nikolaus Pevsner. William's father John Wordsworth, a solicitor, moved into it in 1766 because he was land agent for the wealthy, powerful and corrupt 1st Earl of Lonsdale, whose family seat Lowther Castle (now ruined) was just north of Ullswater at Askham. The visitor today will find

Wordsworth House filled with furnishings that date from the eighteenth century, and some very fine paintings and drawings of the Lake District. There are also some pieces that actually belonged to the poet in later life – a large painted bookcase that came from his Grasmere home Allan Bank, a handsome mahogany writing-bureau, a dinner service, a trunk-case clock and a white and gold inkstand. Portraits of Wordsworth can be seen in the library.

Dorothy, born on Christmas Day 1771, was just twenty months younger than William, and emotionally he was always the closest of her four brothers. Their relationship was the more intense in later life because after their mother's death in 1778, she was sent, aged seven, to stay with relations in Halifax in Yorkshire. She and William did not meet at all for nine years. When they did, at the house of their Penrith grandparents in the summer of 1787, their joy in their reunion was overshadowed by the bullying, impatient treatment they received from their relations. Their father had also died, in 1783, and since his employer, Lord Lonsdale, refused to make over the £5,000 of unpaid salary his heirs were owed, they were charity cases.

William had to be educated to earn a living, and was sent to Cambridge, where he enjoyed himself as a wild young radical. Family disapproval of him meant that Dorothy saw agonisingly little of her favourite brother. 'I cannot help heaving many a sigh of reflection that I have passed one and twenty years of my life and that the first six years only of this time was spent in the enjoyment of the same pleasures as my brothers', she wrote to a Halifax girlfriend in 1792.

It wasn't until 1794 that she managed to get away for a secret meeting with William in Halifax. Shortly after that they escaped together – eloped is the word one biographer uses – to spend two months in the Lakes, based at Windy Brow, near Keswick, the house of old school-friends of William called the Calverts. In 1795 Raisley Calvert, a sickly young man whom Wordsworth looked after for several months, died and left William £900. Despite thunderous expressions of disapproval from relatives, William and Dorothy decided to use it to fulfil their dream of living together permanently. Augmented by allowances for looking after two children, one the son of a friend, the other the love-child of a cousin, this was enough for them to live on and they settled first in Dorset near Lambert's Castle, then, drawn by the infectiously enthusiastic friendship of Coleridge, to the Quantocks, in Somerset, near Nether Stowey. Coleridge, whose own only sister had died three years earlier, and who was shackled more by duty than inclination to his wife Sara Fricker, was as enchanted by Dorothy as he was impressed by William:

Daffodils at Glencoyne on the shore of Ullswater. William and Dorothy were captivated by the flowers when they visited Gowbarrow Park in 1802.

She is a woman indeed! in mind, I mean and heart … In every motion her most innocent soul outbeams so brightly that who saw her would say, guilt was a thing impossible to her. Her information various. Her eye watchful in minutest observation of nature and her taste a perfect electrometer – it bends, protrudes and draws in at subtlest beauties and most recondite faults.

He, William and Dorothy were, he told several friends, 'three people, but one soul'.

Town End (Dove Cottage), home of William and Dorothy Wordsworth between 1799 and 1806; watercolour by Amos Green (1735–1807).

Right: William Wordsworth (1770–1850) by Henry Edridge (*c.*1805).

Below: Sketch of Dorothy Wordsworth confined to a wheelchair, by John Harden, dated 1842.

In 1799, after a six-month tour of Germany with Coleridge, William and Dorothy headed north to stay with relations. In the autumn, Coleridge joined them, and he and William set off on a tremendous tour of the fells which convinced William of the attractions of the Lakes in general and of Grasmere in particular. He and Dorothy settled in a small cottage there, once an inn called the Dove and Grapes, then simply called Town End. Dorothy was blissfully happy, although when William married her old school friend Mary Hutchinson in 1802 she was so emotionally disturbed that, she recorded in her journal, she couldn't go to the church but 'threw myself on the bed where I lay in stillness, neither hearing nor seeing anything'.

Today, Town End, now called Dove Cottage, is the most important shrine to the memory of William and Dorothy in the world, complete with museum, bookshop and a substantial library of Wordsworthiana. It is thoughtfully and convincingly furnished to recreate the outer shell of their lives there between 1801 and 1806, when the growing size of the family made a move, first to Allan Bank and then to nearby Rydal Mount, necessary.

Much as Dorothy evidently adored her brother, one can't help feeling a little sorry for her. As a boy, William was passionately selfish; as a man, he was single-minded in his pursuit of his own genius. It was unarguably

substantial, although far from unflagging. J. K. Stephen (1859-92) summed him up unforgettably in a sonnet in his satirical 'Lapsus Calami' (*Granta*, 1891):

Two Voices are there: one is of the deep;
It learns the storm-cloud's thundrous melody,
And one is of an old-half-witted sheep
Which bleats articulate monotony,
And Wordsworth, both are thine

Having learnt the uses of helplessness early, Wordsworth retained around him a ring of female ministering angels, of whom Dorothy was the most permanently solicitous. He was, however, regarded with some disenchantment by many once close male friends, not least Coleridge, whose poetic confidence was permanently shaken by William's grudging prefatory note to the 'Ancient Mariner' in *Lyrical Ballads*, the book of poetry they were supposed to be publishing together, and his refusal to include *Christabel*, a poem which some critics believe referred to Dorothy.

In later life, Dorothy's mind failed and she was confined to a wheelchair. Meanwhile, Wordsworth continued to enjoy being lionised by hundreds of pilgrims to Grasmere. But he was far from heroic in the eyes of his cook, whose reminiscences of him, together with those of other Grasmere locals, were recorded by Canon Rawnsley some twenty years after the poet's death in 1850. She described him as remote, often critical and totally self-absorbed, and Dorothy as in devoted attendance. 'Mr Wordsworth went bumming and booing about, and she, Miss Dorothy, kept close behint him, and she picked up the bits as he let 'em fall, and tak 'em down, and put 'em on paper for him.' Another servant told Rawnsley that Dorothy 'was a ter'ble clever woman. She did as much of his poetry as he did and went completely off it at the latter end, wi' studying it, I suppose.'

TRAIL **The Poet, the Pike and the Pick-me-up**
2

Samuel Taylor Coleridge's journals and letters describing his experiences in the Lakes are arguably the most amusing and lively Lakeland literature ever written. It helped that his imagination was heightened by a combination of opium and hopeless love. He had married his wife, Sara Fricker, in a spirit of fraternal camaraderie – his fellow poet Robert Southey married her sister Edith – but by the time he decided to move to Greta Hall, Grasmere, to be close to the Wordsworths, he had realised how unsuited he and Sara were. With William a jealous watchdog, Dorothy was out of the question. Instead, Coleridge developed a passion for Sarah Hutchinson, a friend of Dorothy's.

In order to indulge his feelings well away from the mundane domestic round of Greta Hall, Coleridge set out on Sunday, 1 August 1802 on a nine-day 'circumcursion' of the Lakeland hills. The full story is told by Alan Hankinson in *Coleridge Walks the Fells*, an essential guide for those with time to tramp the whole circuit from Keswick to the coast at St Bees, and back via Wastwater, Eskdale, Coniston and Ambleside. Our walk is intended to bring to life the most hair-raising episode of the trip, the poet's descent of Sca Fell by the tricky route known as Broad Stand. Don't worry: no risk is involved. You will be going up the way Coleridge came down, and gazing at Broad Stand with respect rather than moving into Spiderman mode. And the ascent is so gentle (until the last stony stumble up to Mickledore) that you will find yourself within easy reach of the highest mountain in England with remarkably little shortness of breath.

'When I find it convenient to descend from a mountain,' Coleridge later wrote to Sarah Hutchinson, 'I am too confident and too indolent to look around and wind about 'till I find a track or other symptom of safety; but I wander on, and where it is first possible to descend, there I go – relying on fortune for how far down this possibility will continue.'

Left: Samuel Taylor Coleridge, after a painting by James Northcote (1804). Below: Looking towards Sca Fell Pike with the Esk Valley in the middle distance.

Fortune almost failed him on his descent from the top of Sca Fell, which he had approached from Wastwater. He started to descend towards Eskdale, but, having had to hang by his fingers to drop down a sheer slab of rock several times, he 'began to suspect that I ought not to go on. But … tho' I could with ease drop down a smooth Rock 7 feet high, I could not climb it, so go on I must and on I went.' At last, only two drops remained, but the first was quite evidently far too steep to negotiate safely.

'No climber today would tackle the descent of Broad Stand in the Coleridge style', warns Hankinson. But he admires the way the poet kept his head – after a moment of wild ecstasy:

I lay on my back to rest myself, and was beginning after my custom to laugh at myself for a Madman, when the sight of the Crags above me on each side, and the impetuous Clouds just over them, posting so luridly and so rapidly northward, overawed me. I lay in a state of almost prophetic Trance and Delight – and blessed God aloud, for the powers of Reason and the Will, which remaining no Danger can overpower us!

The saving of Coleridge was a narrow cleft in the rock now known as Fat Man's Agony. He seems to have managed – braced no doubt by a pick-me-up from the trusty black bottle of laudanum he carried with him, and certainly more by luck than good management – to slide down the steep rock face into it, and so through to the safe ground of Mickledore.

Despite his wonderful letters to her, Coleridge's wooing of Sarah Hutchinson was in vain. To add insult to injury, she too joined Wordsworth's household of adoring women when her sister Mary married William in October 1802.

Brotherilkeld Farm in the
heart of Eskdale.

Silhouette of Sarah
Hutchinson, Coleridge's
secret love 'Asra'.

MAP
OS Outdoor Leisure 6: The English
Lakes (South-West)

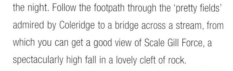

flanked by Ill Crag. Coleridge called it 'the wildest and savagest of all the Vales that were ever seen'.

Rejoin the Esk at Sampson's Stones. Coleridge was very struck by these gigantic boulders, which he thought were hovels when he first saw them from a distance on his descent. You won't get this effect until you return, when to the mirage-prone eyes of the weary walker they could indeed be hovels, one steeply gabled and thatched with moss and grass. The poet also experimented with the echoes, shouting his secret love Sarah Hutchinson's name into a ruined sheepfold and delighting in the 'echo on echo' that resulted.

Above the waterfalls just north of Cam Spout Crag, you'll see, as he did, 'the great triangle-Crag' of Sca Fell and 'the enormous and more perpendicular Precipices and Bull's Brows' of East Buttress. Cross the stream and follow the uphill path close by the falls. It's as steep as a flight of stairs, but flattens out again at the top of the falls, an ideal place for lunch before you ascend a short stretch of steep sharp scree up to Mickledore.

Once you reach it, all is forgiven. Looking over its crest down into Wasdale, you will see what Coleridge, perched high on the northern edge of the mountain to write his beloved Sarah 'surely the first Letter ever written from the top of Sca Fell', called 'the frightfullest Cove that might ever be seen, huge Perpendicular Precipices . . . their height and depth is terrible'. You are, however, a little lower, so will not have to risk life and limb sliding down the giant slabs from Broad Stand into Fat Man's Agony. Slender mortals will be able to explore this narrow cleft in the rock; wise ones will go no further without a mountain guide and climbing equipment.

When Coleridge emerged from Fat Man's Agony, he legged it down into Eskdale with all speed. But having got this far, it is a very easy stroll across the well-trampled scree to the 3,210ft summit of Sca Fell Pike. This is the true top of England, and you can see, even better than Coleridge did from Sca Fell, 'directly thro' Borrowdale, the Castle Crag, the whole of Derwent Water', and, on a clear day, his home, Greta Hall.

Now to descend. Don't be tempted by the vertiginous path through murderous scree in the lee of Ill Crag. It is best to retrace your steps, perhaps varying the route down in the valley by staying east of the Esk all the way back. It is longer and swampier, but the Esk Falls and Gorge are lovely places.

On Foot (*c.*11 miles)

Start at the foot of Hardknott Pass in Eskdale, parking on the broad verge a hundred yards west of the telephone box at Brotherilkeld Farm. Take the footpath that heads north from beside the telephone box and follow the crystal-clear Esk, here thickly wooded, for a hundred yards or so upstream. Take the footbridge across the river and walk through Taw House Farm.

Coleridge enjoyed 'some excellent Salmonlings' here with John Towers and his wife Betty (their names appear on a 1789 datestone over the door), and stayed the night. Follow the footpath through the 'pretty fields' admired by Coleridge to a bridge across a stream, from which you can get a good view of Scale Gill Force, a spectacularly high fall in a lovely cleft of rock.

After a short steep pull, the path levels out. Cross a tiny stream, then aim for a cairn to the right to find the path east of High Scarth Crag, safely west of the swampy moss. This is the heart of a wilderness. The ramparts of the Crinkle Crags stride away to Bowfell on your right, Cam Spout Crag lowers over you on the left, and ahead is the soaring crest of Sca Fell Pike,

THE LILY OF THE VALLEY

The most famous of all Lakeland beauties is the legendarily fair Maid of Buttermere. The story of her bigamous seduction by a confidence trickster posing as a nobleman rocked all England in 1803 and has captured the imagination of essayists, dramatists and novelists, ranging from Samuel Taylor Coleridge to Melvyn Bragg.

It all began when Joseph Budworth sang the praises of Mary Robinson, daughter of the landlord of the Fish Inn, Buttermere, in his *Fortnight's Ramble in the Lakes* (first published in 1792).

> She brought in part of our dinner, and seemed to be about fifteen. Her hair was thick and long, of a dark brown, and though unadorned with ringlets, did not seem to want them; her face was a fine oval, with full eyes and lips as red as vermilion, her cheeks had more of the lily than the rose … After she had got the better of her first fears, she looked an angel, and I doubt not but she is the reigning Lily of the Valley.

Budworth's much-read guidebook brought hordes of visitors to admire Mary, rather as if she were a prize steer. In 1802, aged twenty-four, she accepted the hand of one of her admirers, the Honourable Augustus Hope, MP. They were married on 3 October, and Coleridge wrote the story up approvingly for the *Morning Post* as 'The Romantic Marriage'.

Hope took Mary for a glorious tour of the Lakes, behaving like a princeling and living on credit. But a few weeks later, alerted by real members of the Hope family who had read their *Morning Post*, the police caught up with him and revealed that he was not honourable at all, but a charlatan bankrupt from the south-west of England called John Hatfield. He had been married twice before, first to the natural daughter of Earl Rivers, who had since died, and then to Michilli Nation, who was still alive and by whom he had two children. Coleridge wrote a new article, 'The Keswick Impostor', and Hatfield's infamies resounded all over the country. He escaped for a few months, but was eventually recaptured and taken to Bow Street in London to be charged. The *Newgate Calendar* said of him, 'His manners were extremely polished and insinuating, and he was possessed of qualities which might have rendered him an ornament of society.' His personality won him friends wherever he went, and there was a near riot in Carlisle, where the trial took place in September 1803. There was, however, no doubt of his guilt, and Hatfield was sentenced to death – not for bigamy (though it was distraught letters from past wives that helped to damn him), but for forgery. Postage was then very costly, and one privilege held by real MPs was that of sending letters free by marking them with their own signature as a frank. Since Hatfield was not a real MP, he had been franking his own letters without authority, which was then a capital offence. On the day the trial ended, Coleridge visited him in the condemned cell while *en route* with Dorothy and William Wordsworth for a tour of Scotland. He later described him as a vain hypocrite, but was evidently puzzled by him, adding that 'It is not by mere Thought, I can understand this man.' Hatfield was hanged on 13 September.

What of Mary herself? She bore Hatfield's child, but it did not survive. For a while she became an even greater tourist attraction than before, then she dwindled into a wife, marrying Richard Harrison, a local farmer, and moving to Caldbeck. They had four children, and Mary lived until 22 February 1837. It was a reflection of her fame that her death was reported in the *London Annual Register*:

> Lately, – At Caldbeck, Cumberland, Mary, wife of Mr Richard Harrison of that Place. This amiable individual was formerly the far-famed and much talked of 'Mary of Buttermere' or, as she was more commonly termed, 'The Buttermere Beauty'.

Most of the many retellings of Mary's story (Thomas de Quincey notes in his 1803 diary that he bought one by William Mudworth) have

Mary of Buttermere by
James Gillray (*c.*1800).

deservedly been forgotten. But Wordsworth recorded contemporary
excitement and gave her lasting fame by referring in *The Prelude* to a
melodrama he had seen in London based on:

> … a story drawn
> From our own ground, – The Maid of Buttermere –
> And how, unfaithful to a virtuous wife,
> Deserted and deceived, the Spoiler came
> And wooed the artless daughter of the hills,
> And wedded her in cruel mockery
> Of love and marriage bonds

He recalled how he and Coleridge had visited the Fish Inn and noticed
her 'modest mien / And carriage, marked by unexampled grace' long
before Budworth broadcast her charms.

The most recent and undoubtedly outstanding memorial of Mary is Melvyn Bragg's novel *The Maid of Buttermere* (1987). In it, sexuality and scenery are inextricably entwined. At first, John Hatfield is deliberately made immune to the sublime splendours of the Lakes. He is fascinated only by people, especially women. He comes into his element when making love:

> This was his home, this was his landscape – the paradise of a body, not of earth and woods the contours of flesh, the colours and sensations not of lakes and streams, but of the mouth, the nipples … the tides of love-making, slow clouds of unknowing behind closed eyes, a finger following the rippling path of the spine down from the neck, a sudden bonding of heads, like trees in the lane – as a mouth reached to kiss a vulnerable throat, the swelling and falling susurration of breath itself binding them as the animal bodies moved and turned and locked. This was his dream of nature.

It is only after meeting Mary Robinson that her setting begins to appeal to him, for she and it are inseparable: 'The valley was her, she moved in it as through the natural expression of her mind and feelings'. When he proposes to her by the edge of Buttermere,

> The slap of water on the shore was a mocking sound. Like skin slapping on skin.
> The low rush of the wind in the woods like the low groan of incomprehensible satisfaction.
> The smell of wet earth the exhausted sigh of consummation.

Throughout Bragg's novel, landscape is a mirror of mood, and one sign of Hatfield's redemption is his growing appreciation of the beauties of Nature as well as of women.

Buttermere and
Crummock Water
from Haystacks.

TRAIL
3 **Arthur Ransome's Ideal Mate**

At that moment something hit the saucepan with a loud ping and ashes flew up out of the fire. A long arrow with a green feather stuck, quivering, among the embers.

The four explorers started to their feet.

'It's begun,' said Titty.

Arthur Ransome, *Swallows and Amazons*

The arrival of Nancy Blackett's arrow transforms a sedate tale of four children camping on an island very similar indeed to Peel Island, on Coniston Water, into a hair-raising yarn in the best tradition of Robert Louis Stevenson. Plucky, gallant and ruthless, Nancy Blackett is easily the most vivid and attractive, as well as the most infuriating, of Arthur Ransome's characters. She constantly interferes, insisting on drawing pictures for the stories, manipulating honest Captain John, verging on mutiny in *Secret Water* (1939), dominating even in *Winter Holiday* (1933), when quarantine for mumps leaves her orchestrating from a distance. But Ransome evidently adored her: one can almost hear him chuckling over her escapades. Who inspired her unforgettable personality? This is a voyage rather than a trail, in search of clues to the reality of Arthur Ransome's ideal mate; it is also a celebration of some of the most famous places and incidents in *Swallows and Amazons*.

A convincing source for the crew of the *Swallow* exists: Taqui, Susan, Titty, Roger and Brigit, the five children of Ernest and Dora Altounyan. Ransome taught them to sail on Coniston Water in 1928, when they were staying at Bank Ground Farm, next door to Lanehead, home of their grandfather, W. G. Collingwood. But when asked whom the Amazon pirates were based on, Ransome was always vague, although he did mention seeing two girls in red caps playing by the lake shore.

They could well have been from Tent Lodge, formerly the home of Elizabeth Smith's family, which was owned in the late 1920s by the Rawdon-Smiths. Their two daughters, Georgina and Pauline, were as intrepid as the fell-climbing philosopheress and her sisters. According to Pauline, who later became a sailing instructor, they led lives very similar indeed to those of Ransome's Nancy and Peggy: using semaphore, parachuting from trees into the lake using an umbrella and communicating with each other using bird noises.

But Ransome could also have been inspired by earlier experiences: the years he spent visiting Lanehead as a young man in the 1900s. W. G. Collingwood, formerly John Ruskin's secretary, and a scholar and novelist in his own right, had long been

Top: *Unseen Enemy*, an illustration from *Swallows and Amazons*, which marks the start of the children's adventures.

Above: The real 'Swallows' – Susan, Taqui, Titty and Roger Altounyan, *c*.1928.

Ransome's friend and patron. His daughters, Barbara, Dora and Ursula, were then very dashing and Amazonesque young girls. Barbara and her young brother Robin taught Ransome about sailing, and, when he was camping on Peel Island finishing off a book about French poets, Ursula swam across with a set of proofs on her head.

Another possible Amazon candidate, significantly called Ruth, was Robin's daughter:

> 'Her real name isn't Nancy', said Peggy. 'Her name is Ruth, but Uncle Jim said that Amazons were ruthless, and as our ship is Amazon, and we are the Amazon pirates from the Amazon River, we had to change her name.'

When *Swallows and Amazons* came out, Ruth's grandfather wrote to Ransome: 'Your Ruth-Nancy is more like my Ruth than can be expected unless you had seen her last month being a savage.' But Ransome barely knew this Ruth – she was only born in 1921.

Nancy could also have been a wistful evocation of Tabitha, Ransome's daughter from his first marriage to Ivy Walker, whom he rarely saw. She certainly loved camping and sailing. Another

possibility is Ransome's second wife, Evgenia Shelapina. She was Trotsky's secretary when Ransome met her in Russia in 1918, and those who have read his *Racundra's First Cruise* (1923) will know her as its imperturbable first mate. She certainly had a temper fiery enough for an Amazon pirate, but those who remember her say she was more of a Susan in character: a first-class organiser but not a natural adventuress. By the time she and Arthur came to live on the banks of Coniston at The Heald, Ransome was not a little in awe of her, and often retired to a shack in its grounds that he called 'The Dog's Home' for respite from her energetic housekeeping.

My own conclusion is that Ransome invented an imaginary kindred spirit with elements of all these woman and of himself: the perfect muse, in fact, occasionally stern but essentially generous. In return, Ransome gave Nancy a more enduring immortality than any real muse could have had – both as Nancy, First Class Amazon Pirate and Terror of the Seas, and by renaming the little sloop he bought with the proceeds from his first three books, 'the best little ship I ever sailed in', in her honour. 'But for Nancy', he wrote to a friend, I should never have been able to buy her'. Incidentally, the *Nancy Blackett*, now owned by the Nancy Blackett Trust, is still afloat, and can often be seen at boat shows.

TRAIL
3

View over Tarn Hows, Coniston Valley, one of the most visited spots in the Lake District.

TRAIL 3

By Boat (*c.*12 miles)

If you do not have a sailing dinghy or canoe of your own, do not despair. Go to Coniston Pier where you can hire small motor boats by the hour. There are also two motor launches run by the Coniston Launch Company, *Ransome* and *Ruskin*, which offer tours of the lake, or

MAP

OS Outdoor Leisure 6: The English Lakes (South-West

you can travel in style on the restored lake steam yacht *Gondola* which in part inspired Captain Flint's houseboat. Now owned by the National Trust, it makes regular trips down the lake and back, pausing by Wild Cat Island and stopping at Brantwood.

Begin at Coniston Pier, and head down the lake.

Tent Lodge's square grey shape can be seen opposite Coniston village. Further south on the east bank, you will see a large white house, now an outdoor sports centre. This is Lanehead, home of the Collingwoods. Just south of it, a little closer to the lake, is Bank Ground Farm, a white-painted farmhouse with grey barns. This is the original of Holly Howe, and the steep field leading up to it is the one up which Roger tacks to collect the telegram from his father which will free the Swallows from parental restriction: 'Better drowned than duffers. If not duffers, won't drown'. Today you too can stay at Bank Ground Farm; if in a boat of your own, tie up by the stone boathouse (just next door to the one from which Elizabeth Smith used to row her guests on the lake), walk up Roger's field, and pick up a brochure.

A little further down the lake on the east side is Brantwood. This was John Ruskin's home from 1872 to 1900; W. G. Collingwood worked there as Ruskin's secretary. If you take a walk in its grounds you will find a reconstruction of a charcoal-burner's pitstead.

> High in the darkness they saw a flicker of bright flame. There was another, then another, and then a pale blaze lighting a cloud of smoke. They all looked up towards it as if they were looking at a little window, high up in a black wall. As they watched, the figure of a man jumped from the middle of the smoke, a black active figure, beating at the flames…
>
> 'It's savages,' said Titty.

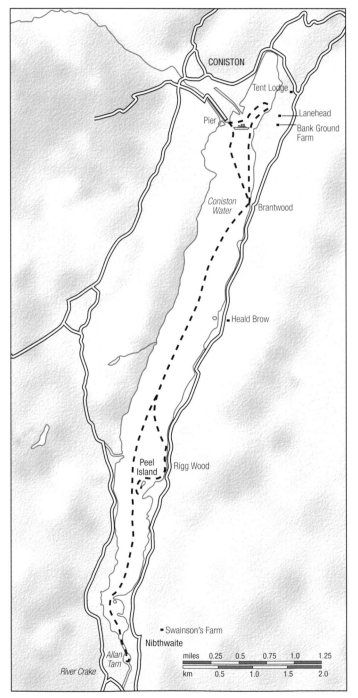

Stephen Spurner's map of Wild Cat Island for *Swallows and Amazons*, and (above, right) the secret harbour drawn by Clifford Webb for the first illustrated edition. Today, Peel Island may be seen from aboard *Gondola* (far right).

Also on this side of the lake is a bungalow almost hidden in the trees: this is The Heald, Ransome's home from 1940-5, and where he wrote *The Picts and the Martyrs* (1943). 'The Dog's Home' is deep in the woods above it.

Now comes the high point of the voyage – Peel Island, immortalised in *Swallows and Amazons* as Wild Cat Island: 'It was not just an island. It was the island, waiting for them. It was their island. With an island like that within sight, who could be content to live on the mainland and sleep in a bed at night?' Those without a boat of their own will have to make do with gazing longingly. Mariners can land in the secret harbour, which is exactly as described in Ransome's story, at the southern end. But your approach has to be directly south to north, just like that of the Swallows. The long slabs of rock that flank its sides run on under water for 20yds or more. Ransome first visited Peel Island as a small boy when his family spent their summer holidays at Nibthwaite, a hamlet at the southern end of the lake.

The hinterland of the island is carpeted with years of fallen leaves – bare feet need to beware of holly. The centre is clearly the place where the Swallows strung ropes between trees to hold up their simple tents – home-made from thin canvas with stones in the hems. The northern tip of the island is a fine lookout, though it has lost its lighthouse tree. But it will have another in time; the Arthur Ransome Society

recently planted a young pine there.

The *Gondola* goes only as far south as Rigg Wood; *Ransome* and *Ruskin* go to the old pier at Water Yeat. If you are in a craft of your own, you can continue down to the very end of the lake. Where it runs into the River Crake, there is a narrow neck of water between the reeds, which, like the Amazon River, swells out into an almost perfect circle. This is Allan Tarn, much better known as the waterlily-filled Octopus Lagoon. Land here is private, but you can look at Nibthwaite village from the water. At the back of the village you will see Swainson's Farm, a four-square grey house where Ransome spent many happy summers as a little boy. From the steep rocks high above he used to watch the *Gondola* approaching.

Sailing back down the lake gives fine views of the Old Man of Coniston (2,631ft), 'Kanchenjunga' in *Swallowdale* (1931). Like Nancy, Ransome frequently climbed it, and used to boast that, having been carried

up it by his father as a baby, he was the youngest person ever to have been at the summit. Again like Nancy, he lost his father when he was a child. One of the most moving incidents in all his books is in *Swallowdale*, when the children discover a little box hidden in the cairn on top of the Old Man. Inside is a Victorian farthing and the proud claim that 'Jim Turner, Molly Turner and Bob Blackett climbed the Matterhorn' in 1901.

'That's mother and Uncle Jim,' said Peggy in a queer voice.
'Who is Bob Blackett?' asked Susan.
'He was father,' said Nancy.

Ransome's father died when he was thirteen, as a result of an injury to his foot when he was fishing. His death marked the end of the holidays at Nibthwaite, leaving memories of them frozen until the time, thirty years later, when Ransome would immortalise them in his books for children.

A Nearly Perfect Little Place

Beatrix Potter (1866–1943) bought the working farm of Hill Top, Near Sawrey, in October 1905. It was a bold move for a thirty-nine-year-old woman on her own; it was also a desperately necessary distraction. Only seven weeks earlier her fiancé, Norman Warne, had died unexpectedly and suddenly from pernicious anaemia. But she had good reasons for her decision. She knew the Lakes well – her wealthy barrister father had been taking the family there for three-month-long summer holidays in large rented houses ever since she was sixteen. She was especially fond of Sawrey – 'as nearly perfect a little place as I ever lived in' – where the family had twice rented a house called Eeswyke, on the shore of Esthwaite Water. And she was a woman of independent means, thanks to the success of the first six of her charmingly written and illustrated books for children. The first, *The Tale of Peter Rabbit* (1902), sold 50,000 copies in two years, and it was with the royalties from it and her other books that she bought Hill Top.

Beatrix told her parents that the farm was just an investment, and she kept on John Cannon, the farmer from whom she bought it, as a manager. For the next few years she continued to live in her parents' house in London's Bolton Gardens like the dutiful daughter they expected her to be, but she visited Hill Top frequently. A new wing was built on to it, so she could stay there to write and draw, and to work in the garden.

Hill Top and its surroundings soon made their appearance in her books. *The Pie and the Patty-Pan* (1905), planned with Norman Warne before his death, shows both Sawrey and Hill Top. *The Tale of Jeremy Fisher* (1906), although started in Scotland, acquired settings on Esthwaite Water. *The Tale of Tom Kitten* (1907) and *The Tale of Samuel Whiskers* (1908) contain such accurate illustrations of Hill Top's interior and garden that they have helped the National Trust in its reconstruction of how things were arranged in Beatrix Potter's day. The beeskip and rhubarb patch beside which Jemima Puddleduck talks to a boy (recognisably John Cannon's son) can still be seen just outside the front gate of Hill Top itself (*The Tale of Jemima Puddleduck*, 1908). *The Tale of Ginger and Pickles* (1909) revolves around Sawrey's old Smithy Lane village shop, and in *The Tale of Mr Tod* (1912), the sinister Mr Tod and the oafish Tommy Brock live

nearby 'at the top of Bull Banks, under Oatmeal Crag'.

Beatrix took a keen interest in the working of the farm, buying new stock and more land. Soon Hill Top had ten cows, fourteen pigs and thirty Herdwick sheep, as well as ducks, hens and a sheepdog, Kep. When buying land, Beatrix used a Hawkshead firm of solicitors. The partner specialising in land contracts was William Heelis, who became increasingly fond of the determined London lady who was getting more and more involved in Westmorland life. In 1912 he asked Beatrix to marry him, but it proved very difficult indeed to get the agreement of her parents, who saw her proper role in life as the mainstay of their old age.

At last, on 14 October 1913, she became Mrs Heelis. She and William lived in Castle Cottage, the house of the Sawrey farm which she had bought in 1909. Hill Top was kept just as it had always been, and Beatrix continued to use it as a study and studio. It was also a convenient place to entertain the number of

visitors who came to express their appreciation of her books.

When her father died in 1914, Beatrix installed her mother in another house in Sawrey – a move that must have been quite a shock for the former Kensington hostess. With the outbreak of war and the general call-up of men, Beatrix was busier than ever, even working in the fields herself at harvest time. After the war, she bought her mother a house on the other side of

Hill Top in Near Sawrey. Beatrix Potter's illustrations for her books reveal much about how the farmhouse was furnished; the dresser shown in the drawing of Anna Maria (above) from *The Tale of Samuel Whiskers* can still be seen in the house.

Windermere: closer to the social delights of Bowness and well out of range of trivial demands on her daughter.

More and more preoccupied with farming, she produced only four books after her marriage. One of them, *The Tale of Johnny Town-mouse* (1918) shows many streets and buildings still recognisable in Hawkshead. But it was, above all, *The Fairy Caravan*, a collection of tales about a travelling circus, that showed not just Sawrey and its surroundings but also the animals of Hill Top and other local farms. It was published in America, where Beatrix Potter had a huge following, in 1929, but she felt it was too autobiographical to publish in Britain. It only appeared in a London edition in 1952, nine years after her death.

Among her many friends in the Lake District was Canon Hardwicke Rawnsley, co-founder of the National Trust in 1895. It was Rawnsley's encouragement that led her to print a private edition of *The Tale of Peter Rabbit* in 1901. The story had begun life as an illustrated letter to Noel Moore, the child of her former governess. Frederick Warne, which had previously turned the story down (as had the four other publishers to whom she had sent it), was so impressed that it offered to publish its own edition. The rest is children's literary history.

Beatrix was an enthusiastic supporter of Rawnsley's campaigns to keep the Lake District from being spoilt. When a strip of Windermere foreshore was under threat from developers, she sold a number of her watercolours to raise money to save it. In 1930, she bought the 4,000-acre Monk Coniston Estate in partnership with the National Trust, and managed it for them until 1941. She died in 1943, leaving her husband a life interest in the by then very substantial estate, which was thereafter given to the National Trust.

Visitors to Hill Top today find it a treasure-trove of Potter memorabilia. As well as many exquisite watercolours and illustrated manuscripts, there are all the props of the stories: the dolls that were the models for Lucinda and Jane in *The Tale of Two Bad Mice* (1904), the longcase clock from the Tailor of Gloucester's kitchen, the dresser past which Anna Maria ran with the stolen dough to make Tom into a roly-poly pudding, and even the Edward VII crown-lidded Coronation teapot from which Ribby pours so proudly in *The Pie and the Patty-Pan*.

Thomas Hardy's Wessex

There are some heights in Wessex, shaped as if by a kindly hand,

For thinking, dreaming, dying on, and at crises when I stand,

Say, on Ingpen Beacon eastward or on Wylls-Neck westwardly,

I seem where I was before my birth, and after death may be

Thomas Hardy, 'Wessex Heights'

Hardy's Cottage at Higher Bockhampton from the path through Thorncombe Wood in a watercolour by Henry Moule (1897). Thomas Hardy's family had lived here since 1800, and Hardy (above, c.1870) remained attached to the cottage all his life.

The novels and poems of Thomas Hardy (1840-1928) are more dominated by a sense of place than those of any other English writer. 'I am convinced', he once wrote, 'that it is better for a writer to know a little bit of the world remarkably well than to know a great part of the world remarkably little.' The little bit of the world that Hardy knew remarkably well was the part of England in which he was born and where he lived almost all his life: Dorset, and its surrounding counties.

He was as interested in its past as in its present; he was also concerned about its future. Rooted by folk memory to the time of the Napoleonic Wars, he was appalled at the hardships endured by the rural poor as the impact of the industrial revolution, the railways and new methods of farming changed the slow-moving certainties of his childhood into the unpredictable and soulless money-grubbing of the present.

His novels and their unforgettably vivid characters are concerned primarily with human destiny, but the inexorable plots unfold against a significant counterpoint: a celebration of country ways, of rural occupations that were fast disappearing, of heredities that stretched back as far as the Conquest, of dialects and folklore.

Hardy had an extraordinarily strong visual sense – which is one reason why his novels make such successful films. Ideas came to him first as mental pictures, 'moments of vision' glimpsed in the 'magic mirror' of his half-waking mind, rather than as subjects for writing down. 'I have no philosophy,' he wrote in his autobiography, 'merely a confused heap of impressions, like a bewildered child at a conjuring show.'

In truth, Hardy was more like the conjuror; it is his readers who often

feel like bewildered children by the time his stories come to a close. His plots are highly ordered, and strongly influenced by classical tragedy. The action may take place in rural Wessex, but Nemesis stalks through the woodland lanes and along the bare high ridgeways. Time and again he hauls the reader up to take an Olympian look at his characters, deliberately drawing them in long-shot, dwarfed against the landscape, reduced to flies with whom the gods sport like wanton boys.

The first mention of Wessex was in his fourth published novel, *Far from the Madding Crowd* (1874). In a preface to a later edition of the book, Hardy expanded on the name's usefulness as a means of giving his stories what we would now call a corporate identity and showed himself a little jealous of what he regarded as a very personal 'trademark':

> The series of novels I projected being mainly of the kind called local, they seemed to require a territorial definition of some sort to lend unity to their scene. Finding that the area of a single county did not afford a canvas large enough for this purpose, and that there were objections to an invented name, I disinterred the old one.
>
> Since then, the appellation which I had thought to reserve to the horizons and landscapes of a partly real, partly dream-country, has become more and more popular as a practical provincial definition; and the dream-country has, by degrees, solidified into a utilitarian region which people can go to, take a house in, and write to the papers from.

When it came to assembling a collected edition of his novels, he suggested to Macmillan that they be called the Wessex Novels. 'I find the name Wessex, which I was the first to use in fiction, is getting taken up everywhere: and it would be a pity for us to lose the right to it for want of asserting it.' He even helped to construct a map of Wessex, which was included in each volume of the collected edition.

Hardy with his bicycle,
*c.*1900.

Although Hardy could take liberties with distance and details in his 'dream-country', the fictional landscape of Wessex parallels reality so closely that, from the very beginning of his fame, literary pilgrims were hotfooting it down to drink up the atmosphere of the places for themselves. Hardy himself entered in on the fun, bicycling around Dorset with Hermann Lea (maker of the first *Guide to Hardy's Wessex* and for ten years tenant of Hardy's old home at Higher Bockhampton), correcting Lea's mistakes and quite often being deliberately misleading in order to protect the privacy of his own especially loved places and the homes of his friends.

Today there are dozens of guides to Hardy's Wessex, to suit all tastes and pockets. The Dorset County Museum in Dorchester is an excellent source of books of all kinds about Hardy, but any Wessex bookshop or even newsagent will have something to offer. There is also a healthy amount of disagreement as to who did what where, regardless of Hardy's plea (to Hermann Lea): 'I have again and again denied that the fictitious places "are" such and such real ones; they are merely ideal places suggested by them.'

Here I have space only to describe the two homes most important to Hardy and to offer (despite his caveats) two trails: one in Cornwall, where he twice fell head over heels in love with his first wife, the other inspired by *Tess of the D'Urbervilles* (1891).

BIRTH OF A WOODLANDER

Hardy was born in an isolated woodland cottage at Higher Bockhampton, three miles outside Dorchester, in 1840. He came of a humble family of builders, although he delighted, as did Tess's father John Durbeyfield, in tracing his heredity back to the Normans – in his case not the D'Urbervilles, but the le Hardi family.

His earliest surviving poem, 'Domicilium', written when he was sixteen is a touching evocation of the house, and the 'long low cottage with a hipped roof of thatch, having dormer windows breaking up into

Hardy's Cottage today is still easily identified as the long low building described in many of his poems.

the eaves' was immortalised as Upper Mellstock in *Under the Greenwood Tree* (1872). It was called Hardy's Cottage before Thomas was born, for it was built by his great-grandfather, John Hardy of Puddletown, in 1800.

It faces west, and round

the back and sides

High beeches bending,

hang a veil of boughs,

And sweep against the

roof. Wild honeysucks

Climb on the walls…

Thomas Hardy, 'Domicilium'

Its deep window seats and leaded panes suggest an earlier date, but country builders change their methods slowly. Today there is still box and laurustinus in the garden and the 'beam bisecting the ceiling' mentioned in the scene of the Mellstock Christmas dance can be seen in the low ceiling of the parlour. The room was originally longer: the wall between the parlour and the 'office', so called because it was in here that Hardy's father did his accounts, is made from a piece of panelling salvaged from a much older and grander house.

Enlarged piecemeal as needs required, the cottage remained Hardy's home for the first thirty-four years of his life, richly endowed with friendly ghosts and the 'meditative solitude' he needed in order to write. 'Those seven little rooms with their chestnut floorboards and bumpy whitewashed ceilings, ancient adze-marked doors from another house, fragile stairs and solid flags exuded it.'

In fact, only the northern, better-built part of the cottage has chestnut floors. The southern end was originally separate, perhaps built to house Mary Head Hardy, Thomas's grandmother, after his parents married and moved into the main cottage. Later, perhaps after Mary's death in 1857, the two cottages were made one, and the copper for washing and brewing which originally stood in an alcove to the right of the hearth was removed and a new entrance made there. The old door became a window, as Hardy records in 'Domicilium':

> Here is the ancient floor
> Footworn and hollowed and thin,
> Here was the former door
> Where the dead feet walked in.

Hardy's own bedroom was in the southernmost attic of the cottage. He lived here while he was serving his apprenticeship as an architect with Hicks of Dorchester. From its window to the west, he could see the far-away obelisk, the Hardy Monument, which had been put up on the crest of Black Down, above Weymouth, in memory of Admiral Thomas Hardy of Trafalgar fame when Thomas was four years old. Admiral Hardy, a remote relative, is mentioned in *The Trumpet-Major* (1880) and *The Dynasts* (1904-8).

When Hardy was a child, wild heathland – the Egdon Heath which recurs so often and with such hefty symbolism in so many of his novels – opened out directly behind the cottage. Much of it has now been planted with conifers by the Forestry Commission. His grandmother used to take him for walks upon it when he was a little boy, telling him stories of bygone days and ways.

Hardy lived at Bockhampton until he was twenty-two, when he got a job as an architect in Arthur Blomfield's office in the Adelphi and rented lodgings in London. But right up until 1874, the year he married, he continued to retreat to the cottage whenever he could, finishing his first novels, *Desperate Remedies* (1871) and *A Pair of Blue Eyes* (1873) there between 1870 and 1871, and making a start on *Under the Greenwood Tree*. The farms and cottages of *Far from the Madding Crowd* were set within walking distance of Bockhampton, and it was while on her way to Mellstock/Stinsford Church that Tess is lifted across the floods in the arms of Angel Clare.

The cottage had nearly two acres of land and its own orchard. A favourite occasion for returning to it was the annual ritual of cider-making. 'The sweet smells and oozings in the crisp autumn air can never be forgotten by those who had a hand in it', Hardy wrote. He also apostrophised cider in verse:

Painting by Thomas Hardy of the house at Higher Bockhampton with Egdon Heath, which in his day backed on to the cottage garden.

> Sweet cyder is a great thing,
> A great thing to me,
> Spinning down to Weymouth town
> By Ridgeway thirstily,
> And maid and mistress summoning
> Who tend the hostelry:

O cyder is a great thing,
A great thing to me!

He remained loyal to the cottage all his life, visiting it weekly on foot
or by bicycle after he moved to Max Gate in 1885. He always walked in
the woods behind it on his birthdays; he also took his aged mother, who
lived there until her death in 1904, for walks on the heath, just as his
grandmother had taken him when he was a child. After she died, he
continued to pay its rent until 1913.

During Hermann Lea's tenancy, Hardy used to visit him and take tea
in the garden under the fruit trees. Even in his eighties, Hardy continued
to take an interest in the well-being of 'the Hardy home', as he called it,
and visited it regularly. He hated to see the cottage look neglected, and in
November 1926, aged eighty-six, he records in his diary that he 'went with
Mr Hanbury [the cottage's owner] to Bockhampton and looked at
fencing, trees, etc., with a view to tidying and secluding the Hardy house'.

The cottage and its ancient unchanged furnishings inspired several
poems. In 'Old Furniture', he describes how when he sits there 'amid
relics of householdry', he sees

…the hands of the generations
That owned each shiny familiar thing
In play on its knobs and indentations,
And with its ancient fashioning
Still dallying:
Hands behind hands, growing paler and paler
As in a mirror a candle-flame
Shows images of itself, each frailer
As it recedes…

Even more haunting, but also for Hardy unusually optimistic, is
'Night in the Old Home'. This conjures up his 'perished people [who]

Right: Manuscript
of the poem 'When I set
out for Lyonnesse',
commemorating Hardy's
visit to Cornwall in 1870.

come and seat them around me in their mouldy places'; however, they counter his desolate mood with advice distinctly reminiscent of Edward FitzGerald's Omar Khayyám:

'– O let be the Wherefore! We fevered our years not thus:
Take of Life what it grants, without question!' they answer
   me seemingly.
'Enjoy, suffer, wait: spread the table here freely like us,
And, satisfied, placid, unfretting, watch Time away beamingly!'

The harbour at Boscastle
where Hardy met his first
wife, Emma Gifford.

"When I set out for Lyonnesse"

When I set out for Lyonnesse,
  A hundred miles away,
    The time was on the spray,
And starlight lit my lonesomeness
When I set out for Lyonnesse
  A hundred miles away.

What would bechance at Lyonnesse
  While I should sojourn there
    No prophet durst declare,
Nor did the wisest wizard guess
What would bechance at Lyonnesse
  While I should sojourn there.

When I came back from Lyonnesse
  With magic in my eyes
    None managed to surmise
What meant my godlike gloriousness,
When I came back from Lyonnesse
  With magic in my eyes.

'Some Strange Necromancy'

Thomas Hardy's most haunting love poems were written in memory of his first wife, Emma Gifford, his 'very West-of Wessex girl, / As blithe as blithe could be'. He was thirty when he met her, sent from London on a chance commission to draw up plans for the restoration of St Juliot's, a remote little Cornish church near Boscastle. Emma was staying with her sister, who was married to the rector, and it was love at first sight. That first meeting, in March 1870, and their wanderings together in the 'wild and tragic' landscape of Boscastle ('Castle Boterel'), the Valency Valley, Beeny Cliff and Tintagel are also detailed exactly in his third novel, *A Pair of Blue Eyes*. 'A region of dream and mystery', he called it in his preface. 'The ghostly birds, the pall-like sea, the frothy wind, the eternal soliloquy of the waters, the bloom of dark purple cast, that seems to exhale from the shore-ward precipices, in themselves lend to the scene an atmosphere like the twilight of a night vision.'

Thomas and Emma also visited Tintagel, Trebarwith and Bude before the young architect set off back from 'Lyonesse' to Higher Bockhampton 'with magic in my eyes' as well as the glory of new love. But despite its promising beginnings, the marriage went sour. Even in *A Pair of Blue Eyes* there are shadows of the miseries to come.

It was only after Emma's death that Hardy returned – for the first time since their marriage forty years earlier. The result was a torrent of poetry dedicated to Emma. 'Much of my life claims that spot as its key', runs the last line of 'A Dream or No', a poem written after a pilgrimage back to Cornwall when he was seventy-two. It was also then that he wrote the wildly romantic poem 'Beeny Cliff, March 1870–March 1913'.

> O the opal and the sapphire of that wandering western
>   sea,
> And the woman riding high above with bright hair
>   flapping free
> The woman whom I loved so and who loyally loved me

Ever afterwards, the calendar on his desk was always set to Monday 7 March, the date on which they met. He died, murmuring brokenly, 'Em, Em'.

Left: Emma Lavinia
Gifford by an unknown
artist.

Right: Hardy's sketch
of Emma searching for
a picnic tumbler in the
River Valency, dated
19 August 1870.

On Foot (*c.*5 miles)

To enjoy this circular walk in the lovers' footsteps, take a picnic with you and cheap editions of Hardy's *Poems* and *A Pair of Blue Eyes*. Leave the A30 after Launceston on the A395 to reach Boscastle, a dramatically located little port which is the only safe haven in forty miles. On his second visit to Emma, in August 1870, Hardy arrived by steamer from Bristol — just as Stephen does in *A Pair of Blue Eyes*. Today it is hard to imagine how the substantial ships that frequented the harbour in the nineteenth century got in and out — in fact they were led in on long ropes held by people on either side of the sinuous little inlet.

Park in the spacious central Boscastle car-park. Walk down to the harbour and take the cliff path on its northward side to the prominent flagstaff on top of Penally Hill. Then look along the coast to see where 'Still in all its chasmal beauty bulks old Beeny to the sky'. Continue along the well-marked cliff path round the 'creamy surge' of Pentargon Bay, past the 120ft waterfall which plunges rapier-thin, crystal-clear, down to the beach below, and up to the summit of Beeny Cliff itself. If you have plenty of time, you could continue along the coastal path for another mile and a half, looking down at what Emma called in her notebook 'the solemn small shores where the seals lived', to High Cliff. This is the monstrous and concave 'cliff-without-a-name' in *A Pair of Blue Eyes*. Here, the resourceful and impulsive Elfride saves the life of Henry Knight, the dry stick she is foolish enough to be in love with, by taking off all her underclothes and making a rope with them. Initially both grateful and amorously stirred by this noble gesture, Knight later condemns it as immodest, and makes it one of his excuses for deserting her. So Elfride joins what a Swedish critic has called the 'procession of dim, doomed figures' that make up Hardy's female heroines.

Otherwise, head inland from Beeny Cliff, first along a footpath and side road to Beeny, then by footpath to Trebyla, then, after crossing the B3263, to Penventon Farm. Here you will join a side road. Turn right towards St Juliot Church, about a quarter of a mile eastwards (nb: the OS map marks this only with a church symbol, and no name). This is the Endelstow Church of *A Pair of Blue Eyes*. Endelstow House does not exist, however; it was an invention, a combination of Lanhydrock near

Bodmin in Cornwall and Athelhampton Hall in Dorset.

Cross the churchyard to where a stile in its south wall will take you on to a footpath which winds down the valley to the sea, first just above the Valency River and then close beside it. It's easy to see how Hardy and Emma fell in love in this leafy valley; there can be few more romantic rambles in Britain.

About twenty yards before you get to the footbridge across the river that gives access to Minster Church (another attractive optional detour, again marked only with a symbol by OS), look out for the 'purl of a little valley fall / About three spans wide and two spans tall / Over a table of solid rock, / And into a scoop of the self-same block'. This is where Thomas and Emma picnicked and lost a tumbler (still reputed to be there): the incident inspired the delightful little poem 'Under the Waterfall'.

Continue on through the thickly wooded valley until it widens out into water meadows and the car-park where you left your car. Visit the Wellington for an opportunity to admire the ruby glass and brass church lamps which Hardy specified for St Juliot Church; they were moved to the inn after the advent of more modern lighting in the church.

MAP

OS Explorer 111: Bude, Boscastle & Tintagel

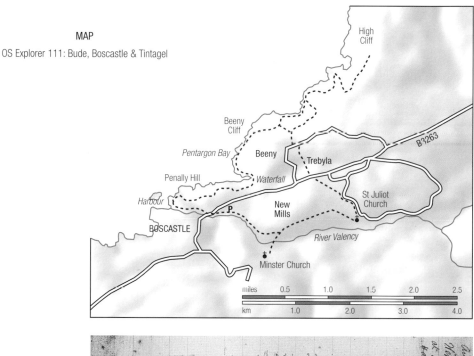

THE HOUSE OF SILENCE

When Hardy finally settled in Dorset in 1883 with Emma, he designed a 'high new house' that could not have been more different from his childhood home. Looking one way to Bockhampton, the other towards Dorchester station and the railway line to London, Max Gate was both a retreat, linked to the past, in which to write, and a base from which he and Emma could sortie forth to London and for trips abroad.

Visually, the house is a shock: a substantial Surbiton villa of crimson brick with all mod cons, set baldly and incongruously on an acre and a half of Duchy of Cornwall wasteland just south-east of Dorchester. Like the jumped-up pseudo-D'Urbervilles' house, it 'rises like a geranium bloom against the subdued colours around'.

But it had a past of its own. Hardy derived its name from Mack's toll-gate, which had once stood there. The excavations for its foundations revealed that the site had once been a Roman graveyard. Hardy was especially moved by the discovery of two skeletons clasped in each other's arms.

> So long, beyond chronology,
> Lovers in death as 'twere,
> So long in placid dignity
> Have you lain here!

Max Gate (*c.*1900), the mansion bought with the proceeds of Hardy's work. Emma and her nephew Gordon Gifford are in the foreground. Thomas Hardy, with his bicycle, is on the left.

But it would take more than an underpinning of ancient history to give the house life and personality. 'The house is bleak and cold / Built so new for me', mourned Hardy. To cut down the blasts of wind that swirled around it, and to protect his privacy from the inquisitive eyes of early literary travellers through his Wessex, he built a high garden wall and planted between two and three thousand Austrian pines around it. They later grew thickly enough to make the house seem in summer to be 'at the bottom of a dark green well'.

Although Hardy spent forty-five years at Max Gate, the entire second half of his long life, the house never warmed the cockles of his heart as Bockhampton did. Though replete with Edwardian luxuries, it was a house of retreating footsteps and closing doors. Part of the gloom was the growing distance between Thomas and the once-adored Emma.

But there is no doubt at all that it was a wonderfully peaceful place in which to concentrate on writing. In a poem called 'The House of Silence', he wrote

'That is a quiet place –
That house in the trees with the shady lawn.'
'If, child, you knew what there goes on
You would not call it a quiet place.
Why a phantom abides there, the last of its race,
And a brain spins there till dawn.'

Streams of stories and novel after novel – including *The Woodlanders* (1887), *Tess of the D'Urbervilles* and *Jude the Obscure* (1895) – were written there. Hardy changed his study three times, always working upstairs, well away from interruptions and with a variety of splendid views. His favourite was the last, looking out over the prehistoric monolith which had been uncovered in the garden and which he always called the Druid Stone, towards Rainbarrow.

In 1913, Emma died. Among her papers Hardy discovered autobiographical jottings that filled him with remorse. Although he remarried quickly, he remained obsessed by Emma, writing poem after poem exploring their first meeting and the decline of their relationship over the years, and insisting on keeping mementoes of his life with her prominently on display all over the house. It must have been a bitter cup for his former mistress and second wife Florence Dugdale to swallow, but she carried out her two most important duties – housekeeper and gatekeeper against unwanted visitors – with good grace.

Pets were an important part of the Max Gate household during both

Hardy in the study at Max Gate with his cat.

Emma Hardy (seated) and her companion Florence Dugdale, who became Hardy's second wife, on the beach at Worthing in Sussex in 1911.

of Hardy's marriages. It was one of Thomas's great regrets that he and Emma never had children and the many dogs, especially Florence's notoriously aggressive terrier Wessex, cats and birds were a kind of substitute. Because of the proximity of the railway line fatalities were frequent, and the pets had a graveyard of their own, which can still be seen tucked away in the shrubbery. 'So like one of Hardy's novels or poems', wrote E. M. Forster to a friend after Florence had shown it to him when he visited the house.

As Hardy's fame grew, there was a constant stream of visitors. They included Edmund Blunden, Walter de la Mare, Siegfried Sassoon, Robert Graves, George Bernard Shaw and Marie Stopes (who had a house nearby, at Portland). Tea was an especially genteel occasion remembered one visitor, Norman Atkins:

Florence and Thomas Hardy at Max Gate after their marriage, *c*.1914, with the irrepressible Wessex.

> the China tea and the microscopic pieces of bread and butter of lace-like thinness, which looked like a collection of pale yellow and brown postage stamps decorating the plate on which they were served; the home-made cakes on a three-tier silver cakestand, and the embroidered table cloth. Mr and Mrs Hardy ate but little and politeness forced me to do likewise.

The favourite of the household was T. E. Lawrence (1888-1935), who had signed up as Private T. E. Shaw in the tank regiment stationed at nearby Bovington Camp in 1923. Once he had, very shyly, ascertained that he was welcome, he became a frequent visitor. He even took Florence, whose life was evidently short on thrills ('they can't laugh together, you know', he later wrote to a friend), out in the sidecar of Boanerges, his motorbike. The Hardys' parlourmaid Nellie Titterington recalled how he dispelled the habitual 'gloom that filled the whole atmosphere' of the house: 'That's why Lawrence's visits were such a joy to me. He brought happiness for a few moments. He also brought pleasure to Mr Hardy, as did several other of his friends…but apart from these occasions it was a house of noiseless gloom.'

'I go there as often as I decently can', Lawrence wrote of his visits in September 1923:

Hardy is so pale, so quiet, so refined into an essence: and camp is such a hurly-burly. When I come back I feel as if I've woken up from a sleep: not an exciting sleep, but a restful one. There is an unbelievable dignity and ripeness about Hardy: he is waiting so tranquilly for death, without a desire or ambition left in his spirit, as far as I can feel it: and yet he entertains so many illusions and hopes for the world, things which I, in my disillusioned middle-age [Lawrence was thirty-five] feel to be illusory. They used to call this man a pessimist. While really he is full of fancy expectations.

The drawing-room at Max Gate.

Hardy died in September 1928, and was buried in Westminster Abbey. Among his pall-bearers (Lawrence was then in Karachi) were J. M. Barrie, George Bernard Shaw, John Galsworthy, Rudyard Kipling, A. E. Housman, Stanley Baldwin and Ramsay MacDonald. But part of him will always rest in Wessex: his heart was removed and is buried with his ancestors in the churchyard of Stinsford where he sang in the choir and played the viol as a little boy.

Melbury and Fontmell Downs are typical of the Wessex countryside that Hardy so loved.

Travels with Tess

The tour can be undertaken on foot, by bicycle or in a car. To enjoy it to the full, buy a guide to Hardy's Wessex and add on a few variant excursions of your own. If walking or cycling, allow several days.

Tess of the D'Urbervilles encompasses the landscapes of Wessex more completely than any other single novel. As Tess roams across Wessex, she is frequently walking along actual watersheds. And her roller-coaster ride to her doom is a story of metaphorical watersheds, a catalogue of accidents, human failings and bad decisions that could, time and again, it seems, almost have taken an alternative course. Most of the momentous events in her life, good or bad, occur in the context of a journey, be it a long traipse across country or a short walk closer to her constantly changing homes.

Most of the route is high on the 'Wessex Heights', from which it is easy to take in the nature of the country that Hardy loved so well. Your take-off point is the 'mountain-town' of Shaftesbury ('Shaston'). Early in the novel, Tess walks there to beg for help from her supposed D'Urberville connections at 'Trantridge' (Pentridge) in Cranborne Chase. This is deep down on the other side of the ridge on the northernmost tip of which Shaftesbury is perched. Park Walk, just south of the ruined abbey in the centre of Shaftesbury, is a fine vantage point. On a clear day, there is a panoramic view of the Vale of Blackmore (Tess's home, the 'Valley of the Little Dairies') to the south-west and of the heights that border Cranborne Chase ('The Chase', the threateningly ancient woodland, dripping with druidical mistletoe, where Tess is raped by Alec D'Urberville) to the south-east. An engraved plaque on a stone pillar lists the hills you can see on a fine day with directional arrows: they include Melbury Beacon (NT), Hambledon Hill, Bulbarrow Hill, Nettlecombe Tout, Gore Hill and High Stoy.

TRAIL
2

By Car, Bicycle or Foot, (*c.*60 miles)

From Shaftesbury take the road south-west to Marnhull ('Marlott', where Tess was born). It is still a long straggling village. Hardy renamed the Crown Inn 'The Pure Drop', the Blackmore Vale Inn may well have been 'Rollivers'. Whether or not Tess Cottage, tucked away in a small cul-de-sac opposite the Lamb Inn, is indeed Tess's birthplace is a matter of dispute among 'topographical itinerarists', as Hardy himself described the pilgrims in search of Wessex certainties.

At Sturminster Newton ('Stourcastle'), the road crosses the River Stour, the biggest of the many waterways that meander along the floor of the enormous Vale of Blackmoor. Hardy lived in Riverside Villa after he married Emma Gifford, and wrote *The Return of the Native* (1878) here. Turn right after crossing the bridge and take the first turning on your left towards Hazelbury Bryan ('Nuttlebury') and Piddletrenthide. Tess passed by the Antelope Inn, a real place, and still there. It was along this road that Tess and her little brother drove a cart loaded with beehives intended for 'Casterbridge' (Dorchester).

After leaving Hazelbury Bryan, take a small turning on the right signposted to Mappowder. It is a peaceful little lane, winding past ancient farmsteads and with fine views of the surroundings hills. But to see the 'Valley of the Little Dairies' to best effect, it is worth gaining height. I stopped at Old Fox Farm, Folly, and walked up the bridleway westwards beside Ball Hill to Church Hill. The deeply rutted track was extremely muddy, but I comforted myself that I was experiencing to the full the distinctive vale clay which signals to Tess on one of her many night-time journeys that she was back in the country of her childhood.

At the top there is an ancient wood of ash and oak trees; before it thickens out there is a small gate to the north of the track which offers a wonderful view over the valley. Carry on westwards to the summit of the hill, where the ancient steading of a prehistoric settlement would make a fine site for Flintcomb-Ash, the high, windy 'starve-acre' farm where Tess toils through the winter after Angel has spurned her. The name has obvious

affinity with Dole's Ash Farm, which can be seen rather more cosily sited in the lap of the combe to the south. On the heights, the clay thins out into grassland, studded with the 'myriads of loose white flints' about whose suggestive shapes Tess's inebriate friend Marian made ribald jokes.

If you are walking, you can make much more direct progress in Tess's footsteps than motorists can. Carry on down to the next valley, turn right along the B3143 for a few hundred yards, and then take the track which climbs the rise opposite to Minterne Parva, as Tess did when she set off from Flintcomb-Ash to contact Angel's parents at 'Emminster' (Beaminster).

At Minterne Parva, turn left down the A352 for a few hundred yards, then take the lane to the right. Cross a stream by the manor house, then take the footpath to the right up East Hill to join the ridge road. Turn left here for Evershot and Beaminster. The views to the north-west are very spectacular, and there is a sense of striding along the very ramparts of Wessex. 'Owlscombe' is, in reality, Batcombe.

Motorists and most cyclists will have to return to Folly, and then follow the road down into the tiny hamlet of Plush. Continue to Piddletrenthide and take the B3143 northwards to Duntish. After Duntish turn left on the B3146. Take the second left turn (signposted Cerne Abbas), which joins the A352, then turn left towards Cerne Abbas. (The magnificently endowed Cerne Abbas Giant – now in the care of the National Trust – is notable by its absence from Tess's story, although it may not be chance that Alec had lodgings at 'Abbot's Cernel'.)

After passing the Lyons Gate Holiday Camp, take the second turning on the right and you will rejoin the walkers on the splendid ridge road to Evershot. The 'Valley of the Little Dairies' is spread out below you to the north. Just after a turning on the right down to the Friary of St Francis, you will see the stone pillar, no more than a yard high, known as the Cross and Hand. This is the ancient monolith on which Alec D'Urberville made Tess swear she would not tempt him any more – an impossible feat, of course, as the obsession was Alec's, not hers.

Evershot ('Evershead') is at the heart of *The Woodlanders* country, but it has a Tess Cottage beside its church, as Tess breakfasted 'not at the Sow and Acorn, for she avoided inns, but at a cottage by the church' on her way to Beaminster. The road slopes downhill, crossing a bridge (note its plaque threatening any malefactor damaging it with transportation) and meeting the A356. Either cross over to continue straight to Beaminster, or make a short detour northwards along the A356, taking a small (unsigned) turning off to the left which will take you to Beaminster via Beaminster Down, from which there are splendid views to the north-west down the Parrott Valley towards Yeovil.

I left Beaminster on the A35 Dorchester Road, but diverted off to the left. This is a single-track road with passing places. It eventually rejoins the very busy main road (A35) which was once 'the straight and deserted Roman Road called Long Ash Lane' along which Tess walked.

Ignore the ringroad and go straight through Dorchester, pausing if you have time to visit the excellent Dorset County Museum. Take the A352 (Wareham) road out of town. Just before the second roundabout you will see, and may wish to visit, Hardy's home, Max Gate (NT), on the right. At the next roundabout take the left fork to West Stafford. On the left at the top of the rise inside a field gate is a round barrow. This is where Angel Clare stood to get a fine view of the Frome Valley, the 'green trough of sappiness and humidity' which Hardy called the 'Valley of the Great Dairies'. It is, despite its name, much smaller than the 'Valley of the Little Dairies'. Tess walks here to make a new start at Talbothays, Dairyman Crick's farm, after having buried Sorrow, her baby, in an unmarked grave in 'Marlott' churchyard. You can also see Stinsford, the 'Mellstock' of both *Tess* and *Under the Greenwood Tree*. It was on their way to church here that Tess and her fellow dairymaids were gallantly carried across the flooded road by Angel Clare. The lane where Angel found them 'clinging to the roadside bank like pigeons on a roof-slope' turns off to the left just after you have crossed the railway line. The churchyard has several Hardy family graves, and Hardy's heart is buried here.

An optional detour can be made to both Stinsford and Hardy's birthplace at Higher Bockhampton by turning left over the railway line.

Continue to West Stafford: Angel and Tess could well have been married in its church. The house on the right called Talbothays Lodge was designed by Hardy and built and lived in by his brother Henry and his sisters (none of whom ever married). It has nothing to do with Talbothays, the dairy farm where the most idyllic scenes in the book take place, but a little further along the road there is a substantial farm called Lower Lewell Farm which fits the book's description in many ways. Hardy's own map had a cross in the field opposite it, which may well have indicated that this was about right as a site for Dairyman Crick's farm. Follow the road along the Frome Valley, enjoying the views to the north over water meadows and the river to the now partly forested heathland above and beyond.

Although the railway did in fact go to Dorchester by 1847, Hardy makes Talbothays the more romantically remote by claiming that the line, modern life's 'steam feeler', did not pass near it. It would have been either to Moreton, a well-established milk collection point, or to Wool, that Tess and Angel take the milk churns on the memorable occasion of Angel's proposal.

At Wool Bridge ('Wellbridge'), you will see the old manor, once owned by the real Turberville family, where Angel and Tess spend their ghastly honeymoon. Cross the railway line, turn left and then take the first left to Bindon Abbey. Among its ruins is the empty stone coffin into which the sleepwalking Angel puts Tess. On the river nearby is the mill, which had lasted, Hardy noted, so much longer than the abbey did.

Return to Wool and head north to Bere Regis ('Kingsbere-sub-Greenhill'), 'a little one-eyed blinking sort of place'. Its high stone cage of a church has a lively carved roof as well as two bleak and desecrated Turberville tombs and the stained-glass window which was perhaps the inspiration for Tess's whole sad story. The Durbeyfields dump bags and baggage and sleep outside and underneath it, in a striking symbol of the downfall of their ancient house. Here, Tess once again meets Alec, who could have been staying at the Royal Oak, the most prominent pub in the high street.

Head east out of Bere Regis along the A31, turning off to the left to Winterborne Kingston.

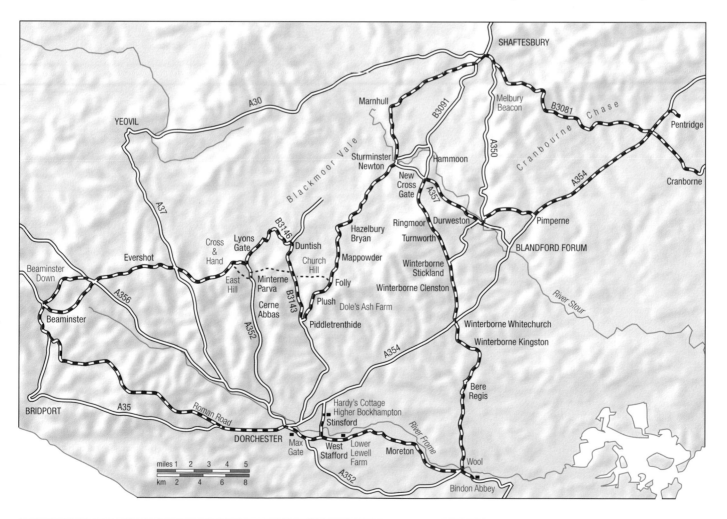

Follow the valley of the Winterbornes up to Winterborne Stickland, and continue north along this fine ridge road. If you have time, park half a mile north of Turnworth village and follow the bridleway up to Turnworth Down and the Romano-British camp of Ringmoor, an oasis of open downland fringed with some fine deciduous woods. There are fine views to Bulbarrow Hill, across the 'Valley of the Little Dairies'. If Tess was following the ancient ridgeway track from Flintcomb-Ash, she would have walked just east of Ringmoor on her way back to Marnhull. Continue up the road to the A357 at New Cross Gate. Walkers, cyclists and motorists in a hurry could cross the A357 and continue through Hammoon, rejoining the B3091 to Shaftesbury just north-east of Sturminster Newton.

More leisured motorists could explore 'The Chase – the oldest wood in England'. At New Cross Gate, turn right along the A357, then left on the A350, just for a few hundred yards, then turn right to Pimperne. Once through the village, turn left on the A354. Follow this to the crossroads with the B3081. Turn right to Cranborne ('Chaseborough'), and visit the Fleur-de-Lis ('Flower-de-Luce') Inn, which is where Tess waits so long for her merrymaking friends, with Alec, menacing and masterful, looming in the background. Return to the main road and turn right. Pentridge, a possible inspiration for 'Trantridge', is down the next turning on the right, a cul-de-sac. Somewhere here was Alec's vulgar redbrick house, so like Max Gate.

Return to Shaftesbury along the B3081, another ridge road with glorious views over the 'soft, azure landscape' of the Chase. These are its thickest woods, and it was into the heart of them that Alec takes the 'inexpressibly weary' Tess to meet her fate. Melbury Beacon, a Spanish Armada beacon site which was bought by the National Trust in 1986, would be a fine spot for a farewell picnic overlooking Tess's country.

MAP
OS Landranger 183: Yeovil & Frome
OS Landranger 184: Salisbury & The Plain, Amesbury
OS Landranger 193: Taunton & Lyme Regis
OS Landranger 194: Dorchester & Weymouth
OS Landranger 195: Bournemouth & Purbeck

Max Gate, Hardy's home until his death in 1928.

'Very Quiet, Very Lonely, Very Bare'

Nothing in Clouds Hill is to be a care upon the world. While I have it there shall be nothing exquisite or unique in it. Nothing to anchor me.

T. E. Lawrence to Mrs Eric Kennington, 1924

In the autumn of 1923, T. E. Lawrence (1888-1935) discovered a semi-derelict cottage, Clouds Hill, hidden among the rhododendron thickets that bordered the narrow gravel road between Max Gate and Bovington. He was immediately attracted by it, and arranged to rent it for half a crown a week, on the understanding that he repair it. 'The cottage is alone in a dip on the moor', he wrote to Jock Chambers in August 1924. 'Very quiet, very lonely, very bare. I don't sleep here, but come at 4.30pm till 9pm nearly every evening, & dream, or write or read by the fire, or play Beethoven or Mozart to myself on the box.'

The cottage, which is signposted clearly off the Wool to Bere Regis road, is still a remote and peaceful place. It was built in 1808 as a labourer's dwelling, and it had no amenities at all. 'As ugly as my sins', Lawrence called it; 'bleak, angular, small, unstable, very like its owner.' He spent much time, and what little money he had, restoring it. To pay for repairs, he raised £120 by selling a much-treasured gold dagger acquired in Mecca. Over the front door, he inscribed the punchline from a story in Herodotus: OU ØPOVTIS – 'why worry?'

At first, he only used the upstairs room. His sofa, chairs and cushions were all covered with undyed leather, now a rich brown. The stainless steel bookstand, the three-part fender and the candle sconces with shiny metal reflectors were made to his design. It was also his idea to fit a 'lazy tongs' to the grate so that toast could be made. Deckchairs provided extra seating when necessary.

Lawrence's gramophone, with its enormous papier mâché horn, is still there. Listening to it in that high wooden space, he must have felt like a Lilliputian inside a cello. He played Boccherini when he felt 'rebellious', Bach's Concerto in D Minor when he was filled with loathing for the barracks. He particularly loved Elgar's 2nd Symphony, which, he wrote in a fan-letter to the composer, 'gets further under our skins than anything else in the record library at Clouds Hill'.

For all his improvements, Clouds Hill always had the feel of a tent. It was the perfect place to write, either at a folding table or sitting cross-legged on the floor, leaning his work on an oak coffin stool given to him by Florence Hardy. He revised *The Seven Pillars of Wisdom* (1926) for publication, finished *The Mint*, a stark account of his first weeks in the RAF, and worked on translations here.

When he was settled, he invited visitors. 'TE was an expert at "mixed grills" where men were concerned', recalled one of them, Corporal Alec Dixon:

He presided over the company, settling arguments, patiently answering all manner of questions, feeding the gramophone, making tea, stoking the fire and, by some magic of his own, managing without effort to keep everyone in good humour. There were many picnic meals (stuffed olives, salted almonds and Heinz baked beans were regular features) washed down with TE's own blend of China tea. Some of us used chairs, others the floor, while TE always ate standing by the side of the wide oak mantelshelf which had been fitted at a height convenient for him.

Besides the Hardys, many great literary figures came to Clouds Hill over the next few years: Robert Graves, George Bernard Shaw and his wife Charlotte and, in March 1924, E. M. Forster. Lawrence took great pains to clean up the cottage before Forster's arrival, repairing the wireless so that he could 'hear Big Ben strike'. Forster enjoyed the visit, and described it in a letter to his mother: 'We worked for a couple of hours on his book, then had lunch on our knees – cold chicken and ham, stewed pears and cream, very nice and queer; a fine log fire.'

In 1925, Lawrence got a transfer into the RAF, and was posted to India. He decided to buy the cottage and keep it as a holiday place. Proceeds from his translation of Homer's *Odyssey* meant that in 1933 a thatched garage could be built and running water installed – Lawrence did much of the building work himself. A hydraulic ram carried water uphill to a reservoir, also used as a plunge pool, and the cottage acquired a bath. It never

The Music Room at
Clouds Hill.

Below: T. E. Lawrence
on his motorbike
'Boanerges'.

boasted a lavatory, although a chemical toilet was borrowed when Lawrence's mother came to stay. Bookshelves were built into the downstairs room, now called the Book Room, to accommodate his substantial library – by 1930 he had around 2,000 books and 200 records.

In 1935 he was discharged from the RAF and was looking forward to the peace of Clouds Hill. But rumours that he was about to be given an elevated government posting were rife, and, to his fury, he was besieged by reporters. Bernard Shaw commented wryly on his 'extraordinary capacity for backing into the limelight'.

The fuss died down, and for a time he had the peace he had craved for so long. He turned down an invitation to Cliveden from Lady Astor, who wanted him to meet the Prime Minister with a view to a job in Home Defence. 'You wonder what I am doing?' he wrote to his friend Eric Kennington. 'Well, so do I in truth. Days seem to dawn, suns to shine, evenings to follow, and then I sleep. Have you ever been a leaf and fallen from your tree in autumn and been really puzzled about it? That's the feeling.'

It was not to last long. In truth, Lawrence was soon restless in the place he insisted was his 'earthly paradise'. He was a great admirer of Henry Williamson, author of *Tarka the Otter*, who had been hugely impressed by what was then seen as the Nazi economic miracle. Williamson believed that Lawrence could be the 'natural leader of that age in England', just as Hitler seemed to be in Germany. He wrote a letter – no one knows quite what

it contained – to Lawrence in May 1938. On 13 May Lawrence went out on his motorbike to send Williamson a telegram inviting him down to Clouds Hill. On the way back he swerved to avoid two errand boys on bicycles. He was thrown over the handlebars and was severely concussed. Six days later he died, without recovering consciousness.

Pilgrims in search of T. E. Lawrence might end their journey at Wareham Church, where Eric Kennington's curiously alert marble effigy of him in Arab dress can be found.

Bloomsbury by the Sea

Virginia in the year of her marriage to Leonard Woolf, painted by her sister, Vanessa Bell.

It has the makings of a most peculiar and I think comfortable, charming, queer resort.

Virginia Woolf, letter to Vanessa Bell, 1926

'How anyone, with an immortal soul can live inland, I cant imagine', Virginia Woolf wrote in 1909; 'only clods and animals should be able to endure it.' Hills only existed to provide 'a wide view from them of the sea, the horizon, & one or two ships between', she thought. 'When you see nothing but land, stationary on all sides, you are conscious of being trapped, on a flat board.' The sea was 'a border of mystery, solving the limits of fields, and silencing their prose'.

Although Virginia was at the hub of the circle of cultured sophisticates named after Bloomsbury, the part of London where most of them lived, she always found that a country retreat within walking distance of the sea was vitally important to her – both as a rural lung and a haven of peace and continuity. Between 1904 and 1940 she lived at eight different London addresses. One of them was Hogarth House in Richmond-on-Thames, rented from 1915 to 1924, and first home of the famous Hogarth Press. But for twenty-two years, from 1919 to her death in 1941, she and Leonard remained faithful to Monk's House in Rodmell, a rural hamlet on the slopes of the Sussex Downs, four miles from the sea at Newhaven and four miles from the pretty little town of Lewes. It became an essential retreat from the social whirl and domestic responsibilities of London, and the place where she wrote the bulk of her best work.

Vistors came – E. M. Forster, Vita Sackville-West, Lytton Strachey, Aldous Huxley, Maynard Keynes, T. S. Eliot and many others. The artist Eric Ravilious settled at Furlongs, halfway between Asheham and Firle. But it was the peace of Rodmell that was its prime delight. 'Back from a good week end at Rodmell,' she wrote in her diary on 13 June 1932:

Monk's House in Sussex, the cottage where Virginia Woolf lived for over twenty years.

a week end of no talking, sinking at once into deep safe book reading; & then sleep: clear transparent; with the may tree like a breaking wave outside; & all the garden green tunnels, mounds of green: & then to wake into the hot still day, & never a person to be seen, never an interruption: the place to ourselves: the long hours.

Drawing of Virginia playing chess with Leonard.

Virginia had long had a deep love for the Sussex countryside. As she wrote to Vita Sackville-West in the winter of 1928:

I have been walking alone down a valley to Rat Farm, if that means anything to you; and the quiet and the cold and the loveliness – one hare, the weald washed away to vapour – the downs blue green; the stacks, like cakes cut in half – I say all this so excited me; and my own life suddenly became so impressive to me, not as usual shooting meteor like through the sky, but solitary and still that, as

I say – well, how is the sentence to end?: figure to yourself that sentence, like the shooting star, extinct in an abyss, a dome, of blue; the colour of night: which, if dearest Vita you can follow, is now my condition: as I sit waiting for dinner, over the logs.

HEAVEN HAVEN: MONK'S HOUSE, RODMELL

Virginia Woolf's first house in Sussex was a brand-new semi-detached villa in the village of West Firle. She called it Little Talland, in memory of her Cornish holiday home. After they were married in 1912, Virginia and Leonard spent their summers and weekends at Asheham House (now demolished), close to Beddingham and the River Ouse. She captures its gentle romantic melancholy in 'A Haunted House', a story published in 1921, in which two ghosts revisit the house they once lived in, looking for their own past in 'the pulse of the house'.

In 1919, the farmer who owned the house decided he wanted it back, and refused to renew the Woolfs' lease. They began to look for another house, even considering a permanent occupation of the little string of Cornish cottages they rented at Tregerthen, near Zennor, once occupied by D. H. Lawrence, later let to Ka Cox and her husband Will Arnold-Forster. But Cornwall was inconveniently far away from London, and Virginia was developing a deep love for the bare, ancient slopes of the Downs. 'Half the beauty of a country or a house comes from knowing it', she would write in her diary nine years later. 'One remembers old lovelinesses: knows that it is now looking ugly; waits to see it light up; knows where to find its beauty; how to ignore the bad things. This one can't do the first time of seeing' (14 August 1928).

Virginia had just bought the Round House, in Lewes itself, for £300, when Monk's House, two miles across the Ouse from Asheham, came up for auction. She and Leonard had often walked to Rodmell, the nearest place to shop, and knew the house from the outside. Virginia bicycled over the next day. She recorded a marvellous crescendo of househunter's self-persuasion in her diary a day or two later:

'These rooms are small, I said to myself; you must discount the value of that old chimney piece & the niches for holy water. Monks are nothing out of the way. The kitchen is distinctly bad. Theres an oil stove, & no grate. Nor is there hot water, nor a bath, & as for the E.C. [earth closet] I was never shown it.' These prudent objections kept excitement at bay; yet even they were forced to yield place to a profound pleasure at the size & shape & fertility & wildness of the garden. There seemed an infinity of fruitbearing trees; the plums crowded so as to weigh the tip of the branch down; unexpected flowers sprouted among cabbages. There were well kept rows of peas, artichokes, potatoes; raspberry bushes had pale little pyramids of fruit; & I could fancy a very pleasant walk in the orchard under the apple trees, with the grey extinguisher of the church steeple pointing my boundary. On the other hand there is little view – O but I've forgotten the lawn smoothly rolled, & rising in a bank, sheltered from winds too, a refuge in cold & storm … There is little ceremony or precision at Monks House. It is an unpretending house, long & low, a house of many doors; on one side fronting the street of Rodmell, & wood boarded on that side, though the street of Rodmell is at our end little more than a cart track running out on to the flat of the water meadows.

On 1 July 1919, the Woolfs bought Monk's House for £700 in the auction, held at the White Hart Hotel in Lewes. The Round House was resold – at a small profit – a fortnight later. In recent years the house had been neglected, but its bones were good: oak-beamed rooms (the pokiness Virginia first noticed was the result of partitioning), an attractive hearth and pointed niches in the dining-room, and plenty of scope for expansion. There were attractive outbuildings in the garden, one of them 'a romantic chamber' containing a very basic earth closet in the form of a cane chair over a bucket. A gate led to the water meadows 'where all nature is to be had in five minutes', she wrote to Janet Case

The Glazebrook family, early owners of Monk's House.

(5 January 1920). In the same letter, which is full of the delights of the landscape around Rodmell, Virginia quotes from Gerald Manley Hopkins, whose poetry she has only just discovered:

I have desired to go
Where springs not fail
To fields where flies no sharp and sided hail
And a few lilies blow

The poem's title was 'Heaven Haven', exactly what Monk's House would prove to be. Even before they had moved in, Virginia wrote to Ka Cox that it would be 'our address for ever and ever; Indeed I've already marked out our graves in the yard which joins our meadow' (12 August 1919).

In time it was discovered that the monks were apocryphal. The house, built around 1707, had first been owned by a family of carpenters, then by the Glazebrooks, the local millers. Among the furnishings which they bought at an auction on the lawn of the possessions of the previous owner, Jasper Verrall (an eccentric who had starved himself to death, according to the local doctor), were three oil-on-wood portraits of the Glazebrook family. 'For myself I dont ask anything more of pictures', Virginia wrote to Margaret Llewellyn Davies (17 August 1919). 'They are family groups, and he began the heads very large, and hadn't got room for the hands and legs, so these dwindle off till they're about the size of sparrows claws, but the effect is superb – the character overwhelming.'

Virginia liked determined colours: pomegranate, yellow, deep blue, and a sea-green for the walls that became her especial signature. The ancient furniture was soon supplemented with throw-outs from Hogarth House, souvenirs from Provence, paintings by Virginia's sister Vanessa Bell, and the products of the Omega Workshops where Vanessa worked with Duncan Grant. Carpets, china, armchairs, tables, lampshades and cushions were all designed by the prolific artists of Charleston, the

Left: The dining-room at Monk's House showing chairs designed by the Omega Workshop.

Right: Cover designed by Vanessa Bell for *To the Lighthouse*, published by the Hogarth Press in 1927.

farmhouse across the downs where Vanessa, Duncan Grant and their unpredictable entourage were based from 1916. It was only a short trip by motor, or an hour-long walk on foot, from Rodmell. The sisters often met halfway at Firle, for a picnic in the park of the manor house, or high on the beacon.

Monk's House, as befitted the name, always remained more austere than Charleston. The walls were barer, the chairs more stiff-backed. It was free of the litter of children. Instead there were animals: a marmoset, a succession of dogs (Grizzle, Sally and Pinker, the model for Flush), fish, both in a tank and in ponds, a swallow that nested in the hall. Innumerable books were stacked in untidy heaps beside chairs and sofas, spilling over on to the floor. Many were rebound by Virginia herself in fancy coloured papers; those she wrote and published at the Hogarth Press had covers designed by Vanessa.

Vanessa Bell's study of Sally, 1939.

There were also pot plants galore. These were Leonard's contribution: he was a keen gardener, and spent long hours nursing and nourishing exotic blooms. The greenhouses that now front the wall of the house were not built until after Virginia's death, but others existed in the garden, and Leonard used to fill the house with relays of plants at their peak of flowering: brightly coloured begonias and gloxinias and heavily perfumed lilies. The eventual shape of design of what Leonard called its

Leonard's flower garden
at Monk's House.

'patchwork quilt' of a garden echoed that of Talland House: open-air rooms, secret corners, unexpected vistas. Hives murmurous with bees flanked the churchyard wall.

As Virginia's earnings from her writings increased, new comforts came to Monk's House. 'I'm out to make £300 this summer by writing, & build a bath & hot water range at Rodmell', she wrote in her diary in April 1925. *Mrs Dalloway* (1925) paid for a hot-water range, a bathroom and a lavatory with running water, and also for opening up the partitioned reception rooms into the 'perfect triumph' of 'our large combined drawing eating room, with its 5 windows, its beams down the middle, & flowers & leaves nodding in all round us'.

The walls of the Woolfs' sitting-room are painted in Virginia's favourite sea-green.

Money from *Orlando* (1928) paid for an extension to the east end of the house. Downstairs was a spacious room (16ft by 18ft) with two great casement windows with 'vast, sweeping views' over the fields. It was originally intended as a sitting-room, but Virginia soon adopted it as a bedroom; in it, she felt she came close to sleeping under the stars. Its fireplace is decorated with tiles decorated by Vanessa: the central motif is a jaunty sailing ship sailing across an impossibly blue sea to a lighthouse. To enter the room, Virginia had to go out of the kitchen, up a short flight of steps and in at its one, outside, door. It was a tiny rite that gave her the separateness from Leonard, from the whole world, which she evidently needed.

In time, they bought the field next door to the house, and also Park Cottages, a few yards down the lane, to provide accommodation for their gardener and his wife, and their cook-general. It was a generous gesture, but it also ensured the peace of a servant-free household.

Virginia Woolf's garden study at Monk's House is one of the most

The tiled fireplace in Virginia's bedroom shows Godrevy Lighthouse.

Virginia's writing lodge.

evocative of retreats. She needed complete separation from the domestic in order to concentrate on her work. She first set up her writing-table in the apple loft, but felt distracted by Leonard's activities in the garden. Eventually her 'lodge' was built at the very far end of the garden, close to the wall between them and the churchyard. Its French windows open out on to a view across the Ouse Valley to Mount Coburn, the huge calm hill above Lewes, and the downs, which 'turn from green to blue, like opals' in the evenings. The Downs 'look so lovely this evening, from my garden room, with the low barns that always make me think of Greek Temples', she wrote to Vita on 27 May 1931. She often spent up to twelve hours of the twenty-four alone.

The Woolfs had a love-hate relationship with village life. At times they were infuriated by the children scrumping apples from the orchard, and their 'cursed shrill voices' as they played in the cricket field. Virginia loathed the sound of church bells ('intermittent, sullen, didactic'). The villagers found them, and many of their visitors, distinctly odd. But as the years went by, the Woolfs became very much part of the place. Old Sussex appealed to Virginia: the shabby old rector, the Revd James Hawkesford, slipping out in the middle of a service for a cigarette; the 'muddy & obsolete' old farmers who 'drink, and lounge about', the 'draggle tail' spinster sisters of the vicar of Southease (where there was a local railway halt on the banks of the Ouse, in the valley below Rodmell).

The 'grey extinguisher' of the steeple of Rodmell village church.

> One of the charms of Rodmell is the human life: everyone does the same thing at the same hour: when the old vicar performs erratically on the bells, after churching the women, everybody hears him, & knows what he's up to. Everyone is in his, or their garden; lamps are lit, but people like the last daylight, which was brown purple last night, heavy with all this rain. What I mean is that we are a community. (*Diary*, 1 October 1920)

She wrote some short stories offering recognisable versions of Rodmell, but the book that most represented it (mixed a little with Firle, her first home in Sussex) was her last, *Between the Acts* (1941). By the time she wrote it, she was on the committee of the village's Women's Institute, attending its Monday meetings regularly. In the last year of her life she agreed to be its treasurer: 'If one lives in a village, one better snatch its offerings.' Leonard became a school governor and treasurer of the local cricket club – a hit into Monk's House garden is still an automatic six.

Rodmell was not only the place where Virginia could work best of all, it was also where she died. On 28 March 1941, distressed by the advent of war and the drone of the flights of bombers heading overhead to London, unsure of the quality of *Between the Acts* and unable to face the prospect of the nervous breakdown she could again feel coming on, she wrapped herself in a heavy fur coat, took up her walking-stick, and set off for the River Ouse. She left letters to Leonard and Vanessa in the upstairs sitting-room.

Leonard, who had been working in his study when she left, read them later that afternoon. They were no surprise: he had been anticipating such an attempt. He called the police, and they helped him search the river. It was twenty-one days before her body was found. It must first have sunk – she had put a large stone in her pocket to make herself as heavy as possible – then risen in the water. How symbolic it was, Jan Morris observes in *Travels with Virginia Woolf*, 'that when she came to end her life, she should do so in the water of the English river that ran within sight of her own house, among the Sussex landscapes that she loved: the human spirit immersed at the end in the spirit of place'.

Her ashes were buried under one of the pair of elm trees that once stood on the boundary between the garden and the downs beyond – they had long christened them Leonard and Virginia. Leonard was desolate. 'They said: "Come to tea and let us comfort you." But it's no good. One must be crucified on one's own private cross', he wrote in a private note. 'I know that V. will not come across the garden from the lodge, and yet I look in that direction for her. I know that she is drowned and yet I listen for her to come in at the door. I know that it is the last page and yet I turn it over. There is no limit to one's own stupidity and selfishness.'

TRAIL 1 Monk's House to Charleston

A walking tour – allow a full day, preferably a fine breezy summer one – is easily the best and most authentic way of exploring Bloomsbury in Sussex. A good alternative is a bicycle; Virginia regularly used one to collect milk and groceries when they lived at Asheham. The speed and seclusion of a car will shut you away from the scent and spirit of the landscape, but the doggedly motor-borne may take comfort in the fact that they too can claim to be following in the tracks of the Bloomsberries. 'What I like … about motoring is the sense it gives of lighting accidentally, like a voyager who touches another planet with the tip of his toe, upon scenes which would have gone on … unrecorded, save for this chance glimpse', wrote Virginia soon after she and Leonard bought their first car, a second-hand Singer, in 1927 for £275 (almost half as much as they had paid for Monk's House nine years earlier). She never learnt to drive properly, but was delighted by their 'nice light little shut-up car … very dark blue, with a paler line round it', and thought it would 'expand that curious thing, the map of the world in ones mind'. In 1935 they graduated to a silver-green Lanchester 18, 'smooth as an eel', Virginia crowed, 'fast as a swift, powerful as a tiger and sealed like a Pulman'. It made her feel 'rich, conservative, patriotic, religious and humbuggish'.

> *I like driving off to Rodmell on a hot Friday evening and having cold ham and sitting on my terrace and smoking a cigar, with an owl or two.*
>
> Virginia Woolf, *Diaries*

On Foot (7 miles)

Take the lane to the church that flanks Monk's House, walk through the school playground past the church and the farm and out on to the flat water meadows to the River Ouse. Follow the raised bank of the river downstream to the swing-bridge at Southease; cross this, the railway line at Southease Halt and the main Newhaven road. Follow the footpath sign to Itford Hill.

As you climb the steep chalk down opposite, mourn the suffocation of Asheham House in cement workings and its final demise under a mountain of landfill. When you reach the summit of Itford Hill, pause to puff and admire the view of the sea, the river winding below, Lewes in the distance and infinite rhythms of downland. Then head over the edge of the escarpment on the South Downs Way, trying to ignore the hideous radio masts on Beddingham Hill by keeping your eyes open for marine fossils embedded in the chalk, to Firle Beacon. The beacon offers an astonishingly commanding view of the countryside below and, on a clear day, of the sea far to the south. An optional variation for those without picnics is to drop down to West Firle village for lunch and a glimpse of Little Talland House (for more details of Firle see By Car section).

Follow the footpath that winds down the north-east face of Firle Beacon to get a glimpse of the farmhouse of Tilton. This was leased in 1925 from Lord Gage of Firle Place by John Maynard Keynes, a regular visitor to Charleston. Unfortunately, the Bloomsberries had taken a thorough dislike to Keynes's new wife, the Russian ballet dancer Lydia Lopokova. Vanessa even considered giving up Charleston when she realised how close Lydia would be living to them. But the Keyneses remained, very happily, at Tilton for the rest of their lives. Keynes was created Baron Keynes of Tilton in 1942 and died there, aged sixty-two, on Easter Sunday 1946. Lydia stayed there until 1977, finally dying at the age of eighty-nine in a Seaford nursing home in 1981. Tilton is now privately owned by Keynes's biographer, Robert Skidelsky, but neither it nor the track to the farmhouse is open to the public. Before you reach it, a left turn in the farm track will take you first west, then north, to Charleston itself.

The Long Man at Wilmington, one of the views over the Sussex Downs.

By Car (*c.*25 miles)

Rodmell is four miles south of Lewes. It can be reached on the road from Lewes, or by turning off the A27 to Kingston, winding through the village, and turning right to Rodmell and Newhaven. As a glance at any road map will show you, now that the A27 ring road gashes its way between Rodmell and Lewes, there is no easy route from Rodmell to Charleston. You have the option of dipping in and out of Newhaven if the traffic from the docks is at an ebb, or winding through Kingston to join the A27 dual carriageway eastbound, or crossing over the A27 and winding through Lewes back to the A27 at the Southerham roundabout. Then turn left (towards Eastbourne).

At the Beddingham roundabout, where the road from Newhaven joins the A27, follow the signs to Eastbourne. After just over a mile, turn off to the right to the village of West Firle, and explore the park where Rupert Brooke once strolled with Virginia. Little Talland House (private property), Virginia's first Sussex home, is one of a pair of three-storey Edwardian half-timbered houses in the main street of the village. In the church there is a radiant John Piper window and a fine 1595 alabaster memorial to Sir John Gage and his wife. The graves of Vanessa Bell and Duncan Grant are in the north-east of the churchyard.

Return to the A27 and, ignoring the perilous right-hand turn to Charleston, continue on to Berwick. Turn right to the village and church. The Church of St Michael and All Angels has some remarkable murals painted by Duncan Grant, Vanessa Bell and her son Quentin Bell. They were commissioned in 1941 by the parochial church council, despite some opposition by those who deplored the fact that Vanessa and Duncan were atheists living in sin and Quentin Bell was a conscientious objector. The department store-owner Peter Jones gave some financial support, and John Christie of Glyndebourne provided large easels for the plasterboard panels, which were painted in Maynard Keynes's barn at Tilton. Friends, family and neighbours were pressed into service as models. The walled garden of Charleston can be glimpsed behind the Annunciation.

On leaving Berwick village, turn left towards Lewes. After about two and a half miles, take the now easily negotiated left turn signposted to Charleston Farmhouse.

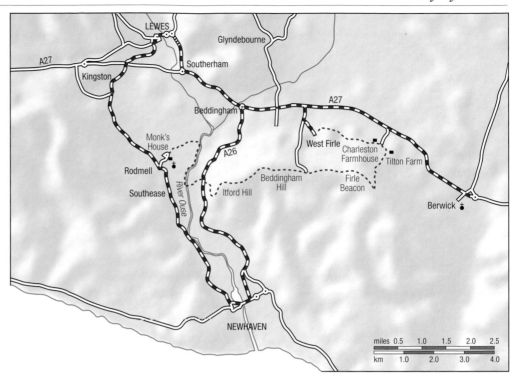

MAP

OS Landranger 198: Brighton & Lewes

OS Landranger 199: Eastbourne & Hastings

CHARLESTON

Charleston is a rambling, unpretentious farmhouse below Firle Beacon, seven miles on foot and twelve miles by road from Monk's House. Vanessa Bell and her household moved there in 1916, when the Woolfs were living at Asheham, four miles away. Duncan Grant and David Garnett, conscientious objectors during the First World War, were granted non-combatant service in the army, and worked for a tenant-farmer of Lord Gage, the owner of Firle Place.

Over the following three years, Vanessa and Duncan decorated almost every available wall surface of the house and much of its furniture. If Virginia's domestic signature was sea-green, Vanessa's was a warm grey. Conditions were primitive: water had to be pumped by hand and heated on the kitchen range, and food shortages meant that there was often little or nothing to eat. Vanessa kept ducks, chickens and rabbits to supplement their diet, and Clive Bell sallied forth with dog and gun to shoot game for the larder.

But the atmosphere of the house was always exciting and warm: home-made scones for tea, classical music on the wind-up gramophone in the evenings, and the enlivening presence of children; Julian, born in 1908, Quentin, 1910, and Angelica, born at Charleston itself at 2 o'clock on Christmas Morning, 1918.

Bicyles, fishing nets and the paraphernalia of painting littered the outbuildings. Everywhere people were intent on making things: books, paintings, furnishings, food. Helen Gunn remembers it as 'a radiant and effervescent place'.

When the war ended, the family returned to London, but continued to spend weekends and long summers at Charleston. After a long period of decline, it has been rehabilitated marvellously by the Charleston Trust, and is now a busy and lively focus for interest and new research into the ever-fascinating world of the Bloomsbury Group.

TRAIL 2 Views of the Lighthouse

Virginia Woolf had a second spiritual landscape that was every bit as important to her as that of Sussex, even though, after her childhood, she visited it only occasionally. The north Cornish coast at St Ives was where she spent every summer from her birth until the age of thirteen, when her childhood ended abruptly with the death of her mother, Julia Stephen, in 1895. When she visited Greece in 1906, she wrote in her diary that the coast of Greece reminded her of the Penwith cliffs, and Athens (inexplicably) of St Ives. 'It is not for the people we crave; it is for the place. That keeps its magic; so strong that it seems to send shocks across the water.'

The summers in Cornwall remained engraved in her memory as an irrecoverable paradise. They began in 1882. That spring, just after Virginia was born, Leslie Stephen was taking one of his habitual tramps across Cornwall when he came across 'one of the loveliest walks imaginable'. It was a gradually sloping moor of gorse broken by masses of primroses and bluebells, and the St Ives Bay and its sandhills in the distance. The air, he reported, was as soft as silk, with 'a fresh sweet taste like new milk'.

On impulse, he asked about houses for rent in St Ives, and inspected Talland House, built in the 1840s. It was a little outside the town, on a hill. There was no furniture, and the cold-water tap didn't work. But there was a glorious view across the bay to the Godrevy Lighthouse. He spent the night there, lying in bed with the blinds open so that he could 'see the Children sport on the shore'. An easy path led to the sandy cove below, down which, he wrote, 'the babies will be able to go quite comfortably'.

From then on, the Stephen family holidays were always spent at Talland House. The unparalleled view was immortalised in *To the Lighthouse* (1927):

> The great plateful of blue water was before her; the hoary Lighthouse, distant, austere, in the midst; and on the right, as far as the eye could see, fading and falling, in soft low pleats, the green sand dunes with the wild flowing grasses on them, which always seemed to be running away to some moon country, uninhabited of men.

Memories of the north Cornwall shore and her parents haunted Virginia all her life. In 1921, she recalled in her diary 'an ordinary summer day in 1890, the sound of the sea and the children in the garden' at Talland House, and concluded that 'all her life was built on that, permeated by that: how much so I could never explain'. She remembered how early one morning, lying in the nursery of Talland House, she heard 'the waves breaking, one, two, one, two … behind a yellow blind'. Lying half asleep, half awake, in her warm bed, she heard that rhythm and saw a moment's light as the wind blew the blind out and knew 'the purest ecstasy I can conceive'. Years later, she wanted the waves' rhythm to sound all through her greatest books, *To the Lighthouse* and *The Waves* (1931).

To the Lighthouse was at first planned as a portrait of her father, but it turned into an elegy for her mother. Mrs Ramsay is Julia Stephen to the life: endlessly loving and dauntingly high-minded, apparently vague but subtly manipulative.

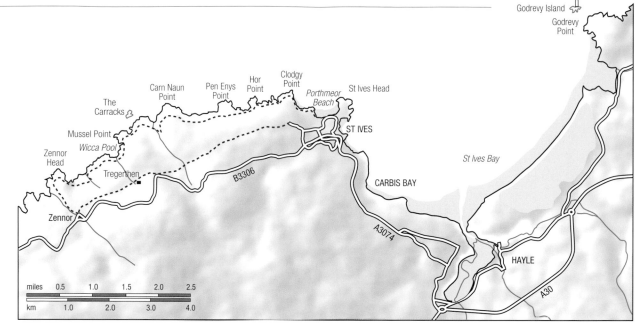

Godrevy Island

Godrevy Point

The Carracks

Carn Naun Point

Pen Enys Point

Hor Point

Clodgy Point

Porthmeor Beach

St Ives Head

ST IVES

Mussel Point

Wicca Pool

Zennor Head

Tregerthen

B3306

St Ives Bay

CARBIS BAY

Zennor

A3074

HAYLE

A30

miles 0.5 1.0 1.5 2.0 2.5

km 1.0 2.0 3.0 4.0

Left: View to the lighthouse from Godrevy Point.

On Foot (c.6 miles)

Looking north from the romantic little chapel on St Ives Head, the lighthouse still dominates the view. It is on Godrevy Island, which is now privately owned although the mainland opposite it belongs to the National Trust. Appropriately, perhaps, it is now as unreachable as it was in the first half of the novel it inspired. Godrevy Point is well worth a visit for a bathe and a picnic, but a suburban sprawl of bungalows at Carbis Bay and Hayle has lessened the attractions of the five-mile traipse towards it along the endless sands of St Ives Bay.

It may seem a shade contrary, but a much more satisfying walk is to do what I did with my daughters In September 1998: turn your back on the lighthouse and take the cliff path from St Ives Head to Zennor. This was a favourite ramble of the Stephen family, and in later years Leonard and Virginia acquired a string of cottages at Tregerthen, very close to Zennor. 'One of them has a tower and great windows', she wrote to Ka Cox on 12 August 1919. 'There are 7 rooms in all: and in the best country in all Cornwall to my thinking, between St Ives and Gurnards Head, a mile from Zennor.'

Do not be deluded by the apparent shortness of this walk on a map, the tameness of the grass across which it first leads or the sunshine in which you will probably set out. Take, as Virginia's family invariably did, stout footwear, sustenance and waterproofs. Cars can be left in the car-park above Porthmeor Beach, a broad golden sweep of sand with snowy-white rollers of surf. If the waves are right, there will be dozens of black shapes bobbing in the water: modern seals, Neoprene-clad surfers, waiting for the Big One.

You are now heading, erratically, south-westward. The tidy municipal Alcohol-free Zone (Clean Up After Your Dog) west of the beach soon gives way to rougher, springier turf, jewelled with tiny flowers. From time to time, turn to see a shifting succession of views of the lighthouse. The path is very rough at times, the local granite implacably resistant to erosion. There are vertiginous views down to turquoise-tinted bays, most of them unreachable except from the sea.

At one point, a local enthusiast has put up a small notice drawing attention to a crag that juts out over the sea fifty yards down from the path. 'The rock below is one of my favourite places', it says. 'Sit there for a moment if you have time.' We did, watching the gulls wheeling below us, absorbing the light, the colour, the air that Virginia's father once described as 'soft as silk, with a fresh sweet taste like new milk'.

If you set out after lunch, especially on an autumn afternoon, the light as you approach Zennor is breath-taking, silhouetting the rocks against a shimmering silver sea. 'Here we spread out our tea, & that finished, walk home again in the dark', Virginia recalled. 'Last night it was dusk when we started, but we had to take a long look at the Gurnard's Head and the misty shapes beyond.'

You can make a ten minute detour to see Tregerthen cottages, but if our experience was anything to judge by, you will by now be more set on getting to Zennor itself. The signpost back at Porthmeor did not exaggerate: it is easily six and a half miles as the foot slogs up and down rather than four as the crow flies. To have succeeded in our original plan, which was to walk back by the inland footpath running straight back to St Ives, linking together the succession of little farms it passes like beads on a necklace, we should have set out after breakfast rather than after lunch. A sudden downpour out of the clear blue sky settled things. At the Tinners' Arms in Zennor, we telephoned for a taxi.

It was, however, all in the spirit of our mentor, who loved motoring. She wrote to Vita Sackville-West in May 1930: 'We had a superb drive from Penzance over the moor to Zennor, all the gorse blazing against a pale blue sea, to St Ives; where I saw my Lighthouse, and the gate of my home, through tears – thinking how my mother died at my age; or next year to it.'

'It was Sleeping Beauty's Castle'

A little statue of an angel is fixed above the arch to the entrance of Vita Sackville-West's tower room at Sissinghurst. Reaching forward, but also looking back, a light-footed listening spirit, it is the perfect symbol of the woman who put it there. Today, Vita's name and that of Sissinghurst are inseparably linked, but it was only the 'technical fault', as she put it bitterly, of being female that brought her there. Had she been a man she would have had her heart's desire and inherited the great house of Knole after her father died. 'I suppose my love for Knole has gone deeper than anything else in my life', she wrote to its new heir, Edward Sackville-West. Many of her books celebrated it: *Knole and the Sackvilles* and her edition of the *Diary of Lady Anne Clifford* directly, *The Edwardians* in fiction. Her friend and lover Virginia Woolf immortalised her wished-for role as its once and future heir in the novel *Orlando*.

But Sissinghurst was some compensation. 'When I first saw it on a spring day in 1930, it caught instantly at my heart and my imagination', she wrote in her diary, 'I fell flat in love with it; love at first sight. I saw what might be made of it. It was Sleeping Beauty's Castle; but a castle running away into sordidness and squalor, a garden crying out for rescue. It was easy to foresee, even then, what a struggle we should have to redeem it.'

Vita's birthplace, Knole in Kent, was central to many of her books, and the inspiration for Virginia Woolf's *Orlando*.

The most prominent feature of the old Elizabethan house of Sissinghurst is the great tower gateway which once fronted the mansion built by the Baker family. Since all that remained of that mansion when Vita Sackville-West and her husband, Harold Nicolson, bought the site in 1930 was the late fifteenth-century service range and stables that had fronted the early Tudor forecourt, the tower had changed its nature: it was a retreat from rather than an introduction to the house.

For their first few nights at Sissinghurst, Harold and Vita slept in the tower on two camp-beds, reading by candlelight. But it rapidly became Vita's private world. Her writing-room was established in the room over its arch. The wide desk faced the wall, looking into an ancient tapestry landscape rather than a real one; a brown corduroy-covered settee flanked the fire. There is a little withdrawing-room beyond it, formed by a second tower, lined from floor to ceiling with books. In 1935 electricity was installed and a sensible brick fireplace was fitted. But even though the room was bitterly cold in winter, Vita rarely bothered to light a fire – preferring to pile more and more coats and blankets on herself, or just to use a single bar of a Belling electric fire.

Vita loved to go up to the roof of the tower, from where she could see the magical garden, which she and Harold had planned from that very viewpoint, take shape. In summer she gardened in the daytime and wrote at night, her only companion was one of her Alsatian dogs. She liked to write by candlelight. No one came up its stairs uninvited, and the invitees were a privileged few. They included, of course, Virginia Woolf.

Vita wrote twenty books in her tower room, including *All Passion Spent* (1931), her best-known novel. She often mentions the tower and the view from it in her writing. Its spectral character at night is celebrated in her poem 'In Absence':

No lights are burning in the ivory tower
Like a tall lily in the moonlight risen . .

In *Family History* (1932), the heroine Evelyn Jarrold visits her lover's castle and finds 'an untidy courtyard, enclosed by ruined walls, and, opposite, a narrow tower springing up to a height

Sissinghurst Castle, Kent

Vita and her beloved 'Sleeping Beauty's Castle' taken from the garden at Sissinghurst, *c*.1940. Her desk (below) can be seen in the tower room, adorned with fresh flowers and photographs.

while working on her last book, *Daughter of France*, are still within reach of her chair, the gardeners still keep fresh flowers in the small white vase that always stood on it.

It was, ironically, not Vita but her husband Harold who wrote most at Sissinghurst – some three million words of daily diary jottings, recorded every day after breakfast on one of his three typewriters (Rikki, Tikki and Tavi). They were consigned to a filing cabinet immediately, 'without thought of publication'. Edited by Vita and Harold's son Nigel, they provide an extraordinary picture of a quite unique relationship.

with lovely, glinting windows'. Later, we read of how 'the heavy gold sunshine enriched the old brick with a kind of patina, and made the tower cast a long shadow across the garden, like the finger of a gigantic sundial veering slowly with the sun'.

Gradually, Sissinghurst and its garden changed Vita's primary literary preoccupations from people and the past to plants and the present. Her long poems, *The Land* (1926) and *The Garden* (1946), now far from fashionable, are the best expressions of her feeling for nature. 'She simply wrote about what she loved, in a way that was familiar to her', says the modern poet U. A. Fanthorpe, quoting a few lines to make her point:

All's brown and red: the robin and the clods,
And umber half-light of the potting-shed,
The terra-cotta of the pots, the brown
Sacking with its peculiar autumn smell.

Between the years of 1946 and 1961, Vita wrote delightfully personal weekly gardening columns for the *Observer*, which, reprinted as *In Your Garden*, are still instructive and inspiring.

She died in 1962. The contents of her room and the photographs on her desk – of Virginia, Harold and the Brontë sisters – remain just as she left them. The volumes she had to hand

The Scene of the Crime

Better if the country be real, and he has walked every foot of it and knows every milestone. But even with imaginary places, he will do well at the beginning to provide a map; as he studies it, relations will appear that he has not thought upon; he will discover obvious, though unsuspected shortcuts and footpaths for his messengers; and even when a map is not all the plot, as it was in *Treasure Island*, it will be found to be a mine of suggestion.

Robert Louis Stevenson, 'My First Book'

Thrillers and crime novels are not necessarily closely connected with real places, but those that linger in the mind tend to be the ones with vivid settings as well as vital characters. Where would Stevenson's *Kidnapped* be without the Scottish lochs and glens, Margery Allingham's *Tiger in the Smoke* without seedy, fog-drowned London, or Colin Dexter's *Inspector Morse* novels without Oxford's ancient spires?

One of the earliest true thriller writers was Robert Louis Stevenson (1850-94). No one was more certain that 'the author must know his countryside, whether real or imaginary, like his hand; the distances, the points of the compass, the place of the sun's rising, the behaviour of the moon, should all be beyond cavil' (*The Art of Writing*, 1894). Stevenson went on to explain that, having been picked up once or twice on matters of verisimilitude, he never wrote without careful research.

With an almanac and the map of the country, and the plan of the house, either actually plotted on paper or already and immediately apprehended in the mind, a man may hope to avoid some of the grossest possible blunders ... it is my contention – my superstition, if you like – that who is faithful to his map and consults it, and draws from it his inspiration, daily and hourly, gains positive support, and not mere negative immunity from accident. The tale has a root there; it grows in that soil; it has a spine of its own behind the words.

The estuary of the Helford River in Cornwall, a favourite haunt of Daphne du Maurier.

The closest follower in Stevenson's footsteps was John Buchan (1875-1940). Such ripping yarns as *The Thirty-Nine Steps* (1915) and *John Macnab* (1925) make use of Buchan's childhood home in the valley of the Tweed, his Oxford house at Elsfield and holidays spent in north Kent, Lochaline and Inverpolly.

Daphne du Maurier (1907-89) was tuned in to a rare degree to the spirit of place. She took Cornwall and all things Cornish to her heart. 'I walked this land with a dreamer's freedom and with a waking man's perception' she wrote in the foreword to *Enchanted Cornwall* (1989), the last of her books. 'Places, houses whispered to me their secrets and shared with me their sorrows and their joys. And in return I gave them something of myself, a few of my novels passing into the folk-lore of this ancient place.'

The American master of the crime thriller, Raymond Chandler (1888-1959), agreed that the mystery novel 'must be about real people in a real world'. The famous modern detective novelist P. D. James also finds that 'it is often the setting that sparks off my creative imagination. A desolate stretch of coast, an old and sinister house, an atmospheric part of London, a closed community such as a nurses' home, a village, a forensic science laboratory.'

Many authors make things easier for themselves and their readers by setting their stories in a part of the country well known for its outstanding beauty. Wilkie Collins's immensely atmospheric *The Woman in White* (1860), regarded by many as the first true detective novel, is set in Cumberland as well as London. Sir Arthur Conan Doyle's *The Hound of the Baskervilles* (1902) is famously set on Dartmoor in Devon; his less well-known story 'Devil's Foot' takes place in a thinly disguised Mullion Cove (the Lizard, Cornwall). Michael Gilbert's *The Empty House* (1979) is set on Exmoor; Mary Stewart's *The Ivy Tree* (1962) is set close to Hadrian's Wall. Edmund Crispin's last and best book, *Glimpses of the Moon* (1977), takes place in a Devonshire village very similar to the one in which he had his writing retreat.

Mullion Cove on the
Lizard peninsula in
Cornwall, the setting
of Arthur Conan
Doyle's story
'Devil's Foot'.

The parkland at Trelissick is among the Cornish settings used by W. J. Burley for his Wycliffe detective novels.

W. J. Burley was fifty-two when his first Wycliffe book *Three-Toed Pussy* was published in 1968. It was set in a village in his home county of Cornwall. Although the action of his very popular Wycliffe series concentrates on the tensions found in closed groups – villages, country houses, businesses – Burley likes to use 'actual locations in Cornwall and Devon, confusing the topography slightly to avoid the need of seeming to represent actual people'. Trelissick is a favourite setting, notably in *Wycliffe and the Dead Flautist* and *Wycliffe and the Four Jacks*. Kiberick Cove appears in *Charles and Elizabeth*. Zennor Head and other places in Penwith appear in *Wycliffe and the Guild of Nine*.

Reginald Hill specialises in Yorkshire settings, and in those of his native Cumberland. *Fell of Dark* (1986) is a Buchanesque adventure, part detective story and part psychological thriller. *The Long Kill* (1996) continues the tradition examined in Chapter Five of men who come to the Lakes and fall in love with both its landscape and its women:

> For the present though the fell tops were clearer. He raised his eyes to them and felt a surge of longing, almost sexual in its intensity, to be up there, to be walking with the wind on his face and his mind clear of all past guilt and future care. He had fallen in love with more than a woman, he told himself. He had fallen in love with a landscape too. The two were linked in a way he did not attempt to analyse further than saying that the woman he wanted was here, and the place he wanted to be with that woman was here also.

Jessica Mann, who has lived in Cornwall for most of her life, has often used National Trust-owned lands as the setting for her novels. *Telling Only Lies* (1992) has scenes at Zennor; *The Only Security* (1973) happens close to Godrevy Lighthouse; and *Private Inquiry* (1996) opens in St Ives. *Hanging Fire* (1997) takes place on Land's End, and *Faith, Hope and Homicide* (1991) at Tintagel.

For Anthony Price, 'looking for, finding and enjoying settings for stories – what might be called "location shooting" – was one of the main pleasures of book production. Many are amalgams or adaptations, but these disguises are not heavy'. Hadrian's Wall, Northumberland, is the location of *Colonel Butler's Wolf* (1973), the story of a middle-ranking intelligence officer who walks it in the line of duty and comes to see himself as a Soldier of the Wall, holding off the barbarians. Price used Rievaulx Abbey, Yorkshire, for the tragic ending of *Tomorrow's Ghost* (1979), and the north Devon coast and Exmoor for both *Our Man in Camelot* (1976) and *For the Good of the State* (1987).

It is the pin-sharp accuracy of such writers' fictional mapping of

England that makes detective novels with evocative settings so popular with exiles and travellers. Cyril Connolly (1903-74) spelt out their nostalgic appeal when he wrote of how, when living in the South of France, he spent his days

> walking with Inspector French round the Mumbles, gazing down winter estuaries, making innumerable railway journeys, exploring Rochester with Thorndike, going with Mr Fletcher to county towns, till I could find my way in any of them to the Doctor's pleasant Georgian home, the rectory, the spinster's cottage, the eccentric lawyer's office.

Hadrian's Wall in Northumberland has played host to numerous crime scenes, including those in Mary Stewart's *The Ivy Tree* and *Colonel Butler's Wolf* by Anthony Price.

Such books were, he believed, 'the last repository of the countryside, their local colour beautiful as well as useful'. Today, Connolly's favourite writers are familiar only to addicts of the detective story genre. Inspector French was the creation of Freeman Wills Croft, Thorndike of R. Austen Freeman. J. S. Fletcher was not a fictional policeman but an author, now largely forgotten, who wrote innumerable novels between the wars. Two of his best books, *The Middle Temple Murder* and *The Charing Cross Murder*, took place in London, but most – such as *The Box Hill Murder*, *The South Foreland Murder*, *The Yorkshire Moors Murder* – had accurate descriptions of real places.

TRAIL **The Road to Manderley**

1

Of all Daphne du Maurier's Cornish novels, none has more resonance, more intensity, more atmosphere than *Rebecca* (1938). Doom-laden Manderley, 'secretive and silent' and veiled in its tangled woods, is as much a character in the story as any of the people. Its setting was inspired by a house three miles west of Fowey called Menabilly, the home of the Rashleigh family. Daphne first discovered it by unabashed trespass, shortly after her parents bought a holiday house in Fowey (Ferryside). The ancient house was shuttered and closed-up, its drive as thickly overgrown as that of Manderley in the dream sequence at the very start of *Rebecca*.

> Last night I dreamt I went to Manderley again ... The drive wound away in front of me, twisting and turning ... The beeches with white, naked limbs leant close to one another, their branches intermingled in a strange embrace, making a vault above my head like the archway of a church ... a lilac had mated with a copper beech, and to bind them yet more closely to one another, the malevolent ivy, always an enemy to grace, had thrown her tendrils about the pair and made them prisoners.

Fascinated by Menabilly's hidden quality, Daphne gained permission from the Rashleighs to wander in its woods. 'The house possessed me from that day, even as a woman holds her lover,' she wrote in a memoir about her first discovery of it. She was then a dreamy twenty-two-year old, who preferred the peace of Cornwall to the hectic pace of social life in London. It was at Ferryside that she wrote her first novel – *The Loving Spirit* (1931), a tale spun from the sight of a wreck on the shore with an extraordinary figurehead. It was an immediate success, and inspired a dashing Grenadier Guards officer known as 'Boy' Browning to come down from London and cruise to and fro in Fowey Harbour in his motor-boat *Ygdrasil* until he could engineer an introduction to its author. Like a prince in a fairy-tale, he married her that same summer, and the couple spent their honeymoon in a remote little inlet on the Helford River known as Frenchman's Creek. Later, this would become famous, in du Maurier's novel of the same name, as the haunt of a French pirate, loved by an aristocratic but tomboyish English lady.

The marriage was long and fulfilling, but not quite a fairy-tale. Browning was a man of the world, with something of a roving eye. Daphne, nine years younger, felt as immature and inadequate as her heroine in *Rebecca*. Browning had been engaged to a glamorous, self-confident debutante called Jan Ricardo, and Daphne recalls how she once found a bundle of her letters, carefully preserved, in one of her husband's drawers. 'The green-eyed monster showed no mercy then, nor would she now.'

Rebecca was written in 1938, when Daphne was in Egypt with her husband. The yearning for Cornwall in its opening pages was real enough, but at that time Menabilly was still derelict and empty. It was well after publication of *Rebecca*, in 1943, that against all advice Daphne arranged to lease the dilapidated house from the Rashleighs and to restore it, making it a home for herself and her family for the next twenty years.

So it is the setting of Menabilly, rather than the house itself, which is exactly that of *Rebecca*'s Manderley. To find 'the mullioned windows ... the great stone hall, the wide doors open to the library, the Peter Lelys and Vandykes on the walls, the exquisite staircase leading to the minstrels' gallery', literary explorers will have to look from afar at another, much grander house – Milton Park (not normally open to the public), near Peterborough, which Daphne visited as a little girl.

By Car, then on Foot (*c.*5 miles)

Menabilly is not open to the public, so please keep to the footpaths. Kerrith, the main town in the story, is, in reality, Fowey, a cliff-hanger of a port, more fitted to seagulls and pedestrians than cars. Admire Ferryside, which overlooks the ferry to Bodinnick, from the window of the Riverside Hotel. Then drive by car out of Fowey on the A3082. After three miles, take the small turning on the left signposted to Polkerris. Ignore two right-hand turns to Polkerris and keep straight on to the farm at Menabilly Barton. Cars can be left in a field ('20p in the milk churn, please. Your honesty will keep prices down.'), and from there you can take a steep footpath, thick with foxgloves, ox-eye daisies and honeysuckle, down to the shore to the twin coves and boathouse cottage of Polridmouth. You can also approach by foot from Fowey, by walking along the well-signposted coastal path.

This is where the *Je Reviens*, Rebecca's ominously named little yacht, was moored or dragged up on the beach (there is still a winch on the foreshore). Rebecca entertained her lovers in the boathouse here, watched through the window by poor simple Ben, the beachcomber. It was in this bay that the sunken yacht with Rebecca's body was discovered, and there are still the remains of a wreck on the far spit of the bay, a ship that Daphne actually saw break its back on the rocks in the stormy January of 1930.

Polridmouth has no curving breakwater; that was borrowed from Polkerris, the tiny hamlet just along the coast. And the novel exaggerated the contrast between the two coves and their approaches: the 'Happy Valley' with its Eden-like paradise of pale virginal blossoms, and the track from the troubled, memory-haunted house, caged within 'glaring rhododendrons, luscious and proud'. Poetic licence, no doubt. Du Maurier uses nature throughout the story to telling effect: the monstrous trees and tangled undergrowth that hold Manderley in thrall like Sleeping Beauty's castle, the wheeling, ominous rooks, the sea in all its changing moods.

Finally, gird your loins to climb the steeply sloping westward coastal path towards the tall red and white mariner's mark on Gribbin Head. From the crest of the hill halfway up it you will get the best legitimate view you are allowed of Menabilly: a long grey roof and a hint of a line of Georgian windows, tucked behind an impenetrable bank of rhododendrons. It seems altogether appropriate that it should remain a house of secrets.

MAP
OS Explorer 107: St Austell, Liskeard, Fowey

Far left: Sunset at Frenchman's Creek, the inlet which lent its name to Daphne du Maurier's novel.

Left: Gribbin Head in Cornwall. The red and white striped tower, the Gribbin day mark, was built to help mariners distinguish the peninsula from the Dodman, nine miles south-west.

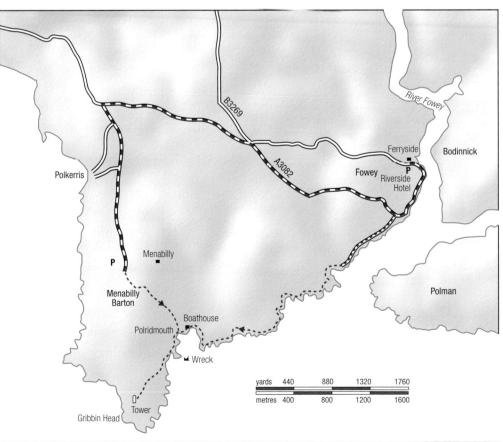

Miss Scarlett in the Library with the Lead Piping

Ever since E. W. Hornung's gentleman burglar Raffles snitched Lady Melrose's diamonds from Milchester Abbey (*The Amateur Cracksman*, 1899), the great house has been a popular setting for what Colin Watson has called 'snobbery with violence'. But there is more to the uses of the closed world of the country house than snobbery. W. H. Auden's essay 'The Guilty Vicarage' – reprinted in *The Dyer's Hand* (1963) – points out that 'a society with an elaborate ritual' is a good take-off point for a successful detective novel. 'The murderer uses his knowledge of the ritual to commit the crime and can be caught only by someone who acquires an equal or superior familiarity with it.' The milieu of the story is all part of this ritual:

> In the detective story and its mirror image, the Quest for the Grail, maps (the ritual of space) and timetables (the ritual of time) are desirable. Nature should reflect its human inhabitants, i.e. it should be the Great Good Place; for the more Eden-like it is, the greater the contradiction of murder.

There is an interesting echo here of the thinking of Henry James, who began to perceive that behind the calm façades and Eden-like parks, all was far from well with English society. The idea that arsenic and old lace, model village and immoral vice, rural idyll and rank evil, could be intertwined to dramatic effect was also voiced early – and with deliberate over-statement – by Arthur Conan Doyle's Sherlock Holmes:

> It is my belief, Watson, founded upon my experience, that the lowest and vilest alleys in London do not present a more dreadful record of sin than does the smiling and beautiful countryside… Think of the deeds of hellish cruelty, the hidden wickedness which may go on, year in, year out, in such places, and none the wiser.

View of the south front of Mottisfont Abbey in Hampshire from G. F. Prosser's *Select Illustrations of Hampshire* (1883). The country house has long been a favourite setting for crime novels, and Peter Dickinson is one of many to have 'borrowed' them.

The closed world of a substantial, self-sufficient house is, of course, a perfect setting for detective puzzles of the 'locked room' variety, as the hugely popular and very English game Cluedo attests. To make plots even more baffling, the action is frequently set in winter, when the risk of footsteps in the snow makes outside interference virtually impossible. Notable examples of classic country house murders include J. S. Fletcher's *Mortover Grange*, Agatha Christie's *The Mysterious Affair at Styles*, Michael Innes's *Appleby's End* and Nicholas Blake's *Thou Shell of Death*.

Today, one of the best exponents of the art of murder in stately homes is Peter Dickinson. Because of his power to create coherent and vivid worlds, Dickinson has been called 'the Tolkien of the crime novel', creating new worlds 'with such conviction, such vividness, such coherence that you come easily to believe that they actually exist'. Many do, he admits.

The unnamed abbey in my short story 'The Spring' in a recent collection *Touch and Go* can only be Mottisfont, though there are minor differences in the layout. Shailwood Castle in *The Last Houseparty* is obviously based on Cliveden, both for the general layout (though there are considerable differences) and the social set-up in the 1930s. And Blatchards in *The Yellow Room Conspiracy* is definitely based on Ickworth, not so much in its appearance, etc, but because I used in the book an episode in my own life when I was a bewildered conscript in a base camp at Bury St Edmunds and was invited out to tea at Ickworth.

CRIME NOVELS AS HERITAGE

Traditionally, the crime novel has reflected the world in which it takes place rather than trying to alter or criticise it. 'The satisfactions of the murder mystery for the reader are those that come from a comforting sense of the familiar, the making of some order out of chaos and a new way of understanding the human condition in which we have all been thrown', says Deborah Bonnetti in her essay, 'Murder Can Happen Anywhere'. Crime writers have on the whole been conservatives at heart, and though their heroes and heroines are often anarchically individualist, they depend on the rule of law. The ultimate aim of their books is to reiterate the values of an ordered society in which evil does not triumph over good and evil-doers are punished. Erik Routley believes the enormous popularity of detective novels since the 1920s is a reflection of the fact that

> [they] served the needs of an age in which increasing numbers of literate people were becoming conscious of the need for honouring the notion of moral and social stability [and for] confirmation of their faith in the rightness of order and peaceful societies…The detective story reader is not a lover of violence but a lover of order …Detective stories don't go with permissiveness; they go with

Chiddingstone in Kent typifies the secluded rural village, with the parish church at its heart, that is so often made the home of amateur detectives such as Agatha Christie's Miss Marple.

convention and style and dogma and assurance; they go with the assumption that a society in which authority is accepted and correction by wiser people of the unwise or the young is permitted is a good society.

It would be going too far to claim that crime novels, easy to read and reassuringly moral, have become in effect a highly diverting substitute for the Sunday sermon. But it remains true that as church-going declines and permissiveness increases, more people pay good money to read fictional accounts of criminals unerringly brought to book and of good overcoming evil. Since the abolition of the death penalty it has also become more allowable for modern heroes and heroines to take the law into their own hands and mete out the ultimate justice themselves.

Besides asserting the triumph of good over evil, English crime novels nurture traditional values of a different kind. 'It is the portrayal of what is real for a particular place and its society that gives the mystery novel depth and resonance', argues Bonnetti. 'The English mystery novel, from Agatha Christie, Dorothy Sayers and others to P. D. James, has symbolized the sense of community and enduring human values in the country village or manor house'. In the first chapter of *Appleby's End*, Michael Innes (1906-94) is celebrating the Englishness of English village names as well as poking fun at them: 'Yatter, A ghastly little place. Yatter, Abbot's Yatter and King's Yatter. Then we come to Drool...I think you said you hoped to change at Linger.' Gladys Mitchell (1901-83) shows the strength of her feelings about the mystical nature of all things British by making ancient earthworks, Arthurian relics, morris dancing and May Day rituals habitual mainstays of her plots. One of her heroes, Timothy Herring, is the chairman of the Society for the Preservation of Buildings of Historic Interest.

John Buxton Hilton (1921-86), whose novels are usually set in the Peak District and the wild countryside between Lancashire and Yorkshire, has said that 'I am less interested in puzzles – and certainly in

Above: The glorious angel
roof of St Wendreda's
Church in March,
Cambridgeshire
(below, right), which
so impressed Lord
Peter Wimsey in *The
Nine Tailors*.

violence – than in character, local colour, folk lore, social history and historical influences, most of which loom large in most of my books.'

Today, the American novelists Elizabeth George and Martha Grimes have out-Englished the English in their re-creations of village life in what Colin Wilson memorably christened the 'Mayhem Parva' school of detection. Although both novelists are writing books with a fashionably ironic and modern feel, George's detective is noble, an earl, and she often weaves English history into her plots. Martha Grimes uses such pub names as The Old Fox Deceiv'd or The Dirty Duck as titles for the series of crime novels she has been writing since 1981. Her aristocratic, apparently dilettante sleuth Melrose Plant has distinct echoes of Sayers's Lord Peter Wimsey and Allingham's Albert Campion; her Detective Inspector Richard Jury is akin to Inspectors Dalgliesh, Alleyn and Grant.

Bell, Book and Angel

The setting of Dorothy L. Sayers's (1893-1957) classic bell-ringing detective novel *The Nine Tailors* is the watery landscape of her childhood, and the tailors in question are church bells, each distinct in character and murderous in combination. Her research into how to ring them was so thorough that, although she

Flat as a chess-board, and squared like a chess-board with intersecting dyke and hedge, the fens went flashing past them.

Dorothy L. Sayers, *The Nine Tailors*

never pulled a bell-rope herself, the *Oxford Dictionary of Music* still recommends *The Nine Tailors* as a lucid exposition of the ancient English art of change-ringing.

The action centres on the village of Fenchurch St Paul, and its sister hamlets of Fenchurch St Peter and Fenchurch St John. The fictional Fenchurches closely resemble the grouping of Christchurch, Upwell and Outwell, twelve miles north of Ely. Dorothy's father Henry was rector of Christchurch from 1917 until his death in 1928. Her mother died nine months later and was buried in the same grave. *The Nine Tailors*, with its gentle rector Theodore Venables and his kindly wife, is undoubtedly a tribute to them. 'It's to be all about a big church in the Fens and a grave which is suddenly found to have an extra body in it!!' she wrote in February 1932.

Although Christchurch's capacious rectory is a possible home for the Venables, its small redbrick church is nothing like the 'young cathedral' of Fenchurch St Paul. For that extraordinary place, with its glorious angel roof, the tour takes a diversion westward to March. Once inside its St Wendreda's Church, prepare yourself for a shock.

> Incredibly aloof, flinging back the light in a dusky shimmer of bright hair and gilded outspread wings, soared the ranked angels, cherubim and seraphim, choir over choir, from corbel and hammer-beam floating face to face uplifted. 'My God!' muttered Wimsey, not without reverence. And he softly repeated 'He rode upon the cherubim and did fly; He came flying upon the wings of the wind.'

Anywhere but in Britain, an interior like this would mean a throng of gaping tourists. St Wendreda's double hammerbeam roof boasts 118 angels and a full complement of apostles, saints and martyrs. Carved between 1470 and 1520, it is an astonishing achievement – some say the finest of its kind in Europe.

The other startling element was borrowed from history. In 1713, Denver Sluice burst under a high spring tide and a violent wind, and tidal water, together with the flood-swollen Bedford Rivers, turned back up the Ouse, drowning the whole area. 'Since, for my story, I wanted a sudden disaster, and the quick release of a considerable volume of water,' wrote Sayers in *The Spectator* (2 April 1937), 'I borrowed the framework of this ancient catastrophe, doing the thing on an altogether more modest scale, with a smaller river and sluice, allowing only a mild flood of a fortnight or so, and drowning only a few isolated parishes.'

TRAIL **2**

By Car (*c.*30 miles)

This is a trip for the car-borne explorer rather than the walker, not only because at least three far-flung churches are involved in the magnificent amalgam of Fenchurch St Paul, but also because a walk which embraced them all would be both tediously long and unrewarding. Since the early 1930s, pylons, telephone wires and nondescript agricultural buildings have diminished the eery Fenland atmosphere the novel evokes so memorably.
If you want to get the atmosphere of the Fens when Sayers was writing, start your tour at the National Trust-managed Wicken Fen, a little south of Ely on the A1123.

Drive from here westwards along the A1123 to Bluntisham. Dorothy Sayers grew up in the vicarage, which has recently been rebuilt as a partly residential, partly commercial development. Drive back from Bluntisham to Earith, where you will see the grey-green greasy waters of the Great Ouse. This is one end of a huge loop of river, highly vulnerable to flooding until the Hundred Foot Drain (or New Bedford River) was constructed, with a sluice at each end. The other end is close to Downham Market at Denver – the name and country seat given by Sayers to the aristocratic family of her hero Lord Peter Wimsey.

Take the B1381 north-east to Sutton, then turn left on the A142 to March. When you get to March, ignore the first church you see and head for the extremely tall steeple of St Wendreda's Church in the northern part of the town. A notice on the door explains how to borrow the key if it is locked. Allow plenty of time to enjoy its fabulous interior, before taking the B1099 eastwards. The road zigzags vigorously over dykes and levels to Bedlam Bridge. After this you must turn sharply to the left (on the B1098) in order to avoid the fate of Lord Peter and Bunter in the opening lines of *The Nine Tailors*:

> The narrow hump-backed bridge, blind as an eyeless beggar, spanned the dark drain at right angles, dropping plump down on the narrow road that crested the dyke. Coming a trifle too fast across the bridge ... he overshot the road and plunged down into the deep ditch beyond.

Searchers after authenticity could, like Wimsey and Bunter, leave their car here, and trudge for a mile and a half alongside the 'slow and unforgiving waters' of the Sixteen Foot Drain, model for the Thirty Foot of the story. They will come to 'a signpost and a secondary road that turned off to the right'. It leads to Christchurch, rather than Fenchurch St Paul. Notice the Dun Cow public house, which appears as the Red Cow in the novel.

Nearby Upwell straddles the ancient course of the River Nene, hemmed into Well Creek in 1290. As you approach Upwell, you cross Popham's Eau, a channel which carries the Nene to the Great Ouse, and becomes Potter's Lode in the story. St Peter's Church also has an angel roof, gilded in places, and its galleries are still in position.

'Hideous cumbersome things they were. They ran right acoss the aisle windows, obscuring all the upper tracery and blocking the light, and were attached to the arcading… If you want to see what they were like,' added the Rector, 'go and look at Upwell church near Wisbech.'

Follow the A1122 to Downham Market. Just before the town at Salter's Lode, you can stop to admire the dramatic meeting of different levels of water at Denver Sluice. The tidal part of the Great Ouse lies to the north, and the higher sluiced section, the Ten Mile River, is to the south. This is where the disastrous flood of 1713 happened.

Turn back here and take the A1101 towards Wisbech. Turn right on the A47 towards King's Lynn. Turn left after two and a half miles to Terrington St Clement and the third church of the trail, the model for the belfry in *The Nine Tailors*. In 1613 and again in 1670, when the river burst its banks and flooded all the marshlands, the people of this village took refuge in the church tower. Its peal of eight bells was rehung in 1925, an event which might well have inspired the bell-ringing heart of Sayers' story. One carries a 1595 legend not dissimilar to those given to the Fenchurch peal: 'Nunc Clemens ego cano vobis ore jocunda' – 'I, Clement, sing to you with joyful voice'.

Left: Wicken Fen in Cambridgeshire in the grip of severe frost.

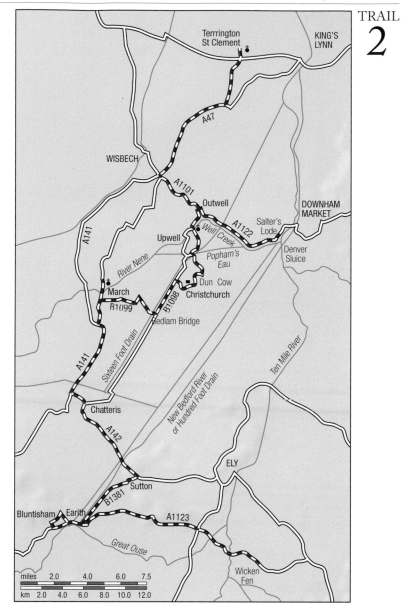

MAP
OS Landranger 143:
Ely, Wisbech

Moving on from Mayhem Parva

In the last two decades, many crime writers have begun to chafe at the boundaries imposed by Mayhem Parva. Especially if a film or television adaptation is hoped for, physical as well as cerebral action is increasingly necessary. Their preoccupations have shifted from a purely individual battle between the good and the evil action to a wider portrait of society.

In 'The Guilty Vicarage', W. H. Auden distinguishes between the settings required for the detective novel and the thriller. The detective novel, he writes, requires a closed world – a country house, a small and tightly integrated village, a train or ship, an institution such as a school or a business. Its members are closely related: everyone within is suspect and one must be guilty. The thriller, on the other hand, 'requires an open society in which any stranger may be a friend or an enemy in disguise'. It ranges across a much wider terrain.

That wider terrain is a feature of books that are in fact successful hybrids of the two genres that Auden explicitly contrasted, the spy thriller and the detective mystery. Anthony Price, some of whose titles are mentioned earlier, excels at such books. 'The setting or background of each story reflected whatever piece of private research (or hobby) I was engaged in at the time', he explains.

Andrew Garve was another a man of action. When his stories don't involve small boats and seafaring, they are set in such dramatic places as Cornish tin-mines or even, as in *The Sea Monk* , a lighthouse. Glyn Carr, an enthusiastic climber, made a name for himself with gripping yarns of skulduggery in very high places: *Death on Milestone Buttress, Death Under Snowdon* and *Swing Away Climber*. He follows in the footsteps of Gwen Moffatt, whose intrepid Melinda Pink is a Justice of the Peace and a mountaineer as well as a novelist. *Persons Unknown* foreshadows many more modern environmentally aware novels with a plot involving the threat to build a nuclear power station on a remote and beautiful part of the Welsh coast.

Ann Cleeves's interest in ornithology is reflected in her recurring

The mountains of Snowdonia provide the perfect sinister backdrop to thrillers such as Glyn Carr's *Death Under Snowdon*.

Blakeney Point in Norfolk,
the setting of novels
by Ann Cleeves and
Jack Higgins.

theme of birdwatchers, but place is always an integral part of the action in her books. Several are set on the coast of her native county of Northumberland. The setting of *Come Death and High Water* is a nature reserve off the Devon coast which evokes both Lundy and Burgh Island. Kinness in *Murder in Paradise* is recognisably Fair Isle, south of the Shetlands. *A Bird in the Hand* includes scenes of birdwatchers on the north Norfolk coast and on the Lizard; it also provides an interesting derivation for the word 'twitchers': 'Twitching is derived from the Wessex phrase "twitching like a long dog", which Hardy used and is still common today in rural counties. A long dog is a greyhound. It could be defined as "straining at the leash", perhaps. So a twitcher is a person who is in that state when he hears news of a bird which he has never seen.'

Crime novelists have always been acute social observers. 'Novelists are unpaid sociologists who make up for their lack of statistical evidence with inspired guesses', wrote Ian Rodger in the *Guardian* in 1967. Pre-war writers concentrated on a rather limited middle-class sphere, but even so, Agatha Christie is already being read for her attitudes as well as her plots. Henry Wade's *Too Soon to Die* and *A Dying Fall* were accurate barometers of the changing values of 1950s society, and P. D. James's books and the numerous writers of feminist sleuth novels will no doubt form the subject of future PhD theses on British mores of our own time.

Such ambitions are conscious agendas for many modern crime novelists. The result can be ponderous and pretentious, but the successful instruct and entertain in equal measure. Colin Watson sets his Flaxborough series not in an idyllic village but in a small, vulgar and lively East Anglian town. Flaxborough, says one of its inhabitants to a newcomer, is 'a high-spirited town ... like Gomorrah' (*The Flaxborough Crab*). His Lucille Edith Cavell Teatime is not the Miss Marple her name suggests but a confidence trickster with a distinctly racy attitude to life. In *The Flaxborough Crab* she sells an aphrodisiac 'Samson Salad' made out of dandelion leaves, and complains that there isn't enough sexual action in the town.

Thrillers also represent both past and present places and people with convincing accuracy. Geoffrey Household's *Rogue Male* (1939) is probably the most memorable of all manhunts, but Jack Higgins runs him close in intensity of suspense. *The Eagle Has Landed* (1975) was, according to Higgins, 'at least 50 per cent documented historical fact'. It was made into a film, shot on location on the north Norfolk coast near Blakeney and Stiffkey. Folk memory in the local pubs there is now a delightful mix of the original wartime drama that inspired it, and the almost equally memorable drama of film-making.

TRAIL 3 The Eagle Has Landed

> It was a strange, mysterious sort of place, the kind that made the hair lift on the back of his head. Sea creeks and mudflats, the great pale reeds merging with the mist and somewhere out there, the occasional cry of a bird, the invisible beat of wings.

> Jack Higgins, *The Eagle Has Landed*

In 1948 Jack Higgins was a young national serviceman in the Horse Guards in Germany. An acute shortage of soldiers meant that many Poles and Germans were recruited into the Allied forces, and one night, conversation turned to the wartime exploits of commandos, including a German plan to assassinate Churchill. 'There was even a specific date and place for it – the autumn of 1943, when they discovered Churchill was spending a few days in Norfolk.' It didn't mean anything at the time. But twenty-five years later, when Higgins was an established writer, he took a family holiday on the north Norfolk coast in the early 1970s. They stayed at the Blakeney Hotel, overlooking the shallow treacherous estuary of the River Glaven and the ever-lengthening forefinger of shingle that makes up Blakeney Point. Higgins was fascinated by the sandy beaches stretching into infinity, the eerie salt marshes and 'the little villages that you can find once in the maze of little lanes, and then never find again'.

There were also tangible relics of the war: pillboxes, tank traps and machine-gun posts. Old photos in country pubs show-ed crashed German planes on the shore, and the locals gossiped of the days when invasion was on everybody's lips and you had to have a pass to travel anywhere twenty miles inland from the Wash, of the top secret units of Americans, Poles and British commandos and – at this point something clicked in Higgins's mind – of a lightning autumn visit by Churchill to the Norfolk bomber stations that were such an important part of the Allied offensive. It wasn't officially reported until the Prime Minister had left – but it was the same year as that of the assassination plan mentioned by the soldiers in Germany.

Research fuelled surmise, which in its turn inspired the plot. How was it that the Germans got hold of the top secret 'Oboe' night bombing surveillance system in 1943, and used it to track and shoot the British bombers as they crossed the North Sea? 'Oboe' was linked with two ground stations, 'Mouse' in Dover and 'Cat' in Cromer. Could there have been a spy with access to the Norfolk station? 'There weren't supposed to be any enemy agents there, but I felt a character like Joanna Grey filled a vacuum, made sense of a genuine mystery.'

There is still a timeless feel about the Norfolk coast. Far away from the rest of England it has been able to hold on to its old traditions and ancient secrets. It is as easy as ever to imagine that the Eagle could land there. But Jack Higgins still doesn't quite know why the story seized people's imaginations in the way it did. 'I'm sure the accuracy was an important part of it,' he reflected. 'But I think it also said something important about what it was to be a soldier – having to carry out orders, even if you didn't necessarily agree with them.' Choice, as Higgins sees it, is illusion, freedom a luxury the true-hearted do not possess.

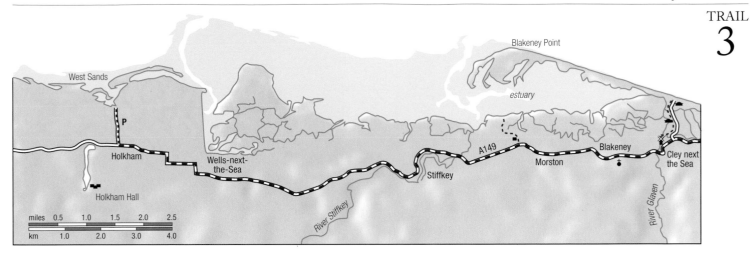

By Car and on Foot (*c.*12 miles)

Most of the novel's action takes place within a few miles of Blakeney, on the north Norfolk coast. Cley, a small village a few miles east, is an ideal place to start re-living *Eagle*. Climb up the beautifully restored windmill and look out across the water meadows to the sea. Take the footpath seawards from the mill along the top of a dyke. About halfway along are the rusty remains of a spherical machine-gun post. Fifteen minutes or so will bring you out at the birdwatchers' car-park at the beginning of Blakeney Point. After admiring the spacious pillbox, a recommended extra is a spectacular four-mile stroll along the Point itself, but as far as the story is concerned, it isn't necessary.

Return to your car and drive westwards along the A149. You will see the grand bulk of Blakeney church, set square in a spacious graveyard. Higgins had Mapledurham, Oxfordshire, in mind as Studley Constable, but the church he describes is unmistakably of Norfolk:

I had expected darkness and gloom inside, but instead, found a medieval cathedral in miniature, flooded with light and astonishingly spacious. The nave arcades were superb, great

Norman pillars soaring up to an incredible wooden roof, richly carved with an assortment of figures, human and animal.

Blakeney's St Nicholas is just like the 'medieval cathedral in miniature'. It has some of the best woodcarving in Norfolk, and ruby red glass lamps glow beneath plaster saints in the north transept.

There are no isolated cottages exactly like Hobs End, the 'marsh warden's cottage' where the wryly philosophical IRA agent Devlin holes up, concealing a jeep and a Bedford truck (for the use of enemy commandos) in its barn. But there may once have been. After you have passed through Morston as you drive westwards along the coast on the A149, you will see a sign saying 'Sailing School, B&B, Fresh Norfolk Oysters for sale' pointing down a rough track. Park your car on the verge and walk down it to a cottage which must once have been suitably simple and tumbledown, but which has since been converted.

Walk past the cottage down to the marshy shore for fine views of the estuary with the point behind. Pick the right moment for weather, and you can imagine Devlin and Ritter shivering in the water, hoping against hope the rescue boat will see them:

Twenty minutes later, the water was up to his chest. He had never been so cold in his life before. He stood on the sand bank, legs apart, supporting Ritter, his right hand holding the luminous signalling ball high, the tide flowing around them.

For the initial parachutists' dropping zone, however, Morston feels a little exposed and open, as does the NT bird-watching reserve at Stiffkey, a little further west. There are no pine trees for Joanna Grey to shelter in, and not much sandy beach for Devlin to lay out his long trail of cycle lights to guide in the laden Dakota.

Drive further west, through Wells-next-the-Sea, to a much more suitable location: West Sands, reached by turning right at Holkham. This is probably the most picturesque beach on the coast, with steep sand dunes knitted with marram grass and a swathe of pine trees, sculpted dramatically by the prevailing north-easterlies. Holkham Hall itself is in about the right position for Meltham, the American Forces' base in the story, though it's a much bigger house, home of the famous eighteenth-century agricultural improvers, the Coke family.

The broad horizons of the Norfolk coast.

MAP

OS Landranger 132: North-west Norfolk;
OS Landranger 133: North-east Norfolk

LORNA DOONE COUNTRY

Left: Old Blundell's School at Tiverton in Devon.

The National Trust's Holnicote Estate in Somerset is at the heart of Lorna Doone country.
Right: Watersmeet.
Below: View to Dunkery Beacon.

R. D. Blackmore's *Lorna Doone* (1869) is one of the earliest English thrillers. The black-hearted Doones, the mysterious and gentle Lorna and the brawny John Ridd are the central characters of a turbulent and extraordinary tale of seventeenth-century Exmoor. It has all the best ingredients of romance – a kidnapped orphan, a dashing highwayman, robbery, murder, near death reunion and, of course, true love.

Few books are more exactly pinned to their home ground; it is a measure of the infancy of the genre that Richard Blackmore (1825-1900) used real names for both places and people throughout the book. Exmoor was his childhood home and he first heard the tales of the marauding Doones and their secret lair in the depths of the moor from his grandfather, rector of Oare, the village at the heart of the story.

Like his hero, John Ridd, and his own father and grandfather, Blackmore went to school at Peter Blundell's School in Tiverton. The original schoolhouse, which Blackmore describes as a 'dark arcade of learning' has been preserved by the National Trust. The great lime trees, the paved causeways and lodges, still exist – so too does the 'Ironing Box', the triangle of grass between two paths and the wall of the school which was the scene of the great fight between John Ridd and Robin Snell.

The little village of Oare is signposted off the A39 halfway between Porlock and Lynmouth. It is still just as John Ridd describes it: 'All above is strong, dark mountain, spread with heath and desolate, but near our house the valleys cove and open warmth and shelter. Here are trees, and bright green grass, and orchards full of contentment.'

Having been killed by the marauding Doones after he saw their watchfire on Dunkery Beacon, John Ridd's father is buried in Oare church. The church also witnesses the climax of the book, when Lorna is shot at the altar by the vengeful Carver Doone. In the graveyard, there are gravestones to Ridds and Snows which testify to the accurate use Blackmore made of local family names. 'Girt John Ridd' was a real historical character, a legendarily strong seventeenth-century wrestler. Blackmore had to make an official apology to a living Nicholas Snow of Oare for implying that the seventeenth-century Ridds were a superior family to their Snow neighbours. Look north from the church across the valley, and you can see the 'pleasant and soft fall of the land round about Plover's Barrows Farm', the Ridds' ancestral home. There is still the wide-awake façade of a house, but it is a later building, Oare Manor (not open to the public).

A little further along the road to the west is 'Lorna Doone Farm', which offers parking, a tea-room and a souvenir shop. This is, in reality, the model for Malmsmead, the home of Farmer Snow and his daughters, the 'fashionable milkmaids' of the story who come up to visit the Ridds 'like fillies trimmed for the fair' when their father and John Ridd make a plan to raise a troop of the militia against the Doones.

What of the secret lair of the Doones, to which John Ridd's mother tramps across the moors to seek satisfaction for the murder of her husband? There has long been dispute as to its whereabouts. James Muirhead, compiler of the 1890 Baedeker *Handbook to Great Britain*, was so struck by the discrepancy between the actual scenery of the Doone Valley and the description of it in *Lorna Doone* that he wrote to the author and complained. Blackmore's reply appeared in the handbook, a frank admission of poetic licence:

> If I had dreamed that it would ever be more than a book of the moment, the descriptions of scenery – which I know as well as I know my garden – would have been kept nearer to their fact. I romanced therein, not to mislead any other, but solely for the uses of my story.

In 1925, Alfred Vowles reported in his guide to Doone Country that he had found the ruins of fourteen dwellings at a point about two and a half miles upstream where Hoccombe Combe joins Badgworthy Water, and positively identified them as the homes of the Doones. 'Fourteen cots my mother counted, and all much of a pattern', says John Ridd. The quick way to approach this is to drive by car to Brendon Two Gates on the

B3223, and then walk across the moors, as Mrs Ridd did, to Hoccombe Water. There are still a few mounds left, and Blackmore may well have been inspired by the sight of then, even though he would have known that they were the remains of a medieval hermit hamlet. Most visitors still accept this as the 'real' Doone Valley. But tucked away to the west of the main stream is, for my money, a much more attractive proposition: Lank Combe.

To find it by John Ridd's accidental route, leave your car at 'Lorna Doone Farm', and take the well-signposted footpath up Badgworthy Water. After Cloud Farm, there is not a house, fence or permanent sign of human life to be seen. Dippers dart along the river, willow warblers warble, swallows swoop, herons rise with lazy, graceful wingstrokes and in the crystal-clear river, fish zip in erratic panic, as prolific as they were when John Ridd wandered up there in search of loaches.

After about a mile, there are two breaks in the hillside to the west. The first is what we literary geographers call a pity, something which is not only not in the story but which rather contradicts the text. Doone Valley was supposed to be all but unapproachable from this angle. Ignore this premature entry, and you will arrive at the second break in the hillside, where a stream cascades down flat slippery rock to join the main river. In wet weather, this becomes a torrent, and the smooth stone slabs of its bed marks it as the famous water slide, the secret entrance to the Doone Valley.

For lo! I stood at the foot of a long pale slide of water [which] neither ran nor fell, nor leaped with any spouting, but made one even slope of it, as if it had been combed or planed, and looking like a plank of deal laid down a deep black staircase.

Today there is a footbridge at this point, which would be another pity, except that most people cross it and disappear upstream to Hoccombe. With luck, you will be left to wander unobtrusively off to the right, clamber up the rocks beside the waterslide and discover the 'deep green valley, carved from the mountains in a perfect oval' of Lank Combe – all by yourself.

Gazetteer

BERKSHIRE

Maidenhead Commons and Cock Marsh: Cookham Dean was the home of Kenneth Grahame, whose *The Golden Age* (1895) and *Dream Days* (1898) celebrated his childhood running wild there. He moved back to Cookham after his marriage in 1899, and the river there became the setting for *The Wind in the Willows* (1908), which was originally written to amuse his son.

BUCKINGHAMSHIRE

Cliveden: The original house was built by George Villiers, 2nd Duke of Buckingham (1666-1696), politician, diplomat, poet and playwright. He was a generous patron to the poet Abraham Cowley, and his dishonourable escapades in the company of the poet John Wilmot, Earl of Rochester, are salaciously recorded by both Samuel Pepys and John Aubrey. Between 1720 and 1751 it was occupied by Frederick, Prince of Wales, under whom it became the hub of an artistic, literary and musical circle. *The Masque of Alfred*, by the poets James Thomson and David Mallet, with music by Thomas Arne, was performed in its cliffside theatre. The most memorable part of this tale of a prince-in-waiting was its climax, a patriotic ode that became immortalised as 'Rule Britannia'. Cliveden became one of the homes of the Astor family in 1893. Under the auspices of the 2nd Viscount Astor and his wife Nancy, it became a fashionable literary and political salon, where Henry James, Rudyard Kipling, George Curzon and Winston Churchill were frequent visitors.

Gray's Monument, Stoke Poges: A classical sarcophagus designed by James Wyatt which stands to the east of the churchyard immortalised by Thomas Gray in 'Elegy in a Country Churchyard'. Gray is buried there, beside his mother. The monument was erected in 1799, twenty-eight years after the poet's death.

CAMBRIDGESHIRE

Wimpole Hall: From 1713-40 Wimpole was the home of Edward Harley, 2nd Earl of Oxford, and the centre of a circle of brilliant writers, scholars and artists including Jonathan Swift, Alexander Pope, and Matthew Prior. Harley's vast and notable library formed the nucleus of the British Library. Wimpole was bought by Rudyard Kipling's daughter Elsie in 1936.

CHESHIRE (INC. WIRRAL)

Alderley Edge: This dramatic sandstone ridge south of Manchester was once a prehistoric settlement. Alan Garner (b.1934) spent his childhood in the village of Alderley Edge and, after leaving Oxford, returned to the area where he wrote his first book, *The Weirdstone of Brisingamen* (1960). Other titles set around Alderley Edge include *Elidor* (1965); *The Owl Service* (1967); *The Old Man of Mow* (1967), the name of a local rock formation; *Red Shift* (1973), and *The Stone Quartet* (1978).

Tatton Park: The model for Cumnor Towers in Mrs Gaskell's last (unfinished) novel *Wives and Daughters*. The nearby village of Knutsford was portrayed in *Cranford* (1853).

CORNWALL

Antony House: Home of the Elizabethan historian Richard Carew, author of the great *Survey of Cornwall* (1602), who witnessed the Armada sweeping up the Channel in 1588.

Bedruthan Steps, Pentire: A precipitous cliff staircase which is mentioned by the novelist Winston Graham as being close to Nampara, home of his fictional hero Ross Poldark. Almost all the books in Graham's *Poldark* saga are set in the triangle of landscape between Padstow, Newquay and Truro. 'Nampara Cove' is based on West Pentire. See also Trerice (below).

Fowey: See p.218. Fowey and the adjacent National Trust coastal holdings are associated with Sir Arthur Quiller Couch (who is commemorated with a granite memorial on Penleath Point) and Kenneth Grahame, who gently caricatured 'Q' as the Water Rat in his *Wind in the Willows*.

Pentireglaze Farm: Scene of Rev. Sabine Baring-Gould's thriller *In The Roar of The Sea* (1892).

Trerice: Exquisite Elizabethan house which appears as Trenwith, the home of Ross Poldark's cousin Francis, in Winston Graham's *Poldark* stories. Graham moved to Perranporth in the 1930s; his former home, Treberran, is now a hotel, Nampara Lodge. See also Bedruthan Steps (above).

CUMBRIA

Acorn Bank: Seventeenth-century walled garden with a famous herb collection. It was restored in the 1930s by Dorothy Una Radcliffe, the Yorkshire travel writer and folk historian.

Borrowdale: The 'immense chaos' and 'dark winding deeps' of Borrowdale were admired by Thomas Pennant (1774) and by innumerable later writers in search of the picturesque. 'Dark rocks yawn at its entrance, terrific as the wildness of a maniac' wrote Ann Radcliffe in 1794. It did not frighten Charles Dodgson ('Lewis Carroll'), whose *Diaries* record that in 1856 he rowed from Keswick to Lodore, then 'walked down Borrowdale and lunched at Seathwaite, where it is said more rain falls in the year than in any other place in England'.

The Hazel Bank Hotel at Rosthwaite stands on the site of 'Herries', home of the hero of Hugh Walpole's novel *Rogue Herries* (1930). Walpole bought Brackenburn in 1923 and spent weeks every year writing there until his death in 1941. The novels of the Herries saga are all set in and around Borrowdale; according to his biographer Rupert Hart-Davis, the house of Adam Paris in *The Fortress* (1932) is set on the site of Brackenburn 'so that much of the scenery could be described straight from his own window'.

Beatrix Potter used Borrowdale as the setting for *Mrs Tiggy-winkle*; its heroine Lucy was inspired by Lucy Carr of Newlands, who she met at Fawe Park, Lingholme, in 1901. Mrs Tiggywinkle was laundress to 'the little lambs at Skelghyl', but the farm illustrated in the story is actually Littletown, higher up the fell towards the ridge of Catbells.

Buttermere: Setting for Nicholas Size's novels *The Secret Valley* (1929) and *Shelagh of Eskdale* (1933), and Melvyn Bragg's *Maid of Buttermere* (see p.158).

Windermere: The inspiration for many poems, the earliest probably being Richard Braithwaite's 'The Fatall Nuptiall' (1636) which recorded the death of forty-seven wedding guests in a ferry accident in 1635. A memorable passage in *The Prelude* records how as a boy, Wordsworth skated on the lake, 'all shod with steel'. Stendhal noted 'fine moonlight with its tender reverie on the shores of Wendermere' on his tour of England in 1826.

Thomas Hardy turned down an invitation to the Coronation of George V because he had already booked a holiday in the Lakes. He later reflected that 'he probably got more satisfaction out of Coronation Day by spending it in Windermere than he would have done by spending it in a seat at the Abbey'. Bowness-on-Windermere is the 'Rio' of Arthur Ransome's *Swallows and Amazons* (1930). Ransome kept his little dinghy *Swallow* on Windermere when he was living at Low Ludderburn, and his own memories of skating on the lake as boy are used in his fourth children's novel, *Winter Holiday* (1933).

DERBYSHIRE

Dovedale: The 1400-acre National Trust holding on the shores of the 'silver shining Dove' is still a place of pilgrimage for admirers of Izaak Walton and Charles Cotton's *The Compleat Angler* (1676). Dr Johnson's Happy Valley (*Rasselas*, 1759) and George Eliot's Eagle Valley (*Adam Bede*, 1859) were both inspired by it. See also p.85-6.

Ilam: Ilam Hall was once a haunt of Congreve, Izaak Walton and Charles Cotton. In 1779 Dr Johnson and Boswell visited to see the egress of the River Manifold after its legendary underground passage through Thor's Cave. Despite the gardener's use of corks to demonstrate this wonder, Johnson was unimpressed. See also p.86.

DEVON

Dartmoor: The pagan poetical Cavalier Robert Herrick (1591-1674) was vicar of Dean Prior near Ashburton from 1629 to 1647 (when he was ousted by the Parliamentarians) and from after the Restoration of 1660 to the end of his life. He frequently said that he loathed both 'the dull confines of the drooping West' and his parishioners, 'A people currish; churlish as the seas;/And rude (almost) as rudest Salvages', but he wrote most of his best verse there, snug in his 'little house, whose humble roof/Is weatherproof/ Under the spars of which I lie/Both soft and dry'. He died in obscurity; his poetry was only appreciated 150 years later.

Dartmoor is most famously the location of Sir Arthur Conan Doyle's detective thriller *The Hound of the Baskervilles* (1902), but the first time that Doyle sent Holmes to Dartmoor was in 'Silver Blaze'. Doyle's Dartmoor is by no means realistic: Grimspound is enlarged into the Grimpen Mire, and Princetown is ruthlessly relocated. R. D. Blackmore wrote *Christowell: A Dartmoor Tale* (1881) as well as *Lorna Doone* (see p. 134), and Holne Woods was the childhood stamping ground of Charles Kingsley (1819-75), who was born there. But the most prolific novelist of Dartmoor was Eden Philpotts (1862-1960), who wrote eighteen novels set on the moor. His most famous book is the tragic tale *The Secret Woman* (1905).

Devon Coast: In May 1798, William Hazlitt and Samuel Coleridge walked along the Devon coast and through Dunster (Somerset), which Hazlitt described as looking 'as clear, as pure, as *embrowned*' as a Poussin landscape on their way to visit the Valley of the Rocks, near Lynmouth. Dunster is Stancy Castle in Hardy's short novel *A Laodicean* (1882).

Killerton: Eighteenth-century mansion which houses the library of the Rev. Sabine Baring-Gould (1834-1924). See also Blackwater Estuary, Essex.

Kipling Tors: The setting for Kipling's *Stalky and Co* (1899). Kipling was educated here at the United Services College from 1878 to 1882. He enjoyed his schooldays, and the book was dedicated to the headmaster. Much of the action took place to the south of the 'twelve bleak houses by the shore', on the rough gorse-covered hill known as Kipling Tors, which was given to the National Trust in 1938 by the Rudyard Kipling Memorial Fund.

Lynmouth: The National Trust's 1600-acre estate here forms part of the setting of *Tarka the Otter*. See also Woolacombe.

Saltram: Built *c.*1750 with a Tudor core. Dr Johnson was an occasional visitor, as was Fanny Burney who wrote of it in 1789: 'The house is one of the most magnificent in the kingdom, its view is noble'.

Westward Ho! and Hartland Point: Part of the 'land of the two rivers', the Taw and the Torridge, which was the setting for both Charles Kingsley's 1855 novel of the same name and Henry Williamson's *Tarka The Otter*. See also Woolacombe.

Woolacombe Beach: Part of the route taken by Tarka the Otter; Henry Williamson's writing hut is close by at Georgeham. The villages of Georgeham and Croyde are renamed Ham and Cryde in the book.

DORSET

Brownsea Island: Visited by Celia Fiennes in 1687; she commented on the manufacture of 'copperice' (green vitriol, used in dyeing, tanning and ink-making), and also mentioned that it was a 'noted place for lobsters and crabs and shrimps, there I eate some very good'.

Corfe Castle: Setting for George Banke's romantic novel *Brave Dame Mary* (1873), a celebration of the heroic Lady Mary Bankes's spirited defence of the castle against the Roundheads between 1643 and 1646. A statue of Lady Mary can be seen at Kingston Lacy. Corfe appears as Corvsgate in Thomas Hardy's first published novel *Desperate Remedies* (1869).

Golden Cap: Mentioned by Dorothy Wordsworth while she and William were living at Racedown House.

Lambert's Castle: Haunt of William and Dorothy Wordsworth when they were living at Racedown House.

Lulworth Cove: Keats composed 'Bright Star' sailing offshore after a day spent exploring Lulworth Cove. Thomas Hardy's Sergeant Troy in *Far From The Madding Crowd* (1874) is apparently drowned at 'Lulwind Cove'.

Whitenothe Cliff, Ringstead Bay: Llewellyn Powys lived for a time in the coastguard cottages at Whitenothe. The steep zig-zag path down to the cove was borrowed for John Meade Falkner's novel *Moonfleet* (1898), although most of the action of the story takes place further west at the ancient home of the Mohun family, Moonfleet Manor (now a hotel), at Fleet.

ESSEX

Blackwater Estuary: The Rev. Sabine Baring-Gould (1834-1924) held the living of East Mersea in Essex for ten years between 1871 and 1881. It was the setting for his spooky tale of treachery and doom *Mehalah, A Story of the Salt Marshes* (1880). The novel, nicknamed 'the *Lorna Doone* of Essex', opens on Ray Island. Paul Gallico's *The Snow Goose* (1941) was also inspired by the 'desolate, utterly lonely' land of mudflats and opalescent skies. Sylvia Townsend Warner discovered the 'melancholy eerie beauty' of the marshes while living in London in the 1920s. She went for a few days and stayed a month, and the fruit of the trip was *The True Heart* (1929). Margery Allingham spent her childhood holidays and most of her married life in the Blackwater area. Both her lurid first novel *Blackerchief Dick* (1923) and her second Albert Campion murder story *Mystery Mile* (1929) were set on versions of Mersea Island.

HAMPSHIRE

New Forest: The Trust looks after properties at Bramshaw Commons and Hale Purlieu within the boundaries of this ancient hunting forest, the setting for Captain Marryat's pro-Royalist historical tale *Children of the New Forest* (1847).

HEREFORDSHIRE

Bredon Barn: This magnificent fourteenth-century barn lies below Bredon Hill, and was fêted by both A. E. Housman ('In summertime on Bredon …') and John Masefield ('All the land from Ludlow town to Bredon Church's spire …').

Malvern Hills: William Langland (*c.*1330-*c.*1400) was possibly the first to celebrate the Malverns in his *Vision Concerning Piers the Plowman*. Langland was educated at Malvern Priory, and began to write his long poem in 1362, when he was about 30; it took him most of his life to complete. A Piers Plowman window in the church at Cleobury Mortimer commemorates the poet's supposed birth there, though the claim is contested by Ledbury and Wychwood. Malvern was also the tramping ground of the poet A. E. Housman (1859-1936), who lived in London but frequently returned to the haunts of his childhood; his ashes lie, appropriately, just outside the door of St Laurence's Church, Ludlow, 'amidst the moonlight pale'. John Masefield (1878-1967) lived in Ledbury as a boy. His children's novels *The Midnight Folk* (1927) and *The Box of Delights* (1935) are both set in the Malvern area.

ISLE OF WIGHT

Culver Down: The high narrow chalk ridge that is the backbone of the island ends in the east at Culver Down, near Bembridge. 'The morning was blue and lovely with a warm sun and fresh breeze blowing from the sea and the Culver Downs [as] I came to Bembridge' wrote Francis Kilvert in July 1875. Algernon Swinburne set himself the challenge of climbing the cliff from the beach, but he only just made it: 'my scanty foothold gave way . . . I swung in the air by my hands from a ledge on the cliff which just gave room for my fingers to cling and held on . . . At the top I had not strength enough left to turn or stir; I lay on my right side helpless. On returning to consciousness I found a sheep's nose just over mine, and the poor good fellow-creature's eyes gazing into my face with such a look of kind pity and sympathy as well as surprise and perplexity that I never ought to have eaten a mutton-chop again'. (*Recollections of A. C. Swinburne*).

Tennyson Down: Tennyson first came to Farringford (now a hotel) in 1853, and lived there for nearly forty years, exiting to a second home in summer to avoid the streams of pilgrims. His visitors included Henry Longfellow, Lewis Carroll, A. C. Swinburne and Edward Lear. After a visit in 1886, Oliver Wendell Holmes, best known as the author of *A Poet at the Breakfast Table* but also founder of *Atlantic Monthly*, described 'seeing the poet to the best advantage under his own trees and walking over his own domain'.

KENT

Dover, White Cliffs of: Ever since the blind Gloucester tries to make his son lead him to the 'high and unbending' cliff in Scene VI ('the Country near Dover') of Shakespeare's *King Lear*, England's springboard to the Continent has attracted poetical and literary notice. Byron roamed there on his last departure from England in 1816 and Matthew Arnold's masterly poem 'Dover Beach' was written after spending a night there on his return from his honeymoon on the Continent in 1851. Charles Dickens knew Dover well: in *A Tale of Two Cities* (1859) he describes it as 'a little, mean, crooked place, which hid itself away from the beach and ran its head into the chalk cliffs like a marine ostrich'. He wrote to Wilkie Collins in 1861 that he had 'walked by the cliffs to Folkestone and back to-day. It was so exquisitely beautiful that, although I was alone, I could not keep silent on the subject. In the fourteen miles I met only twelve people'.

Ightham Mote: Scene of the incarceration of Celia de Bohun, heroine of Anya Seton's historical romance *Green Darkness* (1972). Seton visited the 'lovely and mysterious' moated manor house in the 1960s, soon after its purchase and restoration from ruin by the American C. Henry Robinson, who later presented it to the National Trust.

Pegwell Bay: Scene of the memorable day in Dickens' *Sketches By Boz*, when Mr and Mrs Tuggs and the captain ordered a lunch of 'small saucers of large shrimps, dabs of butter, crusty loaves and bottled ale' in the little garden behind the Pegwell Bay Hotel.

Pilgrim's Way, North Downs: Route taken by Geoffrey Chaucer's pilgrims in his *Canterbury Tales*. The village of Shalford (in Surrey) is reputed to be the model for Vanity Fair in John Bunyan's *The Pilgrim's Progress*.

Smallhythe Place: Sixteenth-century half-timbered farmhouse home of Ellen Terry from 1899 until her death here in 1928. The house is full of theatrical and literary mementoes: Alexandre Dumas's visiting card, Sir Arthur Sullivan's monocle, and a letter from Oscar Wilde begging Ellen Terry to accept 'the first copy of my first play' and hoping 'that some day I shall be fortunate enough to write something worthy of your playing'.

LANCASHIRE

Gawthorpe Hall: Home of Sir James Kay-Shuttleworth, the great Victorian reformer, and his wife, Janet. Charlotte Brontë twice visited 'grey, stately and picturesque' Gawthorpe in 1850 and 1855. The Kay-Shuttleworths also introduced her to Mrs Gaskell when they were both staying at another of their properties in the Lake District.

Rufford Old Hall: The Hesketh family seat from 1420. William Shakespeare is traditionally said to have been in service under Sir Thomas Hesketh in 1581.

LINCOLNSHIRE

Belton House: Built by William Winde, and the home of the Brownlows, a cultured family who were great patrons of the arts. The most notable literary period in Belton's history was during the lifetime of Adelbert, the 3rd Earl Brownlow (1844-1921), who was closely connected with the fin-de-siècle group of idealistic and high-minded intellectuals known as the Souls. The nickname was invented at a dinner given at Belton in 1888, and its members included George Curzon, Arthur Balfour, Margot Tennant and Brownlow's cousin and heir Harry Cust, a poet of some contemporary distinction and editor of the influential *Pall Mall Gazette* in the 1890s. H. G. Wells, one of his contributors, describes a dinner party in just such a house as Belton in *The New Machiavelli*. Belton was greatly admired by the American novelist Edith Wharton, who based the design of her own Massachusetts house, The Mount, upon its classical seventeenth-century proportions.

Gunby Hall: Tennyson, who was born at Somersby, a few miles to the north, may have been thinking of Gunby as the 'haunt of ancient peace' in his poem 'The Palace of Art'. An autographed copy hangs in the hall.

London

The Blewcoat School, Caxton Street: Mentioned by Leon Garfield in his cycle of children's novellas *The Apprentices* (1976-8).

George Inn, Southwark: Dickens mentions this seventeenth-century galleried coaching inn in *Little Dorrit*.

Norfolk

Blakeney Point: Stevie Smith had 'the most glorious bathing I think I have ever had' off Blakeney Point in 1949, when she was holidaying at Wiveton. Richard Mabey's nostalgic memoir *Home Country* (1990) recalls holidays as a child when Blakeney Point seemed 'an enchanted oasis of lagoons and shifting sands, fanned by the coconut and honey scents of tree lupins and sea pinks'. It became his second home in the 1960s, when he lived on a converted lifeboat, the *Dilemma X*, and collected the edible plants that would form the basis for his famous hunter-gatherer manual *Food For Free* (1974). See also p.232.

Blickling Hall: Appears as Bullen Hall in S. T. Haymon's *Stately Homicide*. The ice house inspired that in Minette Walters' novel of the same name.

Felbrigg: The independent and outspoken Whig grandee William 'Weathercock' Windham III (1750-1810) prided himself on being 'a scholar among politicians and a politician among scholars'. Dr Samuel Johnson (1709-84) visited Felbrigg several times, and its library contains many books that were once owned by the famous lexicographer.

Horsey Mere: Visited by the characters in Arthur Ransome's *Coot Club* (1934), which was inspired by the naturalist G. C. Davies's *The Swan and Her Crew* (1876). Rose, the married daughter of the eponymous hero of Ransome's *Peter Duck* (1932), lived at Potter Heigham, a mile to the south of Horsey. Other books set on the Norfolk Broads include Ransome's sequel to *Coot Club*, *The Big Six* (1940); a detective story which might well have been inspired by C. P. Snow's first book, *Death Under Sail* (1932), and E. & M. A. Radford's *Death on the Broads* (1957).

Stiffkey Marshes: Henry Williamson, author of *Tarka the Otter*, bought Old Hall Farm, Stiffkey in 1936. His account of his struggle to make good there, *Story of a Norfolk Farm* (1941) is also a celebration of Norfolk wild life, especially the birds, wild geese and windhovers that were for him, as for T. H. White (see p.58), 'the genius of the place'.

Northumberland (inc. Tyneside)

Allen Banks: Several of Catherine Cookson's novels are set in the Northumberland countryside around Hexham, notably *The Girl*, *A Dinner of Herbs*, *Feathers in the Fire* and *Fenwick Houses*. Her memoir, *Catherine Cookson Country*, is the best guide to the locations of her novels; also informative is her autobiography *Our Kate*.

Lindisfarne Castle: Edward Hudson, owner and founder of the magazine *Country Life*, bought the gloriously situated ruins of Lindisfarne Castle in 1901 and commissioned Edwin Lutyens to fit a 'comfortable modern house into its ramparts'. Many London literati found their way there, including Elizabeth Von Arnim, author of *Elizabeth and her German Garden* and the publisher William Heinemann. Most visitors admired the castle hugely, but Lytton Strachey found it 'very dark, with nowhere to sit, and nothing but stone, over and round you, which produces a depressing effect'.

Wallington: In the nineteenth century Wallington was a centre of cultural debate. Members of the Pre-Raphaelite Brotherhood were attracted there by Pauline, Lady Trevelyan, particularly John Ruskin, whom she jokingly called 'Master'. A. C. Swinburne, whose grandfather lived at nearby Capheaton, first 'breathed the air faintly laden with Pre-Raphaelite incense' at Wallington, and came to regard Lady Pauline as a second mother, such was her encouragement.

Shropshire

Dudmaston: This late seventeenth-century house contains a substantial collection of botanical paintings and notebooks, including examples of the work of P.-J. Redouté (1759-1840) and of the naturalist and botanical painter Frances Pitt (1888-1964) who lived in the area all her life.

Wenlock Edge: A. E. Housman's famous poem *A Shropshire Lad* (1896) is a vivid evocation of the locality. But the lines that open Part L of *A Shropshire Lad* – 'Clunton and Clunbury,/Clungunford and Clun,/Are the quietest places/Under the sun' – are a misquote of a local rhyme; the Cluns, which lie close by Wenlock Edge, were in fact reputedly the '*drunkenest* places under the sun'.

P. G. Wodehouse (1881-1975) used to live not far from Wenlock Edge at Stableford. He had friends at Weston Park, Shifnal, which may have been a model for Blandings Castle. This would make Weston-under-Lizard Blandings Parva, and Shifnal Market Blandings. Other possible models for the castle include Sudeley in Gloucestershire and Corsham Court near Bath.

Wilderhope Manor: A delightfully asymmetrical Elizabethan manor house with mullioned windows and three-storeyed gables overlooking the River Corve. It was the model for Undern Hall in the rural romantic novelist Mary Webb's *Gone to Earth* (1917); the book also features the nearby villages of Hope and Snailbeach. Webb's novels were enjoyed by Rebecca West, Stanley Baldwin and hundreds of thousands of other readers, but were wickedly satirised in Stella Gibbons's *Cold Comfort Farm* (see Fulking Escarpment, Sussex).

SOMERSET (INC. BATH)

Bath Assembly Rooms: See p.88. Eighteenth-century writers who set novels or plays in this fashionable, often somewhat racketty marriage-mart, include Tobias Smollett (*Humphry Clinker*, 1771), Richard Brinsley Sheridan (*The Rivals*, 1775), and Fanny Burney (*Evelina*, 1788). Among later authors inspired by Bath are Charles Dickens, who met a man called Mr Pickwick there and enjoyed Sally Lunn cakes, both immortalised in *The Posthumous Papers of the Pickwick Club* (1836) and Baroness Orczy, whose 'Scarlet Pimpernel' Sir Percy Blakeney was supposed to live in Royal Crescent.

Prior Park: Built by Ralph Allen, one of the creators of Georgian Bath, and immortalised in Henry Fielding's *Tom Jones* (1749) as Squire Allworthy. See also p.91.

The Quantocks – Beacon Hill and Bicknoller Hill: The Trust has substantial holdings in these hills near Minehead where Dorothy and William Wordsworth and Samuel Taylor Coleridge loved to wander; it seems likely that Dorothy was describing Trendle Ring when she writes in her diary of 17 February, 1798 of a walk to 'the top of a high hill to see a fortification'.

SUFFOLK

Dunwich Heath: In his *A Literary Pilgrim in England* (1917), Edward Thomas claimed that it was Swinburne who 'added Dunwich to the poets' country' with such poems as 'Dunwich' and 'By The North Sea'. But in fact earlier poets were fascinated by the dramatic erosion which led the busy medieval port of Dunwich to tumble gradually into the sea. Daniel Defoe noted in his *Tour Through the Eastern Counties* (1724) that Dunwich 'seems to be in danger of being swallowed up; for Fame reports that once they had fifty churches in the town; I saw but one left and that not half full of people'. By the time of George Crabbe (1755-1832), who was born and bred in Aldeburgh and described himself as 'cast by Fortune on a frowning coast', it had become an effective symbol of the rural decay that was the main theme of his poems 'The Village', 'The Borough' and 'Peter Grimes'.

Edward Fitzgerald (1809-83) lived in various lodgings in and around Woodbridge while learning Persian and translating *The Rubáiyát of Omar Khayyám*. Dunwich was a favourite excursion for his visitors, who included Alfred, Lord Tennyson and Thomas Carlyle, when he could be lured from 'the accursed den' in 'his filthy Chelsea'. Jerome K. Jerome spent his annual holidays at Dunwich in the 1890s. In 1907 Edward Thomas took a coastguard cottage at Minsmere to finish his biography of Richard Jeffries; it was while walking on the shore near Dunwich that he met a seventeen-year-old girl who inspired several poems and almost broke up his marriage.

Pin Mill: The mooring of Arthur Ransome's little cutter *Nancy Blackett*, model for *Goblin* in *We Didn't Mean to Go To Sea*; it is also the setting of Patricia Moyes' crime novel *Down Among The Dead Men*.

SURREY

Piney Copse, Abinger Hammer: This 4-acre wood was bought by E. M. Forster when he moved to a leasehold house he inherited in West Hackhurst in 1924. His book of essays *Abinger Harvest* (1936) includes 'My Wood', a wry piece on the corrupting effects of owning property. It was also celebrated in *A Pageant of Trees*, written for Abinger in 1934. Forster lived there until the lease expired, when, to his great regret, he had to move. Essays in *Two Cheers for Democracy* (1951) include 'The Last of Abinger' and the evocative 'Evening walk round by the yew-wood on the Pilgrims Way'. In later years, he often made nostalgic references to Abinger. He bequeathed Piney Copse to the National Trust, to preserve it as open woodland.

Polesden Lacey: The home of the eighteenth-century playwright Richard Sheridan. It was a dilapidated seventeenth-century manor house with 341 acres of land when Sheridan acquired it as part of his wife's marriage settlement. He thoroughly enjoyed being lord of the manor and spent a good deal of money on it – the

Drury Lane stage manager James Aickin threatened to resign, full of 'forebodings of bankruptcy, such things as wood and canvas not to be had, yet three thousand guineas given for an estate'. The only remaining trace of the house in which Sheridan lived is the Sheridan Walk, a terraced avenue of beeches, which he laid out. Sadly, it lost many of its original trees in a storm of 1987.

In the twentieth century, Polesden Lacey was the scene of the high society salon of the vivacious Mrs Ronald Greville who was on intimate terms with most of the crowned heads of Europe and entertained Ribbentrop and other Germans at her table almost until the outbreak of the Second World War. Osbert Sitwell admired her greatly, but according to diarists such as Harold Nicolson, her insistence that English opinion was behind her was a factor in Hitler's assumption that Britain would never attack Germany.

SUSSEX

Black Down: The highest point in Sussex. The Tennysons moved to Aldworth in 1868 to escape from the sightseers who came to gaze at their house at Farringdon on the Isle of Wight. The road along the crest of Black Down is called Tennyson Lane – Tennyson loved walking there and called a group of firs on the ridge's exposed south-east corner the 'Four Winds'. He died at Aldworth in 1892; a glass window depicting Sir Galahad was erected in his memory in the parish church of St Bartholomew in 1899.

Fulking Escarpment: The countryside round the Devil's Dyke and the villages of Fulking and Poynings are plausible settings for the windblasted home of the Starkadders' farm and the village of Howling in Stella Gibbons's *Cold Comfort Farm*. The book was intended as a pastiche of Mary Webb's Shropshire novels *Gone to Earth* (1917) and *Precious Bane* (1924).

Sheffield Park: The patronage of John Baker Holroyd, later Lord Sheffield, was in large measure responsible for the successful completion of Edward Gibbon's *Decline and Fall of the Roman Empire*. Gibbon (1737-94) was made free of the house, and he spent nine months of 1787 there seeing *Decline and Fall* through the presses. He spent the last year of his life at Sheffield Park, and is interred in the Holroyd family mausoleum in Fletching parish church.

WARWICKSHIRE

Baddesley Clinton: Medieval manor house, home of the late nineteenth-century romantic novelist Lady Chatterton.

Charlecote Park: The young William Shakespeare was said to have been caught poaching here and was brought before the owner, Sir Thomas Lucy, the resident magistrate. Shakespeare took his revenge in *The Merry Wives of Windsor* by caricaturing him as Justice Shallow and referring explicitly to the silver pike on the Lucy coat of arms. Many of the furnishings of Charlecote came from Fonthill Abbey in Wiltshire, folly home of the eighteenth-century novelist and man of letters, William Beckford. In *English Hours* (1907), Henry James records his visit to the house 'whose venerable verdure seems a survival from an earlier England and whose innumerable acres, stretching away, in the early evening, to vaguely seen Tudor walls, lie there like the backward years receding to the age of Elizabeth'.

WILTSHIRE

Lacock Abbey: Medieval abbey, and scene of the incident of the Leaping Dame recorded by John Aubrey (1626-1697). Olive Sharington, co-heir of the Abbey, tried to elope by leaping off the battlements into the arms of her suitor John Talbot, a younger brother of the Earl of Shrewsbury, because her father forbade the match: 'She lep't down and the wind (which was then high) came under her coates: and did something break the fall: Mr Talbot caught her in his arms, but she struck him as one dead'. Olive married her suitor and lived on at Lacock until 1646, when she was 'about an hundred years old'. Lacock was later the home of the Fox Talbot family. The museum at the abbey gates is dedicated to the pioneer photographer, scientist and classicist William Henry Fox Talbot.

Mompesson House: Built in 1701, Mompesson House in Salisbury's Cathedral Close evokes the clerical atmosphere of Anthony Trollope's Barchester. Although the town was largely based on Winchester, in his *Autobiography* (1883) Trollope recalls that it was when 'wandering one midsummer evening round the purlieus of Salisbury Cathedral' that he thought up the story of *The Warden*, 'from whence came the series of novels of which Barchester was the central site'.

YORKSHIRE (INC. HULL & MIDDLESBROUGH)

Cayton Bay: Anne Brontë first saw the sea at Scarborough. Her impressions are set down in *Agnes Gray* (1847): 'no language can describe the effect of the deep, clear, azure of the sky and ocean, the bright morning sunshine on the semi-circular barrier of craggy cliffs surmounted by green swelling hills'. In his autobiography *Left Hand, Right Hand* (1945), Osbert Sitwell recalls standing on the cliff at sunset at the age of five and feeling part of the 'boundless immensity of sea and sky'.

Malham Tarn: Spectacular limestone cliff that inspired the setting of Charles Kingsley's *The Water Babies* (1863). Kingsley was staying at Tarn House (now a field studies centre), which became Harthover Hall, 'built at ninety different times and in nineteen different styles'.

Robin Hood's Bay: The childhood home of the novelist Leo Walmsley and the Bramblewick of his first three novels, *Three Fevers* (1932), *Foreigners* (1935) and *Sally Lunn* (1937).

Treasurer's House: Home of Dr Jacques Sterne. His novelist nephew, Laurence, wrote not only *The Life and Opinions of Tristram Shandy* (1760-7) but also *A Political Romance* (1759), a savage satire of the inward looking society of the cathedral close, which was banned because of its outspoken criticism of the ecclesiastical courts.

WALES

ANGLESEY

Snowdonia: Inspired by Thomas Pennant's description of his sunrise ascent of Snowdon (*A Tour in Wales*, 1778-84), William Wordsworth climbed Snowdon with Robert Jones in 1791. He recorded his impressions (much later) in *The Prelude* (1850). To George Borrow, Snowdon was the 'Parnassus of Europe'. He described the view from the top as 'a scene inexpressibly grand'. John Cowper Powys (1872-1963) moved from Dorset to Snowdonia in 1934; he spent the last thirty years of his life there, and wrote two monumental novels set in Wales: *Owen Glendower* (1941) and *Morwyn or the Vengeance of God* (1937).

CONWY

Tŷ Mawr: Sixteenth-century farmhouse in the valley where Bishop William Morgan (*c*.1541-1604) was born. Morgan's Welsh translation of the Bible (still in use today) was published in 1588 and dedicated to the Queen.

GWYNEDD

Bardsey Island/Ynys Enlli: 'The Isle of Tides', one of the most important centres of the Celtic religion in Britain, is off the tip of the Llŷn Peninsula. Three pilgrimages to Bardsey Island were considered the equivalent of one to Rome, and it is said to have 20,000 saints buried there. Among them is St Dubricius, the Bishop of Caerleon, who – according to legend – crowned Arthur king. R. S. Thomas's poem 'Pilgrimages' is marvellously evocative of the island.

Llŷn Peninsula: Home of the clergyman poet R. S. Thomas (b.1913), whose poetry celebrates its pure but bleak beauty.

Plas yn Rhiw: Sir Compton Mackenzie visited the 'remote and ancient little house' in 1950. 'We spent a completely delightful couple of hours . . . the only thing that refused to play its part was the view which sulked in the haze . . .'

WREXHAM

Llangollen: In his *Wild Wales* (1862) George Borrow described his four-month Welsh pilgrimage of 1854 in search of the places connected with such poets as Huw Morris and Goronwy Owen. He started with a visit to Plas Newydd, the home of the famous Ladies of Llangollen, and then visited the hills above Llangollen, including Coed Hyrddyn, or 'Velvet Hill'.

NORTHERN IRELAND

CO. ANTRIM

Giant's Causeway: Famously described by Dr Johnson as 'worth seeing but not worth going to see'. Other literary visitors included William Makepeace Thackeray and Sir Walter Scott.

CO. LONDONDERRY

The Mussenden Temple, Downhill: This spectacular cliff-edge library was built by Frederick Augustus Hervey, Bishop of Derry and 4th Earl of Bristol. Hervey, whose English seat was Ickworth in Suffolk (also National Trust) built the prodigious palace of Downhill in the 1770s. A great traveller, bibliophile and art collector, he was also an avid letter-writer, especially interested in scientific subjects. His acquaintances included Voltaire, Wolfgang von Goethe, Jeremy Bentham, John Wesley, Emma Hamilton and the economist and travel writer Arthur Young, who visited Downhill and described Hervey as 'the most extraordinary man I have ever met'. The Mussenden Temple was named for Hervey's cousin, Frideswide, a captivatingly pretty young girl thirty years younger than he was, whom he met a year after she married the wealthy Derry banker Daniel Mussenden in 1781. Hervey was extremely taken with his 'chère cousine. . . whose dear innocent countenance is sufficient to animate and enliven all around her', and Frideswide frequently visited him at Downhill with her brother Henry, a curate. But in 1784 Mrs Mussenden died, tragically young. The Temple, completed the following year, became a monument to her and was soon filled with fine books and an ingenious heating system to prevent them getting damp. Today only a gaunt shell remains of the vast mansion from which the eccentric Bishop used to organise curates' races along the sands; the winners were rewarded with vacant benefices.

Select Bibliography

*In order to prevent this bibliography from become encyclopaedic, I have
excluded the National Trust guide books for individual properties and places,
although many of them have been founts of information. I have also omitted
titles mentioned adequately in the text, and numerous books used to
substantiate information in the Gazetteer.*

GENERAL

Bird, E. & James, L., *Writers on the Coast*, Windrush Press, 1992

Carpenter, H. & Prichard, M., *Oxford Companion to Children's Literature*,
Oxford University Press, 1984

Drabble, M., *A Writer's Britain*, Thames & Hudson, 1979

Eagle, D. & Carnell, H., *The Oxford Illustrated Literary Guide*, Oxford
University Press, 1981

Earwaker, J. & Becker, K., *Literary Norfolk*, Chapter 6 Publishing, 1998

Gasson, A., *Wilkie Collins: An Illustrated Guide*, Oxford University Press,
1998

Genet, Jacqueline (ed.), *The Big House in Ireland: Reality and
Representation*, Brandon, 1991

Girouard, M., *Life in the English Country House*, Yale University Press, 1978

Greeves, L. & Trinick, M., *The National Trust Guide*, The National
Trust, 1996

Hodges, Jack, *Makers of the Omnibus: The Lives of English Writers
Compared*, Sinclair Stevenson, 1992

Lane, M., *On the Trail of Writers in Sussex*, S. B. Publications, 1996

Legg, R., *Dorset National Trust Guide*, Dorset Publishing Co., 1992

Morley, Frank, *Literary Britain*, Hutchinson, 1980

Perry, R. & Watson-Brownley, M., *Mothering the Mind*, Holmes &
Meier, 1984

Schmidt, M., *Lives of Poets*, Weidenfeld & Nicolson, 1998

Sharp, W., *Literary Geography*, Pall Mall Press, 1907

Shaw, R., *Housman's Places*, The Housman Society, 1995

Somerville, C., *Twelve Literary Walks*, W. H. Allen & Co., 1985

Thomas, Edward, *A Literary Pilgrim in England* (1917), Oxford
University Press, 1980

Tindall, G., *Countries of the Mind*, The Hogarth Press, 1991

Tolhurst, P., *East Anglia: A Literary Pilgrimage*, Black Dog, 1996

Varlow, S., *A Reader's Guide to Writers' Britain*, Prion, 1996

Wallace, A. D., *Walking, Literature and English Culture*, Oxford
University Press, 1993

CHAPTER 1: THE PEN AND THE PLACE – CAMEOS: CARLYLE'S HOUSE; SHAW'S CORNER

Carlyle, Jane, *Letters and Memorials*, ed. J. A. Froude, Longman, 1883

Carlyle, Thomas, *Letters*, ed. C. E. Norton, Macmillan, 1886

Hardwick, Michael and Molly, *Writers' Houses*, Phoenix, 1968

Holme, Thea, *The Carlyles at Home*, Oxford University Press, 1979

Kipling, Rudyard, *Something of Myself*, Tauchnitz, 1938

MacLiammoir, M. & Boland, E., *W. B. Yeats and His World*, Thames &
Hudson, 1971

Lees-Milne, J., *Writers at Home*, Trefoil, 1985

Marsh, Kate (ed.), *Writers and Their Houses: A Guide to the Writers' Houses
of England*, Hamish Hamilton, 1993

Premoli-Droulers, F., *Writers' Houses*, Cassell, 1995

CHAPTER 2: IN SEARCH OF LYONESSE – CAMEO: BATEMAN'S

Alcock, L., *Arthur's Britain*, Penguin, 1971

Alcock, L., *By South Cadbury is that Camelot*, Thames & Hudson, 1972

Anstruther, I., *The Knight and the Umbrella*, Geoffrey Bles, 1963

Ashe, Geoffrey, *The Traveller's Guide to Arthurian Britain*, Gothic Image,
1997

Coles, B. & J., *Sweet Track to Glastonbury*, Thames & Hudson, 1986

De Troyes, Chrétien, *Arthurian Romances*, Penguin, 1991

Duxbury, B. & Williams, M., *King Arthur Country in Cornwall*,
Bossiney, 1979

Field, P. J. C., *The Life and Times of Sir Thomas Malory*, Woodbridge, 1993

Garnett, D., *The White/Garnett Letters*, Jonathan Cape, 1968

Monmouth, Geoffrey of, *Histories of the Kings of Britain*, J. M. Dent &
Sons, 1906

Morris, John, *The Age of Arthur, A History of the British Isles from 350 to
650*, Weidenfeld & Nicolson, 1984

Parini, J., *John Steinbeck: A Biography*, Henry Holt & Co., New York, 1995

Tennyson, C., *Alfred Tennyson*, Macmillan & Co., 1950

Thomas, Charles, *Tintagel, Arthur and Archaeology*, B. T. Batsford, 1993

Steinbeck, E. & Wallsten, R., *Steinbeck: A Life in Letters*, William
Heinemann, 1975

Taylor, Beverley & Brewer, Elizabeth, *The Return of Arthur: British and
American Arthurian Literature since 1800*, Brewer/Barnes Noble, 1983

Warner, Sylvia Townsend, *T. H. White*, Jonathan Cape/Chatto &
Windus, 1967

CHAPTER 3: JANE AUSTEN IN HER LANDSCAPE – CAMEOS: BOX HILL; SELBORNE

Austen, J., *My Dear Cassandra*, ed. Penelope Hughes-Hallett, Collins
& Brown, 1990

Batey, Mavis, *Jane Austen and the English Landscape*, Barn Elms, 1996

Edwards, A., *In the Steps of Jane Austen*, Countryside, 1979

Hammerton, J. A., *George Meredith*, John Grant, 1911

Howard, T., *Austen Country*, Grange, 1997

Kelly, Linda, *Juniper Hall*, Weidenfeld, 1991

Lane, M., *Jane Austen's England*, Robert Hale, 1986

Mabey, Richard, *Gilbert White, A Biography*, Century, 1986

Nicolson, N., *The World of Jane Austen*, Phoenix Illustrated, 1997

Sassoon, Siegfried, *Meredith*, Constable & Co., 1948

Selwyn, P., *Jane Austen: Selected Poems and Verse of the Austen Family*, Carcanet Press, 1996

Tinniswood, Adrian *The Polite Tourist*, The National Trust, 1998

White, Gilbert, *The Natural History of Selborne*, ed. Richard Mabey, J. M. Dent, 1993. An excellent spoken word version, punctuated by appropriate birdsong and other natural sound effects is available from Gilbert White's House.

Tomalin, C., *Jane Austen: A Life*, Penguin, 1997

Chapter 4: Literature and the Country House – Cameo: Lamb House

Bosanquet, Theodora, *Henry James at Work*, Hogarth Press, 1924

Hardwick, Molly, *Mrs Dizzy*, Cassell, 1972

Jackson-Stops, G., *An English Arcadia 1600–1990*, The National Trust, 1991

James, Henry, *Collected Travel Writings*, notes by Richard Howard, Library of America, 1993

Gill, Richard, *Happy Rural Seat: The English Country House and the Literary Imagination*, Yale, 1972

Kelsall, Malcolm, *The Great Good Place: The Country House and English Literature*, Harvester, 1993

Robinson, J. M., *Temples of Delight*, George Philip/The National Trust, 1990

Rowell, C. & Robinson, J. M., *Uppark Restored*, The National Trust, 1996

Sackville-West, Vita, *Knole and the Sackvilles*, Heinemann, 1922

Taylor, D. J., *Thackeray*, Chatto & Windus, 1999

Wells, H. G., *Experiment in Autobiography*, Camelot Press, 1934

Wells, H. G., *Tono-Bungay*, Collins, 1923

West, A., *H. G. Wells: Aspects of a Life*, Random House, 1984

Chapter 5: Muses and Mountains – Cameo: Hill Top

Battrick, E., *Beatrix Potter's Tale*, Ellenbank Press, 1993

Beck, H., *The William Wordsworth Way*, Mainstream Publishing, 1998

Brogan, H., *The Life of Arthur Ransome*, Jonathan Cape, 1984

Coleridge, S. T., *Collected Letters*, ed. E. L. Griggs, Clarendon, 1956-71

De Quincey, T., *Recollections of the Lake Poets*, John Lehmann, 1948

Hankinson, Alan, *Coleridge Walks the Fells*, Ellenbank, 1991

Holmes, R., *Coleridge: Early Visions*, Penguin, 1990

Holmes, R., *Coleridge Darker Reflections*, Harper Collins, 1998

Hughes-Hallett, Penelope, *Home at Grasmere*, Collins & Brown, 1993

Johnston, Kenneth R., *The Hidden Wordsworth: Poet Lover Rebel Spy*, W. W. Norton, 1998

Knight, E. F., *Coleridge and Wordsworth in the West Country*, Elkin Matthews, 1914

Kyros Walker, C., *Walking North with Keats*, Yale University Press, 1992

Lane, M., *The Tale of Beatrix Potter*, Penguin, 1986

Lindop, G., *A Literary Guide to the Lake District*, Chatto & Windus, 1993

Mayberry, T., *Coleridge and Wordsworth in the West Country*, Alan Sutton, 1994

Mitchell, W. R., *Beatrix Potter*, Castleberg, 1998

Murphy, Graham, *Founders of the National Trust*, Helm, 1997

Ransome, Arthur, *Swallows and Amazons*, Jonathan Cape, 1930

Rawnsley, Hardwicke Drummond, *Literary Associations of the English Lakes*, Maclehose, Glasgow, 1894

Rawnsley, Hardwicke Drummond, *Reminiscences of Wordsworth among the Peasantry of Westmoreland* [1882], Dillons, 1968

Stephen, James, *Lapsus Calami*, Granta, 1891

Walker, D. & K., *Wordsworth and Coleridge Tour of the Lake District*, David Walker, 1997

Wordsworth, Dorothy, *The Grasmere Journals*, Oxford University Press, 1993

Wordsworth, W., *A Guide to the Lakes*, Oxford University Press, 1906

Chapter 6: Thomas Hardy's Wessex – Cameo: Clouds Hill

Gittings, Robert, *The Older Hardy*, Heinemann, 1978

Gittings, Robert, *Young Thomas Hardy*, Heinemann, 1975

Harper, C. G., *The Hardy Country*, A. & C. Black, 1904

Hawkins, D., *Hardy's Wessex*, Macmillan, 1983

Hawkins, D., *Wessex: A Literary Celebration*, Century, 1991

Hardy, Evelyn, & Gittings, Robert (ed.), *Some Recollections by Emma Hardy*, Oxford University Press, 1961

Knight, R. D., *T. E. Lawrence and the Max Gate Circle*, Bat and Ball Press, 1988

Lefebure, M., *Thomas Hardy's World*, Carlton, 1996

Pinion, F. B., *A Hardy Companion*, Macmillan, 1968

Pitfield, F. P., *Hardy's Wessex Locations*, Dorset Publishing Co., 1992

Powers, M., *Pub Walks in Hardy's Wessex*, Power Publications, 1997

Chapter 7: Bloomsbury by the Sea – Cameo: Sissinghurst Castle

Bell, Q., *Charleston*, The Hogarth Press, 1987

Brown, J., *Sissinghurst: Portrait of a Garden*, Weidenfeld & Nicolson, 1994

Lee, H., *Virginia Woolf*, Chatto & Windus, 1996

Moore, J., *The Bloomsbury Trail in Sussex*, S. B. Publications, 1995

Morris, Jan, *Travels With Virginia Woolf*, Pimlico, 1997

Nicolson, N. & Trautman, J. (eds), *The Letters of Virginia Woolf*, (6 vols), Hogarth Press, 1975-80

Sackville-West, V., *The Land*, William Heinemann, 1926

Woolf, Virginia, *Orlando*, Penguin, 1928

Woolf, Virginia, *The Widow and the Parrot*, Harcourt Brace, 1988

Chapter 8: The Scene of the Crime – Cameo: Lorna Doone Country

Bonham-Carter, V., *Exmoor Writers and their Works*, Exmoor Press, 1987

Burton, S. H., *The Lorna Doone Trail*, The Exmoor Press, 1975

Cook, J., *Daphne: A Portrait of Daphne du Maurier*, Bantam Press, 1991

du Maurier, D., *Letters From Menabilly*, Weidenfeld & Nicolson, 1993

Forster, M., *Daphne du Maurier*, Chatto & Windus, 1993

Gardner, B., *Lorna Doone's Exmoor*, Brendon Arts, 1990

Gill, G., *Agatha Christie: The Woman and her Mysteries*, Robson, 1991

Reynolds, B., *Dorothy L. Sayers: Her Life and Soul*, Hodder & Stoughton, 1993

Watson, Colin, *Snobbery With Violence*, Eyre & Spottiswode, 1971

Acknowledgements

The extracts reproduced on the pages listed below are taken from the following sources:

p.15 W. B. Yeats, 'My House' from *The Winding Stair*, Macmillan, 1933

pp.19, 193-4, 195, 196, 199, 202, 204 Anne Olivier Bell & A. McNeillie (eds), *The Diary of Virginia Woolf*, Hogarth Press, 1977-84

p.19 Daphne du Maurier, *Letters from Menabilly*, Weidenfeld & Nicolson, 1993

p.21, 183, 190 David Garnett (ed.), *Letters of T. E. Lawrence*, Jonathan Cape, 1938

p.21 Jerome K. Jerome quoted by Jack Hodges in *Makers of the Omnibus: The Lives of English Writers Compared*, Sinclair Stevenson, 1992

p.22 George Bernard Shaw quoted by Michael Holroyd in *Writers at Home*, Trefoil, 1985

p.26 Winston Churchill, *Savrola*, Longmans, Green & Co, 1900

pp.27, 30, 32, 70, 71 Rudyard Kipling, *Something of Myself*, Tauchnitz, 1938

p.28 Hugh Brogan, *The Life of Arthur Ransome*, Jonathan Cape, 1984

pp.29-30, 61, 62, 64, 65 John Steinbeck, *The Acts of King Arthur and his Noble Knights*, Farrar, Strauss & Giroux, 1976

p.33 Sylvia Townsend Warner, *T. H. White*, Jonathan Cape, 1967

p.34 George Bernard Shaw, *The Irrational Knot*, Constable & Co., 1905

p.59 David Garnett, *The White/Garnett Letters*, Jonathan Cape, 1968

p.61 T. H. White, *The Book of Merlyn*, Collins, 1977

pp.62, 66 J. Parini, *John Steinbeck: A Biography*, Henry Holt & Co, 1995

p.67 E. Steinbeck & R. Wallsten, *Steinbeck: A Life in Letters*, William Heinemann, 1975

p.68 Geoffrey Ashe, *The Traveller's Guide to Arthurian Britain*, Gothic Image, 1997

p.68-9 Bernard Cornwell, letter to Christina Hardyment, 1999

pp.70, 71 Rudyard Kipling, *Puck of Pook's Hill*, Macmillan, 1906

p.105 Richard Gill, *Happy Rural Seat: The English Country House and the Literary Imagination*, Yale, 1972

p.117 D. J. Taylor, *Thackeray*, Chatto & Windus, 1999

pp.124, 126 H. G. Wells, *Experiment in Autobiography*, Gollancz, 1934

pp.124, 126-7 H. G. Wells, *Tono-Bungay*, Macmillan & Co., 1909

p.128 T. S. Eliot, *Four Quartets*, Faber & Faber, 1944

p.128 D. H. Lawrence, *Lady Chatterley's Lover*, Penguin Books, 1960

p.129-30 Vita Sackville-West, *Knole and the Sackvilles*, Heinemann, 1922

p.130 Virginia Woolf, *Orlando*, Hogarth Press, 1928. By permission of the Society of Authors and Harcourt Brace Inc.

p.135 E. F. Benson, *Final Edition: Informal Autobiography*, Longmans, Green & Co., 1915

p.158 Melvyn Bragg, *The Maid of Buttermere*, Hodder & Stoughton, 1987

pp.160, 161, 162 Arthur Ransome, *Swallows and Amazons*, Jonathan Cape, 1930

p.163 Arthur Ransome, *Swallowdale*, Jonathan Cape, 1931

pp.182, 190 R. D. Knight, *T. E. Lawrence and the Max Gate Circle*, Bat and Ball Press, 1988

pp.193, 194-5, 197, 201 Nigel Nicolson & J. Trautmann (eds), *The Letters of Virginia Woolf* (6 vols.), Hogarth Press, 1975-80

p.203 Jan Morris, *Travels with Virginia Woolf*, Pimlico, 1997

p.203 Leonard Woolf quoted by H. Lee in *Virginia Woolf*, Chatto & Windus, 1996

p.206 Virginia Woolf, *To The Lighthouse*, Hogarth Press, 1927

p.208 Vita Sackville-West quoted by Victoria Glendinning in *Vita, Life of Victoria Sackville-West*, Weidenfeld, 1983

p.208 Vita Sackville-West 'In Absence' from *Collected Poems*, Hogarth Press, 1933

p.209 Vita Sackville-West *The Land*, William Heinemann, 1926

p.212 Daphne du Maurier, *Enchanted Cornwall*, Michael Joseph, 1989

p.215 Reginald Hill, *The Long Kill*, Collins, 1998

p.216 Cyril Connolly, *Ideas and Places*, Weidenfeld, 1983

p.218 Daphne du Maurier, *Rebecca*, Gollancz, 1938

p.220 W. H. Auden, 'The Guilty Vicarage' from *The Dyer's Hand*, Faber & Faber, 1963

p.222 Peter Dickinson, Letter to Christina Hardyment, 1999

p.222-3 Erik Routley from Colin Watson, *Snobbery with Violence*, Eyre Methuen, 1979

p.225, 226, 227 Dorothy L. Sayers, *The Nine Tailors*, Gollancz, 1934

p.230-1 Ann Cleeves, *A Bird in the Hand*, Century, 1986

pp.232, 233 Jack Higgins, *The Eagle has Landed*, Collins, 1975

List of Plates

Please note that figures in **bold** refer to page numbers.
NTPL – National Trust Photographic Library
NT – National Trust Regional Archives and Libraries

1 Rudyard Kipling's bookplate dated 1909. *NTPL/John Hammond*
2 View over the Lake District towards Buttermere. *NTPL/Joe Cornish*
6 Coniston Water in the Lake District, with the Old Man of Coniston in the distance. *NTPL/Robert Thrift*
8 (Above) George Bernard Shaw at Shaw's Corner in Hertfordshire. *NT*
8 (Below) George Bernard Shaw's writing desk in the study at Shaw's Corner. *NTPL/Geoffrey Frosh*
10 Beatrix Potter and her husband William Heelis on their wedding day in October 1913. *F. Warne & Co*
11 T. E. Lawrence as a cadet on Newporth Beach near Falmouth in Cornwall, painted by Henry Scott Tuke (1858-1929). *NTPL*
12 Caricature of Christina Rossetti by Dante Gabriel Rossetti from Wightwick Manor in the West Midlands. *NTPL/Derrick E. Witty*
14 William Bell Scott's mural of *The Death of Bede* at Wallington Hall in Northumberland, showing the scriptorium at Jarrow Priory. *NTPL/Derrick E. Witty*
17 Portrait of Thomas Hardy, 1923, by Augustus John (1878-1961). *Fitzwilliam Museum, University of Cambridge, © Courtesy of the artist's estate/Bridgeman Art Library*
18 Rudyard Kipling's study at Bateman's in Sussex. *NTPL/Geoffrey Frosh*
20 (Above) View of the North Devon coast from Baggy Point. *NTPL/John Gollop*
20 (Below) Coleridge's cottage at Nether Stowey in Somerset. *NT*
23 Portrait of Caroline Kipling by Philip Burne-Jones at Bateman's in Sussex. *NTPL/John Hammond*
24 (Above) Thomas Carlyle outside his house in Cheyne Row by Henry and Walter Greaves, 1859. *NTPL/Michael Boys*
24 (Below) Robert Tait's conversation piece, *A Chelsea Interior* (1857) showing the Carlyles in their parlour. *NTPL/Michael Boys*
25 Carlyle photographed by Robert Tait at his writing desk in his attic study. *NT*
26-7 Winston Churchill's desk in the study at Chartwell, Kent. *NTPL/Andreas von Einsiedel*
28-9 Arthur Ransome in his workroom at Low Ludderburn in Cumbria. *© Brotherton Collection, University of Leeds*
29 Thomas Carlyle smoking in the garden at Cheyne Row in 1857. *NT*
30-1 Extract from Carlyle's manuscript of *The French Revolution*. *NT*
33 E. F. Benson with Taffy at Lamb House in the early 1930s. *Tilling Society*
34 Shaw's Corner in Hertfordshire. *NTPL/Vera Collingwood*
35 George Bernard Shaw's writing retreat in the summerhouse. *NTPL/Geoffrey Frosh*
36 *La Morte d'Arthur* by James Archer (1861). *Manchester City Art Galleries*
38 The King Arthur Cross, found buried in King Arthur's coffin at Glastonbury Abbey by William Camden, 1607.
39 *The Knights of the Round Table about to depart on the Quest for the Holy Grail* by William Dyce (1849). *National Gallery of Scotland*
40 An anonymous woodcut from Sir Thomas Malory's *Morte d'Arthur* (1498).
41 Illustration by Walter Crane from the 1896 edition of Spenser's *Faerie Queene. Victoria & Albert Museum*
44 Stained glass window showing the Holy Grail descending on Sir Galahad. *© King Arthur's Great Halls, Tintagel, Cornwall*
46 Glastonbury Tor in the evening light. *NTPL/Fay Godwin*
49 *The Winter Smoking Room at Cardiff Castle* by William Burges. *NTPL/John Hammond*
50 Archibald Montgomery, 13th Earl of Eglinton by Edward Corbauld, c.1840. *Victoria & Albert Museum*
50-1 Viscount Alford and the Marquess of Waterford at the Eglinton Tournament. *National Library of Scotland*
51 Alfred Tennyson, painted by Samuel Laurence in 1840. *National Portrait Gallery*